Birgit Braasch,
Claudia Müller (Eds.)

Off Shore

Atlantic Cultural Studies

herausgegeben von

Claudia Schnurmann

Band 12

LIT

OFF SHORE

Perspectives on
Atlantic Pleasure Travel
since the 19th Century

edited by

Birgit Braasch and Claudia Müller

LIT

Cover image: Queen Mary (ship), 2004 – State Library of Queensland

This book is printed on acid-free paper.

Bibliographic information published by the Deutsche Nationalbibliothek
The Deutsche Nationalbibliothek lists this publication in the Deutsche Nationalbibliografie; detailed bibliographic data are available in the Internet at http://dnb.dnb.de.

ISBN 978-3-643-91246-6 (pb)
ISBN 978-3-643-96246-1 (PDF)

A catalogue record for this book is available from the British Library.

© LIT VERLAG GmbH & Co. KG Wien,
Zweigniederlassung Zürich 2020
Klosbachstr. 107
CH-8032 Zürich
Tel. +41 (0) 44-251 75 05
E-Mail: zuerich@lit-verlag.ch   http://www.lit-verlag.ch
Distribution:
In the UK: Global Book Marketing, e-mail: mo@centralbooks.com
In North America: Independent Publishers Group, e-mail: orders@ipgbook.com
In Germany: LIT Verlag Fresnostr. 2, D-48159 Münster
Tel. +49 (0) 2 51-620 32 22, Fax +49 (0) 2 51-922 60 99, e-mail: vertrieb@lit-verlag.de
e-books are available at www.litwebshop.de

Table of Contents

1. Introduction *Birgit Braasch and Claudia Müller*	7
2. By Water *Casey Orr*	13
3. The Superliner and Liminal Space *Emma E. Roberts*	29
4. Frocks versus Guns: Sailing the South Atlantic in the 1982 Falklands/Malvinas Conflict *Jo Stanley*	61
5. "Even being idle has to be learned" – Overcoming Liminality on Atlantic Passenger Ships, 1840-1920s *Dagmar Bellmann*	99
6. War Crossings: The American GI as Transatlantic Traveler during the Second World War *Mark D. Van Ells*	129
7. The Experience of a Lifetime: Lydia DeGuio's Journey across the North Atlantic *Birgit Braasch*	161
8. A Floating Carnival: P. G. Wodehouse and the Atlantic Crossing *Eric Sandberg*	199
9. Menageries at Sea: Animals and Trans-Atlantic Travel in 1940 *Stephanie Beck Cohen*	229
10. Innocence Aboard *Lynn Bloom*	263
11. Conclusion *Birgit Braasch and Claudia Müller*	275
List of Figures	281
List of Archives	283
Selected Bibliography	285
List of Contributors	291

1. Introduction

Birgit Braasch and Claudia Müller[1]

When the *Queen Mary 2* completes her transatlantic crossing in Hamburg, Germany, in the early hours of the morning, the liner is regularly greeted by a large number of people.[2] Both parties, those on the ship and those on shore have gotten up early to participate in this event. Some people who wait and wave from the shore have already travelled on the ship and enjoy being reminded of their experiences. Others fantasize about being a passenger on such a liner with luxurious amenities. The tourists on deck wave back at a mainly unknown crowd that welcomes them at five o'clock in the morning.
Travel on ocean liners goes back to the 19th century and since then tourists' practices which were specific to ocean liners were continuously developed, like the welcoming described in the scene above.
This practice relates to the tourist setting of transatlantic crossings. Compared to cruise ships the departure and the landing were important for transatlantic crossings. In contrast to cruising trips, e.g. in the Caribbean, Atlantic crossings were a long non-stop journey across the ocean. For example, in the late 1930s the ocean liner *Queen Mary* departed in New York and landed about four to six days later in Southampton.[3] During this journey passengers did not have the chance to leave the ship. In contrast, during a classic cruise tourists had the opportunity to go on land frequently.[4] The structure of the Atlantic crossing with its one departure and one landing thus constituted a very specific tourist setting which shaped practices on board.
In addition, the scene nicely portrays how practices on board and on shore relate to each other. The ocean liners have been and still are bade farewell by friends, relatives and local onlookers and are constantly discussed in local newspapers.[5]

---

[1] We would like to thank Fenja Heisig for proofreading the whole manuscript.
[2] Antje Blinda, "Zehn Jahre 'Queen Mary 2' und Hamburg: Ein Hafen und seine Königin" *Spiegel Online*, 18 July 2014, http://www.spiegel.de/reise/aktuell/kreuzfahrt-queen-mary-2-und-hamburg-zehn-jahre-hafenliebe-a-81381.html, accessed 16 Nov 2014.
[3] Card: Cunard Steam Ship Company Ltd., "Abstract of Log of the Queen Mary", Aug 1966, University of Liverpool Special Collections and Archives (UoLSC&A), D42/PR3/24/43.
[4] Peter Quartermaine and Bruce Peter, Cruise: Identity, Design and Culture, London 2006, p. 23.
[5] See e.g. Axel Tiedemann and Edgar S. Hasse, „Die Queen - Milliardengeschäft für Hamburg", *Hamburger Abendblatt Online*, 19 July 2014,

The practices of waving on board and on shore gain their full sense only in relation to each other. For example, the practices would be different if people on shore waved to the ship, but passengers did not answer the waving because they were already having dinner.

Following from these considerations, the contributions to this collection all aim to explore different experiences and practices[6] and their changes over time which seem to be specific to tourists' Atlantic crossings. The articles all provide answers to the following questions:

1. What informed and shaped practices on board an Atlantic liner? We would like to explore the change of those practices over time by including into the analysis (on shore) reference points, like the architecture of luxury hotels, for example.

---

[6] http://www.abendblatt.de/hamburg/article130332329/Die-Queen-Milliardengeschaeft-fuer-Hamburg.html, accessed 20 Oct 2014; „Royal send-off: 20,000 gather in Liverpool to see Queen Victoria sail out of her ‚spiritual home'", *Mail Online*, 2 June 2014, http://www.dailymail.co.uk/travel/article-2646042/More-20-000-gather-Liverpool-Cunards-Queen-Victoria.html, accessed 20 Oct 2014; „Three Cunard Queens in Southampton", *Daily Echo Online*, 9 May 2014, http://www.dailyecho.co.uk/photographs/news_galleries/three_cunard_queens_in_southampton/view/gallery_404778.The_Three_Cunard_Queens_in_Southampton/, accessed 20 Oct 2014. In the following introduction the terms "practice" and "experience" are used as interrelated. The term "practice" as it is used here is based on Bourdieu's concept as outlined in *The Logic of Practice* (Pierre Bourdieu, *The Logic of Practice*, Cambridge 1992, p. 52.) With this concept Bourdieu aims to incorporate historical change. At the same time he criticizes the concept of 'lived experience' (Ibid., p. 25). His critique is taken seriously by Bruner and Turner (Victor W. Turner and Edward M. Bruner (Eds.), *The Anthropology of Experience*, Urbana/Ill. 1986) who develop their concept of experience and incorporate this critique by interrelating practices and experience. They describe an experience process as being divided into five different moments: "the perceptual core, the evocation of past images, the revival of associated feelings, the emergence of meaning and value and finally the expression of the experience. [...] It is only in the fifth moment of 'expression' that the 'structured unit of experience' can be said to reveal itself" (Jason C. Throop, "Articulating Experience", in: *Anthropological Theory* 3 (2003) p. 219-243: 223.). In their concept the dynamic of the experience process is conceptualized through the influence of the immediate situation (Bourdieu's "lived experience") as well as by the historical experiences, interpretations and expressions. The latter ones can be conceptualized as practices.

2. How did tourists appropriate those practices? We would like to understand how tourists shaped those practices and at the same time understand their gain from appropriating certain habituses.

3. Finally, how have on-board tourist practices been appropriated in other contexts of travel, every day routines or leisure activities?

Since experiences and practices on ocean liners have not yet been systematically analyzed, this collection draws from very disparate bodies of literature.

An existing approach to tourists' experiences on ocean liners constitutes the literature on the age of the liners which is characterized by a certain type of nostalgia.[7] The nostalgia evident in these histories mostly refers to the style in which passengers, mainly in first class, could travel.[8] This style of travel is usually connected to the design of ocean liners and the stories about rich and famous people who travelled on these liners.[9] Those stories focus on ocean crossings and emphasize a contrast to modern cruising, which corresponds to discourses about a shift from travel to tourism.[10]

In an attempt to break with the nostalgic writing about the ocean liners, academics analyze the development of the ships' designs and styles over time and connect them to wider developments in the history of art and design.[11] Similarly, the contributions to this collection aim to keep the focus on passengers' experiences and analyze them in relation to the historical context – how it shaped these experiences and how they were shaped by it.

---

[7] See e.g., David L. Williams, *Cunard's Legendary Queens of the Seas*, London 2004; Neil McCart, *Atlantic Liners of the Cunard Line: From 1884 to the Present Day*, Wellingborough 1990.

[8] See e.g., John Malcom Brinnin and Kenneth Gaulin, *The Transatlantic Style*, New York 1988, p. 181ff.

[9] See e.g. William H. Miller, *SS United States: The Story of America's Greatest Ocean Liner*, Sparkford 1991, p. 136ff.

[10] Paul Fussell, *Abroad: British Literary Traveling between the Wars*, Oxford 1980, p. 37ff.

[11] Quartermaine and Peter, *Cruise: Identity, Design and Culture*; Bruce Peter and Philip Dawson, "Modernism at Sea: Ocean Liners and the Avent-garde", in: Lara Feigel and Alexandra Harris (Eds.), *Modernism on Sea: Art and Culture at the British Seaside*, Oxford 2009, p. 144-157; Philip Dawson, *British Superliners of the Sixties: A Design Appreciation of the Oriana, Canberra and QE2*, London 1990.

Literature on the ocean-liner industry with its emphasis on technological and economic developments [12] constitutes the companion piece to the nostalgic writing. While the passenger experience in this literature is absent, the analysis of the economic and technological developments can still help to understand tourist experiences and practices. The analysis can show how by striving to generate income and build their business, shipping companies accounted for the tourist experiences on board and aimed to shape it.

Interestingly, literature on crews does not focus on the white male captain, but very much takes other historical actors into account.[13] The literature on ships' crews helps to widen our perspectives on historical actors. For example, Lorraine Coons and Alexander Varias analyze female crew members on transatlantic liners in the interwar years.[14] Similarly, Paul Baker and Jo Stanley consider the question of the sex and gender perspective by describing the life of gay sailors on board ocean liners after the Second World War.[15] Adapting these perspectives for this collection means to relate different tourists' experiences and practices to other sailing historical actors in order to understand the changes in these practices.

Finally, this collection draws on ideas which relate the experiences and practices on the ocean liner to practices on shore. In his general history of the construction of an image of the world ocean, geographer Philip Steinberg focuses on how the shore societies represent the ocean and for what purpose. He relates these representations back to changing capitalistic needs.[16] Coming from the other direction, Bernhard Klein and Gesa Mackenthun in their collection about oceanic spaces draw attention to the sea as a space that is experienced by a variety of

---

[12] See e.g. Terry Coleman, *The Liners: A History of the North Atlantic Crossing* London 1976; Stephen Fox, *The Ocean Railway: Isambard Kingdom Brunel, Samuel Cunard, and the Revolutionary World of the Great Atlantic Steamships*, London 2004; McCart, *Atlantic Liners*.

[13] Since crew members had very close relationships with the tourists, their accounts can as such be essential to understand their experiences and practices. Baker and Stanley, for example, critically assess the life of the crew, inter-crew relationships, and their relationships with passengers. Paul Baker and Jo Stanley, *Hello Sailor! The Hidden History of Gay Life at Sea*, London 2003, p. 201.

[14] Lorraine Coons and Alexander Varias, *Tourist Third Cabin: Steamship Travel in the Interwar Years*, New York 2003, p. 107ff.

[15] Baker and Stanley, *Hello Sailor!*

[16] Philip E. Steinberg, *The Social Construction of the Ocean*, Cambridge 2001, p. 209.

travelers and how this experience feeds into literature.[17] For example, historian Claudia Schnurmann shows the importance of the relation between technologies, such as ships, and the image of the ocean by following the change of oceanic images especially in Early Modern Times in Europe.[18]

The multidisciplinary contributions to this collection all follow a historical approach. All contributions, from literature and literature studies, from photography as well as design history and from general history, capture how different tourist practices related to other practices on shore and how they and their relationships changed.

The collection pairs contributions which are dedicated to understanding practices on ocean liners with those which take up similar practices in another context. Pairing such different views shall also give the opportunity to understand specificities of tourists' travels across the Atlantic.

In order to introduce the topic and allow the reader to reflect his or her own ideas on crossing the Atlantic, the collections begins with a photographic essay by Casey Orr who recounts in her photographs her crossing of the Atlantic on a container ship between Leeds/Liverpool (UK) and Chester, Pennsylvania (USA). The pictures not only reflect her personal experience but give first tentative insights into the topics which might be related to the crossing of the Atlantic, like danger, industries and transport, childhood games or even boredom.

The first block consists of the contributions of Emma Roberts and Jo Stanley. Both contributions engage with the interior design of ocean liners and how passengers engaged with this design from two very different perspectives: while Emma Roberts starts off with her analysis of tourists on a superliner, Jo Stanley looks at the relationships between the ocean liners and its passengers during the Falkland war when most of the passengers were soldiers and only some of the ocean liners' original crew stayed onboard. While the situations the authors look at could not be more disparate, it is interesting to see how practices and discourses related to the design are very similar.

The second block consists of contributions by Dagmar Bellmann, Mark van Ells and Birgit Braasch; this section continues this narrative with another topic: the

---

[17] Bernhard Klein and Gesa Mackenthun, "Einleitung: Das Meer als kulturelle Kontaktzone", in: Bernhard Klein and Gesa Mackenthun (Eds.), *Das Meer als kulturelle Kontaktzone: Räume, Reisende, Repräsentationen*, Konstanz 2003, p. 1-16: 10.

[18] Claudia Schnurmann, "Frühneuzeitliche Formen maritimer Vereinnahmung: Die europäische Inbesitznahme des Atlantiks," in: Bernhard Klein and Gesa Mackenthun (Eds.), *Das Meer als kulturelle Kontaktzone: Räume, Reisende, Repräsentationen*, Konstanz 2003, p. 49-72: 49.

time structure on board. Dagmar Bellmann analyzes the establishment of activities and routines for the passengers. Mark van Ells does the same for American soldiers on board ships during the Second World War. In the war context they also adhered to those established tourist routines and van Ells carefully explores the relationship between tourist crossings and those of soldiers in his article. For the time after the Second World War Birgit Braasch focuses on one woman and her experience of these tourist practices.

The role shore societies had in transatlantic travel is the focus of the third part. The essays analyze the mutual influences of these shore societies and transatlantic travel. Stephanie Beck Cohen describes the network on both sides of the Atlantic which enabled the married couple Mann to organize animal transports between Liberia and the USA. The article contributes to an understanding of the personal networks which were formed through travels across the Atlantic. In his analysis of P.G. Wodehouse's novels, Eric Sandberg also explores explicitly the public view the shores had of Atlantic crossings. He points out how Wodehouse in his novels relied on and played with images of Atlantic crossings as a space free from national or gender constraints as they existed in the US and England in the 1920s. Building on this image, Sandberg argues that Wodehouse at the same time contributed to a transatlantic narrative.

The last contribution by Lynn Bloom brings the arguments put forward by the authors together in a personal essay about four transatlantic crossings. Lynn Bloom describes her transatlantic crossing between the US and Europe in the 1950s, the images and practices she recounts as well as the meanings those crossings still have in her life-story.

2. By Water

Casey Orr

In the summer of 2006 I travelled from Leeds, England to Delaware, USA, where I'm from. I rode my bicycle down the old path by my house leading to Armley Mills and then the 127 miles along the Leeds-Liverpool Canal to Liverpool, where I boarded a container ship. Nine days and 3000 miles later I arrived in the small port town of Chester, Pennsylvania, my birthplace. By Water is a series of photographs about this journey, about how water connects us, how it linked us historically through wool, cotton, tobacco and slavery and how it links us now through the often invisible movements of goods.

The Leeds-Liverpool Canal is 127 miles long. It winds through cities that change to countryside, where industrial landscapes merge with farms and longboats slowly chug past. There are abandoned mills, dogs and people riding bikes, along with breathtakingly quiet, rolling hills where there's no sound except for sheep and moving water.

It was through the port of Liverpool that goods were brought back and forth from England to the rest of the world. The plantations in the US exported cotton through Liverpool into the mills of Lancashire and Yorkshire. Liverpool was not only a trade centre for cotton, tobacco and other American goods, but also where the ships that were used to fight the American Civil War were built. It was also one of the main ports of the slave trade. Hundreds of thousands of European people left for America through Liverpool, including my ancestors from England and Northern Ireland. Migrants from Europe docked in Hull and traveled across land to Liverpool. Much of the cargo would have used the canalways.

Containerisation changed the culture of port cities. Waterfront workers and their communities were replaced by high-speed cranes as containers revolutionised the way cargo was shipped; as goods became anonymous and impersonal. The ship I sailed on – *The Independent Pursuit* – was part of a fleet of ships that sailed weekly. Container ships transport 90% of the world's non-bulk cargo and some 18 million containers make over 200 million trips every year; yet ocean journeys are a thing of the past for most people.

The Independent Pursuit had a crew of 22. The officers and engineers, who are mostly Eastern European, from Romania, Russia and The Ukraine, work on six month contracts. The oilers, cook, steward, and maintenance workers are Filipino. When I sailed with them they had just heard that their contracts had been extended to nine months.

The weather began to settle when we approached Canada and the air became warm. As we turned towards the Delaware River, 300 miles away from the coast, there were signs of land – in the form of trash, from paper cups to plastic bags, a woollen hat, everyday flotsam and jetsam. One large, bobbing shape was a turtle, swimming on its own. Then there were tree branches washed away from a recent storm and finally the oppressive heat of an East Coast summer and flies, lots of flies that boarded the ship around 100 miles from the coast.

Marcus Hook, Pennsylvania was an early shipbuilding centre. In 1901 Sun Oil purchased 82 acres in the town as a site for refining crude oil. Along with the prison and a new race track, the oil refineries are the main employer in Marcus Hook.

The people of the river towns and cities along the Delaware River join the flows of water, shipping channels and currents through the state of Delaware.

The river opens into the Delaware Bay where fresh water mixes with the salty waters of the Atlantic Ocean.

Rehoboth Beach, Delaware sits below the estuary outlet of the Delaware Bay. From here the lights of ships can be seen, hundreds of miles out in the Atlantic Ocean.

3. The Superliner and Liminal Space

Emma E. Roberts

Introduction

By the start of the twentieth century, crossing the Atlantic by ocean liner was imbued with nostalgic and romantic notions. The transport was one between an old and a new world, and passengers in either direction felt hope, excitement and the thrill of ritual. They were indeed experiencing a rite – a transition overlaid with meanings that had changed the lives of many who went before. Central to this is that the Atlantic was encountered as a place almost without time, and as an 'other world': "travelers experienced the transatlantic voyage as an initiation of transition into another world, both imaginative and physical."[1] Upon embarkation, travelers had little option but to enter what could almost be proposed as an alternate reality for five days or more. It has been noted that

> "[m]any people who have commented on traveling have noticed in passing that, in traveling for an extended period of time on a ship, ocean voyages enter a unique space [...] But few people have tried to make sense of this 'world between worlds' and how it might affect those who enter it."[2]

The purpose of this article is to try to make sense of the "unique space" that was the transatlantic 'superliner' and its effect upon participants.

This chapter argues that ocean liners themselves were vessels to transport people into 'liminal space' where they could, temporarily, be free of their usual roles and relations. The concept of the liminal is explained by Arnold Van Gennep, who is credited with first using the phrase, albeit in ethnographical terms. He writes, "I propose to call the rites of separation from a previous world, preliminal rites, those executed during the transitional stage liminal (or threshold) rites, and the ceremonies of incorporation into the new world post-liminal rites."[3] These rites and stages are therefore central to an understanding of the liminal. Passengers crossing the Atlantic in either direction can be assumed to have traveled into an unknown world and to have left their old lives behind, even if only temporarily.

---

[1] Mark Rennella and Whitney Walton, "Planned Serendipity: American Travelers and the Transatlantic Voyage in the Nineteenth and Twentieth Centuries" in: *Journal of Social History*, 38 (2004), p. 365-383: 377.
[2] Ibid., p. 367.
[3] Arnold Van Gennep, *The Rites of Passage,* Chicago, London 1972, p. 21.

This was often a great attraction: "For many of the transatlantic travelers, physical distance from family and community was almost a pre-requisite for articulating a sense of self."[4] Van Gennep's original observations on tribal societies led him to ascribe a "magico-religious aspect [to] crossing frontiers:"[5] "thus the 'magic circles' pivot, shifting as a person moves from one place in society to another."[6] The effect of this is thought to be that persons traversing through such rites of passage undergo a 'rebirth' of sorts: a spiritual experience. They have been transported between worlds, both physically and psychologically. It is important to note that, despite Van Gennep's anthropological approach and subjects of focus, stressing "the importance of transitions in any society, Van Gennep singled out rites of passage as a special category [...] The ritual pattern was apparently universal: all societies use rites to demarcate transitions."[7] This universality of the rituals that evoke the liminal sanctions justifies the use of Van Gennep's concept of the liminal in the present article which discusses the late modern period and Atlantic cultures.

Van Gennep's observations about rites of separation and the liminal were later examined further by Victor Turner. He explained that the liminal stage is uninhibiting and even 'transformative'. He writes, "during the intervening liminal period, the state of the ritual subject '(the passenger)' is ambiguous; he passes through a realm that has few or none of the attributes of the past or coming state;" he is not in this middle, liminal, stage, "expected to behave in accordance with certain customary norms and ethical standards."[8] Again, like Van Gennep, Turner uses a tribal society in order to test and confirm his ideas so "how exactly can we employ the concept of liminality towards an understanding of social, cultural and political processes in modernity?"[9]: in this case, passengers' experiences on board transatlantic liners? In short, "Turner repeatedly identified parallels with non-tribal or 'modern' societies, clearly sensing that what he argued for the Ndembu had relevance far beyond the specific ethnographic context."[10] Again, this is

---

[4] Rennella, Walton, "Planned Serendipity".
[5] Van Gennep, *Rites of Passage*, p. 15.
[6] Ibid., p. 13.
[7] Bjørn Thomassen, "Revisiting Liminality: The Danger of Empty Spaces" in: Hazel Andrews and Les Roberts (Eds.), *Liminal Landscapes. Travel, Experience and Spaces In-Between,* Abingdon 2012, p. 21-36: 23.
[8] Victor Turner, *The Forest of Symbols. Aspects of Ndembu Ritual,* New York, London 1967, p. 94.
[9] Thomassen, "Revisiting Liminality", p. 27.
[10] Ibid.

confirmation that the concept of the liminal can have applications for interpreting twentieth-century cultures.

As this article proposes that crossing the Atlantic by liner enables the travelers to experience the transformative rites of passage, the elements that helped to construct these rites will be examined, as well as evidence of passengers' thoughts. In order to contain the discussion within reasonable parameters, attention will focus on the Cunard line which has the longest history of transporting travelers across the Atlantic.[11] Again, in order to narrow the focus, the experiences of upper-middle and upper-class passengers on early twentieth-century 'superliners' will dominate. Passenger diaries and letters stored in the Cunard Archive at the University of Liverpool and in the Merseyside Maritime Museum Archives in Liverpool will be analyzed.

The Floating Hotel

The phrase 'superliner' was defined neatly by William Francis Gibbs, the designer of the *S.S. United States*: "A superliner [...] is the equivalent of a large cantilevered bridge covered with steel plates containing a power plant that could light any of our larger cities, and with a first-class luxury hotel on top."[12] This quotation shows that superliners were extraordinary vehicles and therefore demand extra critical attention. In itself this extraordinariness is a key component in creating conditions that enable liminality for "liminal spaces are attractive. They are the places we go to in search of a break from the normal."[13] The liminal experience that the superliner could provide was seemingly enhanced by the exceptional facilities on board the ship - at least for the passengers who are the focus of concern in this article. This is central to the argument here. For the wealthier travelers, their time on board was distinguished by the sensory experiences of partaking in exotic and elaborate meals, parading fine clothes, indulging in diverse conversations and relaxing with varied leisure activities. For the continuing development of ocean liners as well as the initial development of cruise ships it is important also to note the impact of having been free of US-American prohibition for passengers from that continent: "it soon became apparent to ship owners that there was a market gap they could meet [...] 'Booze' cruises alone would not have led to the first great growth of the cruise industry

---

[11] Cunard was granted the contract to deliver mail and to transport passengers across the Atlantic in 1847.
[12] John Malcolm Brinnin, *The Sway of the Grand Saloon. A Social History of The North Atlantic,* New York 1971, p. 474.
[13] Thomassen, "Revisiting Liminality", p. 21.

but coupled with the flamboyant style of the age, cruising became a more intense experience than the leisurely pre-war operations and one, for Americans at least, where you could enjoy a legal drink."[14] Alongside this temporary liberation, there was the frisson of meeting people from multiple countries and backgrounds with the possibility of forming new business, friendship or romantic relationships. Despite being a vehicle which very much contained those within, the superliner experience was one that was highly aestheticized, freeing and overlaid with multiple possibilities; therefore "uncanny feelings inspired by ocean voyages"[15] could be experienced. Although, first and foremost, crossing the Atlantic by liner was a necessary and practical endeavor for each ship's many passengers, one argues that the journey – often unexpectedly – provided a transformative experience. As Andrews and Roberts state, liminal places "are generally held to be those which play host to ideas of the ludic, consumption, carnivalesque, deterritorialisation, and the inversion or suspension of normative social and moral structures of everyday life."[16] Leaving behind the strictures of everyday life meant that existence on a transatlantic liner, even for just a few days, could feel more uninhibited – a "psychic space of potentiality."[17]

Frequently, the phrases 'floating hotel' or 'floating town' were used by both passengers and cruise line publicity materials to explain the sense that people were bound together in a contained, communal space, but that this was yet a highly luxurious and heady experience with multiple amenities. For example, first-class passenger, Washington Dodge, spoke of his Titanic dining experience: "It was hard to realize, when dining in the large and spacious dining saloon, that one was not in some large and sumptuous hotel."[18] In one Cunard publicity brochure of c. 1912, the use of the word 'hotel' occurs on many occasions within just a short space:

> "The passenger is perhaps, more directly concerned with the comfort which his floating hotel provides [...] [liners are] certainly not

---

[14] Roger Cartwright and Carolyn Baird, *The Development and Growth of the Cruise Industry*, Oxford, Auckland, Boston, Johannesburg, Melbourne, New Delhi 1999, p. 24.

[15] Rennella, Walton, "Planned Serendipity", p. 370.

[16] Hazel Andrews and Les Roberts, "Introduction: Re-Mapping Liminality" in: Hazel Andrews and Les Roberts (Eds.), *Liminal Landscapes. Travel, Experience and Spaces In-Between,* Abingdon 2012, p. 1-19: 6.

[17] Ibid., p. 1.

[18] Rick Archbold and Dana McCauley, *Last Dinner on the Titanic*, New York 1997, p. 62 (At the time of the *Titanic's* build and sailing, the White Star Line was the company behind the liner, however Cunard and White Star Line merged in 1934).

surpassed by any of the leading hotels ashore. In short, the highest and best in hotel life are adapted to the ships [...] the more attractive features of hotel life are strikingly present in the ménage of the *Lusitania* and *Mauretania* [...] equaled only at the very finest hotels ashore."[19]

Perhaps this connotation that Atlantic liners were floating hotels was partly to mitigate against the reputation that they held of causing seasickness but, undoubtedly, it emphasized the exceptionally high standards and the aestheticisation of daily life that was to be found on board by upper class passengers. From the turn of the nineteenth-century onwards, shipping lines began to employ renowned hotel designers to create fantasy spaces in the dining saloons and other public spaces on board the superliners. These include Charles Mewès, the architect of the Paris and London Ritz hotels, who designed spaces for HAPAG's *Amerika*, German contemporary architects, Bruno Paul and Rudolf Schröder, who worked on Norddeutscher Lloyd's *George Washington* and James Miller for Cunard's *Lusitania*. Miller, and other designers employed by Cunard, were greatly conscious of the impact of details in the appearance of rooms and thought was given to providing varied spaces with different functions and effects. Attention was paid to the psychological impact of the signs that were intended to be observed by passengers from the interior design and rooms presented clear 'signs' of their very specific functions. These signs, in turn, presumably promoted passenger behaviors. Indeed, Hart notes that, once the Cunard liners *Lusitania* and *Mauretania* adopted 'hotelism' in their interior design, there was a perceptible impact upon passengers' actions. He writes of the consequence of the addition of the luxurious lounge space to liners:

> "While press accounts of the lounge studiously avoided the implication that the new space might lead to a blurring of gender-based social norms, the room, in fact soon witnesses behavior that challenged the boundaries. As Lady Duff commented to reporters regarding her conduct on the Adriatic, 'On board a steamship, there is more license than on shore.'"[20]

Hart makes explicit the links between the interior architecture and the liberation of passenger behavior. Other accounts of the themed, decorative spaces also indicate that the carnivalesque was authorized as a result of interior design. Timothy Green expresses this effectively: "Where else have ships had Byzantine chapels and Pompeian swimming pools, dining rooms styled like the palace of

---

19 Brochure: *Cunard Line. Luxury Afloat*, c. 1912, UoLSC&A, D884.
20 Douglas Hart, "Sociability and 'Separate Spheres' on the North Atlantic: The Interior Architecture of British Atlantic Liners, 1840 – 1930" in: *The Journal of Social History* 44, (2010), p. 189-212, p. 202.

Versailles, lounges decorated in mock Inigo Jones, and Turkish baths like Egyptian harems?"[21] In fact, Green even points out that, as early as 1879, with the launch of Cunard's Gallia, "the saloon was decorated in Japanese style, the walls being in panels of jasper-red lacquer, with delicate Japanese designs in gold and soft colours portraying birds and flowers. There was even a fountain spouting in the centre of the smoking room."[22] These hedonistic and evocative themed environments must have been striking but, when experienced as a compressed conglomeration of spaces in a vessel moving through both time and a vast ocean, it is no wonder that Foucault and Miskowiec write of a ship as a 'heterotopia' – a floating place that enables floating dreams and ideas. They call "this floating piece of space, a place without a place, that exists by itself, that is closed in on itself and at the same time is given over to the infinity of the sea […] simultaneously the greatest reserve of imagination."[23]

Jonathan Culler writes that "tourists are the agents of semiotics: all over the world they are engaged in reading cities, landscapes, and cultures as sign systems."[24] There was a proliferation of signs within Cunard superliners for the passengers to read and which, for Foucault and Miskowiec, provide a "reserve of imagination" for floating dreams.[25] In the *Aquitania* the main drawing room was based on Robert Adam's plans for Lansdowne House in Berkeley Square, London, and the first-class dining room featured a minstrels' gallery that "was supposed to convey to passengers that they were eating in the palace of the Sun King at Versailles."[26]

---

[21] Article: Timothy Green, "Samuel Cunard's Floating Palaces" c. 1967, p. 65 UoLSC&A, D42/PR12/61/16.
[22] Ibid., p. 67.
[23] Michel Foucault, "Of Other Spaces", in: *Diacritics* 16, (1986) p. 22-27: 27.
[24] Jonathan Culler, "The Semiotics of Tourism" in: Jonathan Culler, *Framing the Sign: Criticism and Its Institutions,* Norman/OK 1990, p. 1-10: 2.
[25] Foucault, Miskowiec, *Spaces*, 27.
[26] Green, "Floating Palaces", p. 67.

Figure 1: Aquitania First Class Lounge with Clock

A shipbuilder's journal recorded the eclectic juxtaposition of signs that were colliding within *Aquitania*: "a faint echo only of Tudor times and the days of Hans Holbein will be found [...] From this we pass to the days of Sir 'Anthonie' van Dyck and Inigo Jones, but [...] most completely illustrated in the ship are those which lie between the Restoration of Charles II and the middle of the reign of George III."[27] Presumably passengers perceived these scenes as spectacle. It is known that the interior architects and ship owners intended them to be viewed as such. Certainly, writers commenting on crossing the Atlantic by liner refer to the experience as "an important site of the imagination – a place that allowed people to think and act in ways that they might not allow themselves to do otherwise."[28]

---

27 Brinnin, *Sway of the Grand Saloon*, p. 393.
28 Rennella, Walton, "Planned Serendipity", p. 369.

Transformation

The use of themed rooms that were carefully and consciously constructed to alter one's state of mind can be understood as being instrumental on the rites of passage as described originally by Van Gennep. It is clear that, with reference to "the Sun King" and "minstrels' galleries", the themed rooms offered fantasies. Surely these fantasies would reinforce the sense that routine daily life was, even temporarily, being left behind. That some passengers, at least, perceived this unreality shows the comment of one traveler: "The blissful isolation of a cruise [...] [without] local, contemporary reality to disturb our detachment."[29]

The various rooms in first-class areas also each demanded different patterns of behavior and dress from their users. Passengers' intensified awareness of their appearance and demeanor is likely to have heightened the sense of liminality – the awareness of being in a removed world but one with potentiality and the possibility of transformation. One might wear sporting apparel for deck games, afternoon dresses or flannel trousers for the Writing Room, but white tie and tails or evening dresses for the dining room. Garments could be changed as many times as five times in each day. The regular adoption of different clothes would contribute to the changing state of mind, as would the corridors and portals between the rooms which would emphasize transitions through space and the need to change mood or behavior. Edington states, "Much time was spent changing clothes [...] Several of the liners has staircases that seem designed entirely for grand entrances [...] It was all highly time-consuming." [30] Photographs from the *Aquitania* indicate that staircases, long galleries and corridors were intended to be 'transgressive' spaces that allow the mind to adjust as one traverses the route; for example from the Edwardian Orangery-style Smoking Room Gallery to the Tudor-style Grill Room.[31] It is not insignificant that Van Gennep wrote much about the deep impact and significance of portals, doorways or thresholds. He states that "to cross the threshold is to unite oneself with a new world" and continues, "It will be noted that the rites carried out on the threshold itself are transition rites. 'Purifications' (washing, cleansing etc.) constitute rites of separation from the previous surroundings; there follow rites of

---

[29] Brinnin, *Sway of the Grand Saloon*, p. 500 (Parentheses added).
[30] Sarah Edington, *The Captain's Table: Life and Dining on the Great Ocean Liners,* London 2005, p. 16.
[31] See, for instance photographs of interiors from the *Aquitania*, UoLSC&A, D42/PR2/1/17/D118-128.

incorporation (presentation of salt, a shared meal etc.)."[32] In this context, perhaps the rituals of washing and dressing for dinner, sharing a pre-dinner drink in the purpose-designed reception rooms whilst being serenaded by a quintet from the ship's orchestra and making introductions at a dinner table, could all be considered 'rites' that are transformative.

Often, in a quite literal sense, other on-board activities enabled passengers to undergo 'transformations' and indulge the imagination. Ship games regularly demanded that travelers become 'other' in the service of humor and entertainment, as they called for people to wear fancy dress or to utilize ordinary objects for anachronistic purposes.[33] Some passengers even planned ahead with their costumes. For example, on one voyage were "two men dressed as Marilyn Monroe and Diana Dors, both massive. They must have brought the wigs with them specially for the occasion and you should have seen their huge red lipsticked mouths. They both look as though they are loving every minute."[34] On some of these occasions, wearing 'drag' and caricaturing the opposite sex or another race was probably overlaid with titillating frissons for both wearers and viewers.

For other, less fortunate, passengers the rites of separation and inclusion that are part of the liminal experience could be unpleasant. Commonly, emigrants in steerage watched as the mattresses that they had brought with them were thrown overboard on approaching New York, in case they contained lice and disease. Similarly, Peter Lawson's diary from his travels across the Atlantic on the *Etruria* in 1890 records "Was surprised to see all steerage passengers being collected together today and being examined by the doctor. Those who showed no sign of vaccination had to be re-done."[35] Such activities could also be considered as rites of separation and inclusion when crossing the Atlantic but were presumably overlaid with fear rather than amusement.

Wealthier passengers, however, often took interest and delight in the spectacle of some of the rites of separation and inclusion. For instance, "Staying up late or

---

[32] Van Gennep, *Rites of Passage,* p. 20 (Parentheses in the original).
[33] See, for example, photographs from the *Berengaria* that depict "A group of prize-winners showing the wonderful effect that can be obtained from odds and ends collected on the ship." These included: photographs of someone dressed as an Arab and 'blacked up', holding a melon; women dressed as men in the roles of a newspaper boy and a pageboy and men dressed as women in evening gowns. UoLSC&A, D42/PR2/1/33/F1-F2.
[34] Edington, *Captain's Table,* p. 43.
[35] Transcript of a diary written by Peter Lawson whilst travelling on the *Etruria* from Liverpool to New York, October 1890. 28 Oct 1890, p. 9. Merseyside Maritime Museum, Maritime Archives and Library, Liverpool, (MMM MAL) DX/2355.

rising early to watch the ship land at Plymouth became a ritual"[36] that many shared. Another diarist wrote vividly of the disembarkation and mail and luggage removal processes upon arrival in New York:

> "140 sacks, London to New York, Chicago and Shanghai and all over the world, made up and sealed. These having been sent off, the great bulk of passengers' luggage was hoisted by ropes, and only one portmanteau fell, some forty feet, into the water: instantly, a Boatswain's Mate on the Scotia jumped over after it and made it fast, and then was hauled out himself."[37]

He was clearly entranced by the spectacle of the arrival processes at New York. Similarly, an anonymous 'School Inspector' travelling across the Atlantic with Cunard from the United Kingdom to New York in the 1930s, also wrote with fascination about what one suggests are the rites of separation and inclusion. He even seems to make the link clearly that these are rites of passage in the sense that Van Gennep would propose by stating: "A real holiday should also afford a striking contrast to the life of ordinary workdays, and an ocean voyage emphasizes these contrasts in many unexpected details. There are, for instance, the interesting formalities before the journey begins, and at embarkation. At the start, there is a comfortable cabin in which to rest, or a deck from which to view the amusing bustle of departure [...] This dower of new impressions, whether it be of the first pale green valley, or of New York on the skyline, is given to the voyager, whatever his grade, if he be sensitive to receive it."[38] He described the sense of being secreted into a contained, heady world that is provided by ocean liner travel. On either side of this journey are pre-liminal and post-liminal rites such as embarkation and disembarkation; these stages, combined with the central journey, cumulatively comprise the liminal experience and all phases have an important function.

Many of the sights absorbed during the journeys whilst crossing the Atlantic were necessarily unique, and would contribute to the sense that the voyage was removing one from routine experiences: either temporarily or for ever. This sense of the uncanny as a result of being "betwixt and between"[39] is a key condition of

---

[36] Rennella, Walton, "Planned Serendipity", p. 375.
[37] Microfilm of a diary by Unknown Writer, travelling on the *S.S. Scotia* from Liverpool to New York, September-December 1874. 21 Sept 1874, p.25. UoLSC&A, D170.
[38] Booklet: *From the Old World to the New. Notes on an Atlantic Trip by a School Inspector,* c. 1930-2, p. 5 & p. 14 UoLSC&A, D42/PR12/5/26.
[39] This is the title of Turner's chapter "Betwixt and Between: The Liminal Period in Rites of Passage" in his 1967 *The Forest of Symbols.*

liminality. Victor Turner, whose seminal writings have laid much of the theoretical foundations for understandings of liminality and ritual, describes liminality as "'cunicular' – like being in a tunnel between the entrance and the exit."[40] The vista of the New York skyline looming up on the horizon would signal the end of the 'cunicular' experience and indicate the post-liminal stage. Diarists, whose accounts exist in the Merseyside Maritime Museum Archives in Liverpool, write of seeing whales, strange birds, butterflies and atmospheric conditions during their Atlantic crossings. In 1949, a lady wrote of her voyage to Canada on *R.M.S. Nova Scotia* saying, "There was a most lovely sunset […] In the evening a whale passed us, spouting regularly […] on the way out, we passed a school of porpoises, quite close to the ship. They were most lively, jumping out of the water continuously."[41] Even more dramatically, the *Scotia* diarist reports: "lightning ran along the deck. The First Officer was on duty and told me that the electricity played around his feet in a wonderful way; an Electric Ball, three feet in diameter was at the mast head; and Electric Balls that they called corpuscles, studded the booms and rigging."[42] The specificity employed by both writers signifies their wonderment and awe at natural phenomena that they had never before experienced. These sights are markers of the singularity of ocean travel. When observed for the first time, sights such as a nearby whale or rare, transient weather conditions can induce emotion and even appear mystical. In fact, such sights confirm Van Gennep's concept of the 'magico-religious' quality of the 'territorial passage' which is fundamental to liminality. Although, of course, Van Gennep first formulated his theories after working with tribal groups, liminality has now been adopted in fields such as Management Studies, Health Studies, Sexuality and, as is pertinent in this case, Tourism Studies[43].

Dining as Ceremonies

Meal times, as mentioned previously, are important stages within the rites of passage for all civilizations, and often act as rites of incorporation. Archival research demonstrates that passengers spend much time relating their experiences of dining on board Atlantic liners, and publicity materials from Cunard and other

---

40	Van Gennep, *Rites of Passage,* p. 15, note 1.
41	Transcript of a diary of a holiday to Canada by an Unnamed Teacher, possibly a Miss Davies, or Miss Anderson, on R.M.S. *Nova Scotia*, September 1949. 4 Sept 1949, p. 4 and 21 Sept 1949, p. 69 and 22 Sept 1949, p. 70. MMM MAL, DX/1868.
42	Diary by Unknown Writer, on the *S.S. Scotia,* 15 Sep 1874, p. 15.
43	Van Gennep, *Rites of Passage*, p. 69.

lines emphasize meals greatly. Van Gennep states that new residences are always 'taboo' until the appropriate rites have been conducted to lift that burden. These are the "rites of incorporation: libations, ceremonial visiting, consecration of various parts of the house, the sharing of bread and salt or a beverage, the sharing of a meal […] These ceremonies are essentially rites identifying the future inhabitants with their new residence."[44] Passengers on board ship have always used the dedicated periods for sharing meals and drinking beverages together in order to progress their relationships and to enhance their shipboard experiences. Although, of course, the tribal societies studied by Van Gennep differ so greatly to the clientele of ocean liners, the universality of eating and drinking to all societies links modern people to ancient. As Morgan writes, "Because ritual is an articulation of solidarity and table manners are a form of ritual, by extension, table conversation can be seen as ritual as well."[45]

The spectacle, quality and range of food and drink on superliners made the journeys memorable for passengers as archival collections attest. Much of the food and drink was exotic and almost all was spectacular and noteworthy. Even before the existence of 'superliners', the *S.S. Scotia* diarist wrote with evident delight at the opportunities afforded him to try new delicacies on offer at that time: "If thou wants to know our dinner, I may say there was Mock Turtle and Julienne soup, all sorts of joints, cutlets, stewed kidney, curries and roast Turkey, Chickens, Pies, Tarts, Puddings, puff pastry, three kinds of cheese, and dessert. This is the daily provision."[46] He wrote also of the novel spectacles surrounding dinner that were practiced by Cunard serving staff: "which is a sight for thee to see,- the row of Stewards: the clash as every cover is taken off at the same instant: and the rapidity with which the joints are cut up by the Stewards, and every one served […]"[47] "The waiters form a line all down the Saloon between the rows of tables, and the dishes are rapidly handed from one to the other without any running about: about 16 waiters to 8 tables, with 14 passengers to each."[48] Similar comments were made by passengers writing home from liners in the 1920s and 1930s: "The meals are a scream. Everything is served as a different course and they keep giving you clean plates and forks all the time […] We always have

---

[44] Van Gennep, *Rites of Passage*, p. 23f.
[45] Linda Morgan, "Diplomatic Gastronomy: Style and Power at the Table" in: *Food and Foodways: Explorations in the History and Culture of Human Nourishment*, 20 (2012), p. 146-166: 158.
[46] Diary by Unknown Writer, on the *S.S. Scotia*, 7 Sept 1874, p. 4.
[47] Ibid., 9 Sept 1874, p. 11.
[48] Ibid., 5 Sept 1874, p. 4.

cheese with every meal. They give you a lot to eat, but you can never eat more than a third of it because the other two-thirds are so very strange."[49]

Although, at first, even first-class passengers were expected to eat in large groups on long lines of tables with fixed chairs, by the early twentieth-century, Cunard had found it necessary to target the homogeneity of this experience. The *Scotia* diarist described the rigidity of former practices: "Two bells ring at 7; and one at 9 there is a second brew of tea: fair work. Breakfast [...] 8.30 [...] Lunch 12.0 (soup, meat, potato, stewed prunes, cheese) Dinner 4.0 [...] Tea 7.0 [...] Supper gong 9.0 [...] The cabin lights are put out at 11., and the lights in the berths at 11.30."[50] Instead of this earlier mandatory schedule, later liners like the *Aquitania* and *Mauretania* could facilitate relatively impromptu private parties with tailor-made menus and specially printed personal menu cards.[51] Increasingly, publicity material emphasized Cunard's ability to respond to individual taste or needs. They trumpeted that "the elasticity of hotel life as existent on the *Lusitania* or *Mauretania* is further exemplified by the dining arrangements [...] passengers can dine table d'hôte or à la carte, and that without extra charge. Furthermore, he who desires to dine his friends can do so, selecting his own menu etc."[52] The changing daily lists of activities like model 'horse' racing, 'housey-housey' (bingo) and quoits also indicates that, with the launching of superliners in the twentieth century, Cunard intended to offer a choice of events that could pander to individual tastes and thereby enable a sea passage to be-come more memorable. This option was clearly popular and was something replicated by other cruise lines: David Padmore, Purser on the Union-Castle Line recalled "A huge proportion of First-Class passengers didn't choose from the dinner menu but placed individual choices in advance with the Maître D'."[53]

It is clear from examining Cunard archival materials that the company was, very early on, conscious of the transformative effects of their dining rooms and meals, and great thought was given to planning menus. Archbold and McCauley criticize the menus of the *Titanic* in purist terms, for the inspiration was Ritz chef, Escoffier's, many courses and yet the meat of the 'removes' course tended to have no separate, individual garnish that enhances its character as one would find

---

[49] Rennella, Walton, "Planned Serendipity", p. 373.
[50] Diary by Unknown Writer, on the *S.S. Scotia*, 12 Sept 1874, p. 18.
[51] See for example, annotated menu from the *Aquitania* of 3 July 1939. UoLSC&A, D891/1/14. "Neptune's Farewell Dinner to the 'Old Shellback,' 'Mr. Stanley Bell', Otherwise known as 'Dingle'".
[52] *Cunard Line. Luxury Afloat.*
[53] Brinnin, *Sway of the Grand Saloon*, p. 85.

in France.[54] However, by the 1930s, the menus offered by the Cunard superliners were highly complex, exotic, sensory extravaganzas. The *Mauretania* dinner menus of 1930 offered delights such as "Roast Long Island Duckling [...] Bird's Nest Soup [...] Boar's Head Aux Pistachesm[...] Succotash,"[55] or "Potage de Volaille Creole [...] Crème Derby [...] Suprême of Boston Sole au Vin du Rhin [...] White Squash au Gratin."[56] Even breakfasts were complicated and gave passengers the chance to experience the food of the country to which they were travelling. British families might have been bemused and confounded by "Boiled Hominy [...] Maple Syrup and Waffles" whereas the American clientele might have thought the same about "Curried Prawns and Rice" or "Yarmouth Bloaters" for breakfast.[57]

From examining the menus, it is apparent that Cunard was aiming simultaneously to please customers from both sides of the Atlantic, as well as to provide them with unusual and diverting experiences. On occasions, the selections seem almost polarized and caricatured in their attempts to provide pan-Atlantic cuisine. A 1938 dinner on the *Queen Mary* offered "Consommé de Volaille au Riz [...] Homard Thermidor [...] Roast Turkey and Ham [...] Sauce Mousseline" but then the contrasting "Plum Pudding, Brandy Sauce, Mince Pies."[58] Both Homard Thermidor and Plum Pudding had been served on the fateful Titanic journey, therefore showing their staying power as delicacies esteemed by the Cunard White Star Line. The desire to satisfy simultaneously the native appetites of the two major consumer groups on board was also unchanging. As has been reported of the menus offered on Titanic, "It also represented a clear marriage of British and American food tastes, plum pudding sharing space with American ice-cream."[59] Magee states that, although food has been studied, there has been

---

[54] Archbold, McCauley, *Last Dinner on the Titanic*, p. 69. The authors state, "Here, the removes course has veered perilously close to the meat, potato, and vegetable main dish of a more middle-class dinner. Undoubtedly, these slight vulgarisations reflect the less-educated palates of the *Titanic's* predominantly Anglo-American clientele." (Rather than French).

[55] Dinner Menu from the *Mauretania*, Friday, 26 Sept 1930. UoLSC&A, D885/1/C.

[56] Dinner Menu from the *Mauretania*, Sunday, 28 Sept 1930. UoLSC&A, D885/1/G.

[57] Breakfast Menu from the *Mauretania*, Monday, 29 Sept 1930. UoLSC&A, D885/1/H.

[58] Dinner Menu from the *Queen Mary*, 20 Dec 1938. UoLSC&A, D891/1/12.

[59] Archbold, McCauley, *Last Dinner on the Titanic*, p. 96.

"relatively little on the rhetoric of food."[60] An examination of Cunard menus would prove enlightening in this respect.

Nostalgia

The same drive to please inhabitants of both continents on either side of the Atlantic is noticeable with shipboard entertainment. The 1938 booklet of licensed popular songs for communal singing on board the liners contains an idiosyncratic mix of American and Anglo-Irish music- almost all of which were nostalgic and even nationalistic. The titles include: Dear Little Shamrock; Home Sweet Home; The Irish Emigrant; John Brown's Body; Little Grey Home in the West; My Old Kentucky Home and Rose of Tralee.[61] It is clear that Cunard was aware of its role in the construction of national identity and the sentimentalizing of the homeland that its passengers leave behind, and even encouraged this. It is probable that Cunard was aware relatively early on that consolidating its position as a crucial force in the mass emigration of nationals would guarantee its place in public affection and thereby its continued economic success. However, the playing and singing of these songs occurred throughout all classes on board the liners, and was not just restricted to Steerage.

By 1946, Cunard further signaled consciousness of its role as a maker of history when the first guests of the *Queen Elizabeth* were provided with their own 'log book'. The recipient was left in no doubt that future historians and cruise aficionados would note their historic attendance on board this ship: "This, the first civilian voyage of the *Queen Elizabeth* from Southampton to New York (and contra wise), makes you a momentous passenger. We hope you have no objection. As you are thrust into this not unenviable position, we thought you would like to record a true navigational log of your own voyage."[62] Passengers were asked to understand and engage with the historicity of the company through their interaction with the log book. This is a relatively early example of the cultivation of brand identity and

---

[60] Richard M. Magee, "Food Puritanism and Food Pornography: The Gourmet Semiotics of Martha and Nigella" in: *Americana: the Journal of Popular Culture*, Vol. 6, (2007) Available at: http://www.americanpopularculture.com/journal/articles/fall_2007/ magee.htm.

[61] Booklet: *Popular Songs for Community Singing for use by Passengers Aboard Cunard White Star Liners*. May 1938 UoLSC&A, D891/1/25.

[62] *Elizabethan Log Book*, c. 1946, UoLSC&A, D647/13. Although R.M.S. *Queen Elizabeth* was launched in 1938 she did not serve as a passenger liner until 1946 as a result of being deployed as a troop ship during World War II.

loyalty and, in particular, the concept of its superiority; all of which was intended to reflect back on to the discerning consumer and his or her ego.

Figure 2: Cunard Menu Card – Gilded galleon scene.

Cunard also encouraged the collecting of menu cards by producing new examples for each meal and all with different imagery. The collections of individual passengers' journey souvenirs in the Cunard Archive at the University of Liverpool demonstrate that passengers frequently collated all the menu cards from their transatlantic crossings. By saving and storing such ephemera it seems likely that these passengers valued their elaborate meals and perhaps recalled them with nostalgia. The dining rooms of liners were always the most opulent and sensational spaces on board ship but Cunard did not neglect small touches such as these menu card designs. Each evening's menu exhibited a new art work and the images spoke their own story in terms of the messages that were being broadcast through them about Cunard and its place in history. In one week's collection of menu cards from the *Mauretania*, illustrations on the covers included: a print of London's Peter Pan Memorial, an illustration of Windsor castle, a gilded scene of an Elizabethan galleon-style sailing ship's arrival, examples of historic figureheads, a British fox-hunting scene, an heraldic lion and an illustration of an English country cottage garden in full bloom.[63]

Figure 3: Cunard Menu Card – Cottage Garden.

These romanticized images were, of course, designed and selected for use consciously, and it is interesting to speculate on their roles as signifiers to the largely British and North American passenger groups on board. For the British, scenes such as galleon ship arriving in port and the heraldic lion probably signified the long-held conception that the United Kingdom was a major international power with established traditions. For the North Americans, it is likely that the depiction of Windsor castle and the historic figureheads rehearsed beliefs about the cultural richness and superiority of the 'Old World', and the cottage garden could signify twee and romantic notions. Indeed, Cunard has been "accused of pandering to the American fantasy of The Old Curiosity Shop and Ye Olde England."[64] This is hardly surprising when one considers that a reason

---

[63] These can be seen in a folder of *Mauretania* menus, UoLSC&A, D885/1/A-J.
[64] Philip Dawson, *The Liner. Retrospective & Renaissance*, London 2005, p. 127.

behind many passengers' journeys was indeed to seek out the cultural artifacts of Europe. Renella and Watson refer to "literary Americans [who] went to meet with leading writers and thinkers of their day [...] visual artists [...] eager to learn from the example of the masters of Renaissance Italy or classical Greece, whose works were largely unavailable for close inspection in America." [65] It is possible that the imagery on the menu cards might perhaps be both a reflection of conventional beliefs about cultures and simultaneously fuelling such ideas. In any case, these menu cards are just a small example of the overwhelming signification at work throughout the interiors of superliners – most of which indulged travelers' attraction to nostalgic themes and imagery.

Interior Design

As well as providing visual pleasure with nostalgic and spectacular decorations, the interior design of the Cunard liners also showed much sensitivity to passengers' need to feel pampered as first-class customers. If at all possible, at least in the 'Cabin Class' grade, any signals of standardization were minimized or abandoned in architecture and interior design. As with the dining experience, there was also a drive to offer a personal, unique atmosphere in the design of the cabin accommodation with the advent of the superliners. The range of *Queen Mary*'s first or 'Cabin Class' sleeping environments were designed with many differences – particularly in terms of interior decoration. Photographs from about 1956 show that one cabin was notable for its African-style sculptures sited within alcoves and Chinoiserie-effect wallpaper; yet another, which was adjacent, featured contemporaneous Lucienne Day Calyx fabric and tub chairs.

---

[65] Rennella, Walton, "Planned Serendipity", p. 369 (Parentheses added).

Figure 4: Chinoiserie Room with African Sculptures.

This willingness by Cunard to provide individually-styled cabins was "probably rooted in the belief that a ship must herself provide a greater sense of diversity and individuality to those aboard for a crossing of five days or more than is expected of a hotel, where one is free to come and go at will and to experience its surrounding vicinity as a natural extension of its own facilities."[66]

Also significant in the list of reasons for sanctioning the design of non-standard cabins is that Atlantic travel, like many forms of tourism, "involves a fantasy of achieved upward mobility, and it has favored models of the aristocratic good life."[67] In 1956, when these photographs were taken by esteemed Liverpool photographer, Stewart Bale, the United Kingdom had only recently ended rationing after the Second World War and it was uncommon for people to have access to newly-fashioned satinwood and full carpeting as in these images. Also, the connotations of objects such as the African-type sculptures were still that they were of avant-garde, glamorous and esoteric taste. This is despite the fact that British Modernist sculptors like Barbara Hepworth and Henry Moore had been inspired by such imagery as far back as in the 1920s as a result of their studies of original tribal artifacts in the British Museum's collection and because of their

---

[66] Dawson, *The Liner*, p. 83.
[67] Ibid., p. 147.

contact with artists like Picasso and Braque. It is significant that, "by 1900, more first-class Americans were traveling back to their 'Old Countries' than there were first-class Europeans sailing to the United States."[68] This latter statistic suggests that the American passengers wished to reconnect with Europe- or at least with a concept of a cultivated Europe that they had formed over years and from a distance. With the assistance of such decorative features in the staterooms and public areas across the superliners, assumptions of European history and culture were confirmed – at least by superliner travel – even if the reality of Europe itself in the post-Second World War period would often disappoint.

Figure 5: Bedroom with Lucienne Day 'Calyx' Fabric.

The interiors of the liners certainly did not disappoint. They conjured up various fantasies: for example, of an ideal English country house. A Cunard brochure of around 1907 describes the luxurious finishes that were about to be unveiled with the launch of *Lusitania*:

> "The First Cabin Smoke Room [...] is in the Georgian style [...] There are two open fireplaces and the walls and pillars are in Italian walnut

---

[68] Anonymous, "Pioneers of the Sea. The Story of the Cunard Line: The Super-Ships" in: *Look and Learn Magazine,* 483 (1971), p. 4-6: 6.

with carvings after Grinlin [sic] Gibbons in lime tree. The First Class Lounge and Music Room [...] Above the fireplace proper is a classic picture in enamel, the largest enamel ever made. The picture is framed in silver and between the frame and the space between picture and the marble pillars is filled with gold mosaic work."[69]

Much detail is provided about the materials and their quality. In this brochure, as well as in countless other Cunard publicity documents, extensive descriptions of features, workmanship and decorative effects are provided. Even in Cunard brochures or reports without images to pique one's interest, the prose is always vivid and aids the imagination. Writers employed by Cunard emphasize repeatedly the historical precedents of the company, the accuracy of interior design replications and the quality of craftsmanship throughout the liners. The promotional materials, and the fixtures and fittings on board the liners offered various nostalgic blends of imagery. As Frow explains, this satisfied a need inherent in many travelers: "nostalgia for lost patterns of everyday life and for auratic objects that seem to be inherently meaningful 'surely forms a powerful motivation even for fairly high cultural tourism.'"[70] Therefore Cunard's success as a brand could, at least in part, be a result of its willingness to supply "lost patterns of everyday life" and "auratic objects." Cunard realized that they already had what is known in today's cruise industry as a valuable brand identity [...] These (ships) were British institutions, the daughters of the Clyde, Tyneside and Belfast-Queen's Island where they were built, and of their Empire home ports."[71] In the context of Frow's remarks then, the superliners of the first half of the twentieth century could be read as a necessary respite to modernity and the alienating Modernist environments of Europe and North America with their absence of restorative and reassuring signs of 'heritage' and 'stability'. One suggests that it is partly the presence of heavy signification throughout the liners that enables liminal experience for passengers to occur. Indeed, as Berger states, "Cruise ships are paradise for semioticians since they are, in effect, sign systems – full of signs designed to convey certain meanings and feelings to passengers."[72]

---

[69] Brochure: *Cunard Line. Royal Mail Express Turbine Steamer 'Lusitania', 32,000 Tons.*, c. 1907 D885/1/A-J, D163/4.
[70] John Frow, "Tourism and the Semiotics of Nostalgia" in: *October*, 57 (1991), p. 123-151: 133.
[71] Dawson, *The Liner*, p. 127.
[72] Arthur A. Berger, 'Sixteen Ways of Looking at an Ocean Cruise: A Cultural Studies Approach' in: Ross K. Dowling (Ed.) *Cruise Ship Tourism*. Oxfordshire, Cambridge/Mass 2006, p. 124-128: 127.

One argues that the result of the meanings and feelings is that the passengers experience the liminal.

Figure 6: Tourist Class Smoking Room.

Although some might counter that the uplifting signification was only available to the moneyed few, it should be noted that even in the lowest-grade areas on the *Franconia II*, for example, photographs record that plush, themed designs proliferate. For example, the Tourist Class Smoking Room contained an Inglenook fireplace, oak-effect beams on the ceiling, leaded light windows and pewter tankards.

The effect created is, one imagines, of the appearance of a sixteenth-century English public house. The First Class equivalent does not differ in terms of the extremity of the theming offered, but only in that it more personalized: it is more like an individual's room in a Victorian country house.

Figure 7: First Class Smoking Room.

In the latter, the Smoking Room contains a china cabinet, complete with ornaments, a Victorian-style open fireplace and a mantle clock. The effect is that the room is traditional, comfortable and intimate and it offers a narrative. It is a space where one who had never before experienced the reality of a Victorian country house in England could enjoy spending time and imagining what it would be like to inhabit such a room permanently as an owner. The subliminal messages that differ between the two spaces might be simply that the fantasy suggested by the Tourist Class space was the more communal experience of 'the pub', whereas that offered to First Class passengers was more intimate and of 'the home'. Both were particular to the liner and often very different to life known to the passengers on shore, and both would have contributed to the ocean crossing being an occasion when the traveler encounters a liminal experience – an "interstructural situation [...] with its scarcity of jurally sanctioned relationships [...] People can 'be themselves,' it is frequently said, when they are not acting institutionalized roles."[73] In either the First or Tourist Class Smoking Rooms, a passenger could enjoy individuality and a sense of self, and fulfill his "quest for an experience of signs."[74]

The link between nostalgia-inducing signage and the liminal experience on board superliners was understood clearly by the Cunard Public Relations department. In an advertising brochure entitled *The New Art of Going Abroad*, the writer emphasized that the protected hedonistic space of the superliner would induce a liminal experience. He wrote, "the transatlantic week, from pier to pier, can be – should be – one of the gala weeks of life [...] of those rare and preciously perfect intervals, snatched from the grudging gods."[75] Although littered with hyperbole, the text does highlight the significance for the journey of being between the dock piers – the "perfect interval" – which is key to a liminal encounter. The piers function to the writer as thresholds which frame the experience, in the manner that internal entrances or corridors act, as it has here been argued, to demarcate states of mind. Other writers also focus attention on the point at which the ship and the land are separated and, again, imply that this aids the liminal experience: "They walk over the first-class gang-plank, are greeted by a band, are waited upon, deferred to, bowed to, coddled, and the rest."[76] Although the entire Atlantic passage can be referred to as the liminal stage which is framed by the 'pre-liminal' and 'post-liminal' stages on the land, within the central liminal stage can be observed small versions of the cycle too. The uses of the spaces on board, such as doors and corridors, and interaction with the rituals such as communal meal taking are, themselves, miniature versions of the total cycle that is in operation. As Van Gennep observed, "in certain ceremonial patterns where the transitional period is sufficiently elaborated to constitute an independent state, the arrangement is reduplicated."[77] In other words, the cycle of rites of passage can, within itself, contain smaller cycles of rites of passage. So, in between the experience contained within the large thresholds of the piers, there are other thresholds which also frame liminal experiences.

As has been argued in this chapter that there is a potential for a liminal experience on board the superliners, Brinnin also implies that the author of Cunard's promotional The New Art of Going Abroad is suggesting this likelihood. When discussing this pamphlet, Brinnin states,

---

[73] Turner, *Forest of Symbols*, p. 101.
[74] Culler, "The Semiotics of Tourism", p. 9.
[75] Quoted in: Brinnin, *Sway of the Grand Saloon*, p. 463 (Italics in the original).
[76] Ibid., p. 437.
[77] Thomassen, "Revisiting Liminality", p. 11.

> "The social ton and spiritual aura of both the *Mauretania* and the *Berengaria* were, it is clear, comprehensible and communicable. But in the case of the *Aquitania* an evanescent, almost subliminal soupçon of distinctiveness defied the rude adequacy of words [...] The meaning lay between the lines [...] and the burden of it seemed to be that she was a ship of such quintessential sophistication that only life as it was lived in the stately homes of England could provide a serviceable metaphor."[78]

Without using the word 'liminal', Brinnin observes that the brochure promises a transformational experience on board the Cunard ocean liners, and notes that the passenger is offered a themed, fantastical experience which could be felt even as alternative reality.

Indeed, the brochure writer's text reads rather as an advertisement for a Disney attraction than an ocean passage. He offers a distinct experience or – in contemporary words – a 'lifestyle':

> "You may [...] sleep in a bed depicting one ruler's fancy, breakfast under another dynasty altogether, lunch under a different flag and furniture scheme, play cards or smoke, or indulge in music under three other monarchs, have your afternoon cup of tea in a verandah which is essentially modern and cosmopolitan, and return to one of the historical periods experienced earlier in the day for your dinner in the evening at which meal, whatever may be the imperial style or the degree of colonial simplicity, you will appear in very modern evening dress."[79]

This contrast can be seen in the *Aquitania* Dining Room and the *Aquitania* Soda Fountain in Garden Lounge.

---

[78] Brinnin, *Sway of the Grand Saloon*, p. 447.
[79] Ibid., p. 394.

Figure 8: Aquitania Dining Room Ceiling.

Figure 9: Aquitania Soda Fountain Garden Lounge.

For an early twentieth-century document, the suggestion that the consumer is able to enter and exit realities via themed environments on board ship is surprising. In the postmodern society of today it is quite usual to encounter such 'hyperrealities'[80] as a result of visiting places like Disney's Epcot theme park in Florida, in which one may eat lunch in 'Paris' and dinner in 'Fez' but this brochure, remarkably, was written circa 1912.

There is an uncanny similarity in the writer's vocabulary to the often-quoted definition of Postmodernism by philosopher Lyotard. He defined Postmodernism, as "Eclecticism [...] one listens to reggae, watches a western, eats McDonald's food for lunch and local cuisine for dinner, wears Paris perfume in Tokyo and 'retro' clothes in Hong Kong."[81] Of course, such eclectic activities are possible as a result of multiple lifestyle choices in contemporary society; indeed, the advanced consumer society of which we are a part today has necessitated such freedom. However, in the early twentieth century, a vast array of options – be it in terms of clothes, food, travel or social activities- were not generally expected and were certainly not demanded – even by the average first-class passenger. This is one reason why it is possible to argue that the effect of pursuing all these different activities in one day was a liminal experience for the passenger in the first half of the twentieth century.

Having such a plethora of choice would, in itself, contribute towards making the experience liminal and not just memorable or special. As mentioned, choice was liberating and enabled passengers to escape routine strictures. This escapism is essential for enabling the liminal state. Even first-class passengers would not normally expect within a compressed space to confront a "Pompeian" swimming pool and then, a few feet further, a dining room that evoked Versailles, or an Art Deco cocktail bar. In the face of such visual stimulation along with evocative themes, a great sense of liberation and euphoria would undoubtedly comprise the first-class experience on board these superliners. Berger calls this "'carnivalization' [...] There was, unquestionably, a sense of joyousness and celebration that was found, Bakhtin explains, in Mediaeval carnival periods. So that was an element of the appeal of ocean cruises [...] There is also an element of fantasy involved in cruising and, perhaps, a mythic element to it."[82] In one day, the passengers' experience of foods from around the world, varied leisure

---

[80] This phrase is linked, amongst others, to the philosopher, Jean Baudrillard, who observed it to be a key characteristic of Postmodernism that emerged simultaneously with the movement.

[81] Jean-François Lyotard, *The Postmodern Explained. Correspondence 1982-1985*, Minneapolis 1993, p. 8.

[82] Arthur A. Berger, "Sixteen Ways of Looking at an Ocean Cruise", p. 125. With this in mind, it is interesting to note the name of the contemporary American cruise line company, Carnival Cruise Lines.

activities and themed visual environments would induce this sense of the carnivalesque, the fantastic and the mythic.

Earlier, this article discussed the issue of choice as being important and, indeed, novel at the time. The opportunities to arrange private dining, to personalize menus, to select from a range of individual cabins,[83] to collect menus and record an individualized passage in the 'log book' were highlighted. Indeed, it is asserted that having choice in itself contributed greatly to the experience becoming liminal. The fact that spaces throughout the ships were themed also made it appear that the traveler had options, as he or she could ascertain which spaces on board would make them comfortable or, in other words, which expressed the person's identity most effectively. The consciousness of personal identity is well understood as a burgeoning characteristic of postmodern life, but would have been rarer in the first half of the twentieth century before 'lifestyle choices' were conceptualized. Time spent on board liners crossing the Atlantic would have been very liberating as a result of the multiple options for every part of the day.

The importance of choice was seen by Cunard to be highly important: not only within individual liners, but as a fundamental philosophy underpinning the company. Cunard was highly conscious of the need to develop itself as a brand and, within that, to offer sub-brands that each represented different things to the consumer. This was reported within the company to the employees via the newspaper, Cunard News: "It is common knowledge that the modern liner must be tailor-made for her trade. Each and every trade has its own special needs to be constantly watched and translated into ships that will exactly fulfil those needs."[84] Cunard seem to have developed the concept that their ships were individual components of a large whole, but also that the components each performed different functions. Again, to the company workers, the management explained, "All the ships of the group, small and large, are fitted for their own particular job. Together in their different ways, they contribute to the unity of the team, and are part of the Cunard Associated Lines and yet retain their all-important individuality. Here, surely, is that flexibility which is one of the many sources of real strength."[85] Today, this is a well-understood business and branding concept with applications in most industries, and has much relevance especially in the

---

[83] On the *Aquitania*, some suites were named after historic famous painters, such as Thomas Gainsborough (1727-1788), and reproductions of their key works hung within the rooms. Undoubtedly, some passengers would identify more with one artist than another and this would reinforce the ego positively.

[84] Anonymous, "Bermuda Calls Next Winter" in: *Cunard News* (110th Anniversary Issue) 3 (1950), p. 1, UoLSC&A, D42/PR9/2.

[85] Ibid.

cruising trade,[86] but was an innovative mode of thinking in 1950, when the above comments were written.

Advertisements for the clientele articulate this approach to the brand and emphasized choice: "The initiate takes pains to choose the ship that suits him or her as carefully as a prima-donna chooses a gown or an actress her background."[87] Of course, the assumption is that the crass uninitiated might choose a ship based on less 'worthy' criteria: for example, on price. Choosing an Atlantic passage on the basis of price, rather than how it aided in the construction of one's sense of identity, would clearly impact upon the individual's ego and thereby probably reduce the intensity of the liminal experience.

In fact, the reputation and standard of the selected Atlantic liner had a very significant impact upon the status of not only the individual passenger, but also of the backing nation, which is, of course, much of the reason behind the notorious Blue Riband competition.[88] As Green states, "The splendour of the ships became a matter not just of commercial pride but of national prestige [...] Governments were frequently persuaded to subsidize luxury liners far beyond their economic value."[89] There was much to be gained for the parent nation if their ship was the most esteemed in the world for beauty, size, facilities or speed. Indeed, some of the early twentieth-century publicity brochures use the tactic of displaying, in graphic clarity, the lengths of the new ships in comparison to the length and height statistics of the world's iconic structures, thereby emphasizing both the size of the ships and their correlation as icons.

---

[86] Dowling states of contemporary cruise lines: "Cruise companies are increasingly promoting and positioning their brand names to enable customers to identify the products as competition grows... For example, Carnival Cruise Lines associates the characteristics of 'fun' ships with its brand name, while the 'QE2' suggests a more exclusive image and unique experience." Ross K. Dowling, "The Cruising Industry" in: Ross K. Dowling (Ed.), *Cruise Ship Tourism.* Cambridge/Mass. 2006, p. 3-18: 3.
[87] Quoted in Brinnin, *Sway of the Grand Saloon*, p. 444.
[88] The Blue Riband was a competition to ascertain which ocean liner could cross the Atlantic with the fastest average speed. The formal award of a trophy for success in this endeavor was offered from 1935 however the unofficial competition had been in existence since around 1910.
[89] Green, "Floating Palaces".

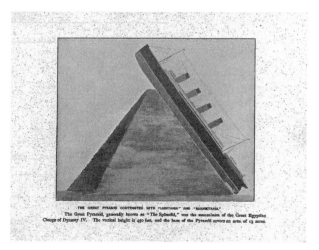

Figure 10: Pyramid, 1907 Cunard Brochures.

The government subsidies would have helped greatly to effect the production of these mammoth vessels with pretensions to vie with structures like the Eiffel Tower. It is interesting to note that even ordinary employees of the company were quite clear about the British government's sponsorship of Cunard's line, were proud of this fact and showed great employee loyalty. It was related by a diarist that

> "I stood with the First Officer [...] He was a very nice intelligent man, had been 25 years with Cunard, and was proud of the service. He said they didn't allow swearing on board, and in port, send all the men to Church accompanied by Officers [...] Thus the Cunards have carried the mails for 35 years and never lost a letter or a passenger. The subsidy is £75,000 per annum."[90]

Even in times of economic hardship, such as during the Great Depression in the 1930s, the British, French, and American governments still found it necessary to subsidize the superliners that transported passengers across the Atlantic. The reputations of the supporting nations were advanced considerably when progress in some aspect or other was reported from within the liner trade. The benefit to the national economies was also great in terms of revenue from business, shopping and tourism, not to mention the impact of the liners on the progress of

---

[90] Diary by Unknown Writer, travelling on the *S.S. Scotia*, p. 9-10.

the Second World War.[91] However, this article has been concerned with impact of Atlantic travel on the individual and, of that being deep and lasting, there is a vast array of evidence.

Conclusion

This article has shown that the person "who steps on shore down the gangway is not the same person who embarked a few short weeks before. The Atlantic holiday deals generously with its devotee; it gives him permanent recollections of happy hours. Like Ulysses, it makes him 'a part of all that he has met,' and it weaves indelible colors into the fabric of his memories."[92] Being framed by the gangplanks on either side of the journey, the Atlantic crossing can be, and often was, a liminal experience which licensed passengers to find concealed but essential parts of their identities. They could relish the 'carnivalesque' joyous microcosm of the liner in which normal patterns of behavior and responsibilities could be forgotten temporarily. This state was stimulated and sustained by the themed environment and plentiful food and leisure activities which were provided by the ship designers and staff. As Turner writes of the liminal stage, "the phenomena and processes of mid-transition […] paradoxically expose the building blocks of culture."[93] We revert back to a more primal state when the body, instinct and emotional responses are to the fore – as when travelling by superliner with all its facilities and visual splendors. This explains why, for several generations of passengers who crossed the Atlantic Ocean by liner, "we are, psychologically, back in the Garden of Eden and […] there is a paradisiacal element to cruising."

---

[91] The issue of the Atlantic liners and war is outside the realm of this chapter but is covered elsewhere in this book. However, one may note that Winston Churchill credited the Cunard liners with shortening the length of the Second World War. See John Maxtone-Graham, *The Only Way To Cross: The Golden Era of the Great Atlantic Liners*, London, New York 1972.
[92] *From the Old World to the New*, p. 19.
[93] Turner, *Forest of Symbols*, p. 110.

4. Frocks versus Guns: Sailing the South Atlantic in the 1982 Falklands/Malvinas Conflict[1]

Jo Stanley

Introduction

The South Atlantic voyages revealed in this chapter were a complex mix of bellicosity and tourism. Their stories offer insights into the way 'femininity' was unexpectedly presented and changed on what might have been expected to be hyper-masculine wartime troopships.[2] In 1982 troops and civilian crew sailed from a flag-waving UK to what Britons call the Falklands Islands and Argentineans call Las Malvinas. Voyagers were concerned with ice cream and beer as well as weapons. Military operations were planned in liners' hairdressing salons. Helicopter pads replaced swimming pools. Ships' decks normally more accustomed to large dollops of Ambre Solaire sunscreen were instead slippery with WD40 lubricant and Avcat aviation fuel.[3] Romance and sex, cross-dressing and homophilia/phobia were an integral (if small and overlooked) part of the story of voyages to and from a ten-week conflict that had unprecedented media

---

[1] This article is dedicated to the women and LGBT people involved in that war. I thank the many people who have helped me with this essay, particularly those who worked so hard to put me in touch with GBT men who'd sailed in the conflict. I also appreciate John Johnson-Allen, Ted Scaplehorn and Graham Wallace for suggestions and technical advice. Most of all I am grateful to my interviewees, some of whom prefer to be anonymous. The term 'Falklands/Malvinas' irritates some British participants who see it as 'The Falklands Conflict.' But as an act of respect to both sides I have used the term 'Falklands/Malvinas' and interchanged it with 'Malvinas/Falklands' to indicate there were two parties involved with two opposed ideas of the islands (which the Argentineans call the Malvinas).

[2] My work on women at sea in wartime reveals a somewhat different picture of troopships in the Second World War, where women passengers (female crew were rare after 1942) might be outnumbered by 4,000 to one by male troops and expected to take a much more traditional position: mending men's socks and acting as acquiescent eye candy while accepting 'masculine' attitudes such as the denial of fear.

[3] John L. Muxworthy, *The Great White Whale Goes to War,* London 1982, p. 164. WD40 is a multipurpose water-displacing spray used in most British households; people use it free jammed locks in doors. Avcat is aviation carrier turbine fuel.

attention. Ships had an extraordinarily gendered send-off: girlfriends on Southampton docks bared their breasts in farewell, throwing off bras and blouses with no public outcry. 'Our boys' (not 'our people') were welcomed home in scenes so festive that it was like 1945 Victory in Europe Day celebrations.

Figure 11: QE2 in the Falklands: The Neptune Ceremony takes on a new form when hundreds of troops are involved. (Right: Nursing Sister Jane Yelland).

The War that Wasn't

The ten-week-long Falklands Conflict / Guerra de las Malvinas was an expression both of long-standing but intermittently-expressed Argentinean claims for sovereignty and of anomalous British assumptions that the islands[4] were British overseas territory, not least because the 1,800 islanders considered themselves British. It's called a conflict, not a war, because no declaration of war was actually made. The conflict arose because on 19 March 1982 Argentinean forces suddenly crossed the 480 kilometers of ocean and invaded 'las Malvinas' to finally establish Argentina's sovereignty. Failing dictator General Leopoldo Galtieri annexed the territory in a bid to win public support by appealing to nationalist sentiment. Failing UK prime minister Margaret Thatcher, mobilizing nationalist

---

[4] The disputed territories also included South Georgia and the South Sandwich Islands.

sentiment, retaliated by sending a Task Force 13,000 kilometers to 'our Falklands'. The British aim was to retake the islands by sending in commandos in landing craft, fast patrol boats, zodiacs and mini-submersibles the following month.

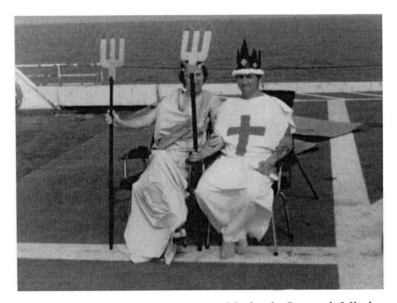

Figure 12: Neptune ceremony on Norland: Steward Mimi poses as Queen Amphitrite.

After naval and air battles, the British Task Force landed at San Carlos Water on 21 May. The two sides fought on land, until the Argentineans surrendered on 14 June 1982 after 74 days. Conflict resolution expert Nora A. Femenia plausibly contends that it was not a simple conflict over sovereignty. Rather it was about the two sides seeking to satisfy emotional needs for affirmation and national self-esteem, which necessitated utilizing (if necessary, creating) a dramatic predicament to enable this to development.[5]

Because the islands are so far from Britain, vast amounts of troops and equipment needed to be transported long distances and by amphibious assault and had to be enabled by the most intensive naval action since the 1940s. So "The Biggest Armada since World War Two", according to the London-based red-top press, set sail. Much depleted by defense cuts, Britain's Royal Navy no longer had sufficient

---

[5] Nora A. Femenia, *National Identity in Times of Crisis: The scripts of the Falklands-Malvinas War,* New York 1996, especially p. 3.

ships for the task, let alone at such short notice. Therefore 52 of the 100-strong fleet were Merchant Navy vessels STUFT (Ships Taken Up From Trade).[6] Over 20,000 military and naval men were sent by sea, not air. So too was all the machinery of war, and the stuff of life to support participants. For example, among the *Uganda* supplies were seven tons of ice cream and seventeen tons of potatoes.

Between 4,000 and 7,000 merchant seafarers were involved.[7] At least half were on Royal Fleet Auxiliary ships, which service Royal Navy vessels, and some ferry crew had experience of transporting British troops to and from Germany. Others were on unhedonistic tankers, cargo vessels and tugs. The several thousand Merchant Navy crew and officers on passenger ships, who are mainly the focus of this article, were far more accustomed to making pleasure trips around Europe and the world's more urban tourist attractions, such as New York and Bangkok. Their metaphorical baggage was definitely vacation-oriented, and fun-focused. The habitat of these hosts culturally opposed the military habitus of their guests.

It cannot be said that that particular area of sea *per se* was significant to the voyagers; for all that Britons had been there for over a century because of the islands' militarily strategic location and the whaling possibilities. The much more important point is that the South Atlantic was so far away, so unknown to most seafarers. Cunard and P&O passenger ships usually went across the Atlantic, to the Pacific, and 'around the world', which actually meant around popular parts of the globe, not the South Atlantic. For merchant seafarers this far-off location meant three main things. First, that voyages were long, around 40 days. "It felt like a very long way away indeed" Kevin Smith, a gay steward on the *Canberra* Second, ruefully remarked. Those waters were traversed with geo-political innocence. Like the troops, until the conflict most merchant seafarers had never heard of the Falklands. "We thought they were somewhere off northern Scotland," like the Hebrides or Orkneys, laughed *Norland* gay steward Roy 'Wendy' Gibson.[8] And no-one had any aid such as a "*Lonely Planet*" guidebook. Third, the vessels used were not necessarily suited to such cold conditions.

---

[6] John Johnson-Allen, *They Couldn't Have Done It Without Us*, Woodbridge 2011, p. 20. Other experts claim there were 49 Merchant Navy ships.

[7] Johnson-Allen in *They Couldn't Have* contends there were 7,000. Lawrence Freedman, who wrote *The Official History of the Falklands Campaign, Vols. 1 and 2*, London 2005, offers the 4,000 estimate, based on those awarded the South Atlantic Medal.

[8] Author's interview with Wendy Gibson, 2 May 2012. The exception is mainly those few who'd been to the Falklands on R.F.A. (Royal Fleet Auxiliary) ships serving the British base there.

Figure 13: "One of our war's leading characters": Roy 'Wendy' Gibson at the Falklands.

Everyone had expected diplomats to end the conflict long before the Task Force reached even halfway there. Therefore crews were not prepared for the harsh winter they found at their destination. (Britain's Ministry of Defence signaled ships that supermarket chain "Tesco are offering free thermal underwear to ladycrewpersons and embarked QARNNS [nurses]. Ships with women [on board are] to send total number in three groups for sizes small/medium/large." The goods never arrived).[9] Crew made do, and were sometimes supplied with company-monogrammed fleeces.

---

[9] Muxworthy, *The Great White Whale*. QARNNS stands for Queen Alexandra's Royal Naval Nursing Service. Naval, not army or air force, nurses went out on these ships as 'passengers' like the troops.

That far South Atlantic and those Unheard-of Malvinas

In what non-tourist zone did this extraordinary phenomenon take place? Although the Atlantic Ocean's 82 million square kilometers are the most intensely travelled waters of the earth's four oceans, the South Atlantic is scarcely used by vacationers. This is not least because since 1914 the Panama Canal enabled vessels going east and west to avoid venturing far south round the infamous Cape Horn, the site of so many shipwrecks. Antarctica and the 700 under-populated rural and rugged Malvinas/Falklands Islands are mainly, now, the focus of recreational voyagers. They go there because of what the Antarctic Convergence – the meeting point of warm, sub-Antarctic waters and the colder Antarctic waters that flow north – has created: distinctive and prolific wildlife. This area of the Atlantic is known for its unspoiled wildness, clear light and abounding rare birds and animals, from elephant seals to Black-chinned Siskins and Magellanic Oystercatchers.

Britain is the main European country associated with the area, even though few Britons knew the islands existed until 1982. That knowledge came from arguments about the Falklands Islands rights to self-determination, which Argentina refused to recognize. The war occurred because Argentina invaded the Falkland Islands. It was a conflict that, for the late twentieth century, was extraordinarily sea-based, as well as extraordinarily charged by a British patriotism that many thought no longer existed and that was utilized by Thatcher to distract attention from domestic issues. Indeed, journalism expert Robert Harris held that the media converted the events into an egotistical "national drama with all the cathartic effect of a Shakespearean tragedy," where, for examples, storms were "grandiosed out of all proportion."[10] Certainly the heroic British bulldog spirit was evoked as never before since the Second World War, except in B-movies. Indeed, some participants read the conflict like the black-and-white war movies they had, as children, seen on television. But this time it was in color. And they, bizarrely, now found they were acting in it instead of watching a potted and glorifying version of it through a small square of T.V. glass in their living rooms at home.

---

[10] Robert Harris, *Gotcha: The media, the government and the Falklands crisis*, London 1983, p. 146.

Figure 14: ways of going to war. (RSM means Regimental Sergeant Major).

Surreality at Sea

"It was surreal, really" is a phrase merchant seafarers repeatedly used for describing the situation. On the *Canberra*, purser Lauraine Mulberry wrote in her diary about the incongruity of fine dining while a string quartet was playing, yet being involved in conversations about the cold storage of corpses and then, the next minute, about W.B. Yeats' poetry. The ship, she wrote, was full of "sharp contrast: warship/cruise ship; helicopter pad/swimming pool, operating theatre/nightclub. This is so totally real and yet surreal."[11] There was the frivolous façade of the cruise, yet men were gearing themselves for fighting, killing and even dying. The battle of us versus them (that is Brits v Argies) was colored by the rhetoric of sexism and racism, with some British troops conceiving of

---

[11] Johnson-Allen, *They Couldn't Have,* p. 36, citing Lauraine Mulberry's typescript.

themselves as "real men" and "righteous warriors for justice" against "pansy dagoes". Yet ironically those "real men" also sunbathed, camped around in frocks during on-board shows, were capable of being tearful, and were often moved by the extreme youth and vulnerability of some Argentinean conscripts.

Figure 15: Paratroopers sunbathing en route to the Falklands on North Sea ferry Norland.

Songs sung on board show how much tourism and war co-existed (although they fail to reveal the tensions around gender). Rod Stewart's *We Are Sailing* is the standard cruise song on recreational voyages. But these war trips' musical soundtracks included Meatloaf's punk-Wagnerian *Bat out of Hell*. Seemingly it was as central to war build-up as *The Ride of the Valkyrie* was to the 'Let's-bomb-Vietnam-to-smithereens' sequence in the movie *Apocalypse Now*. Voyages were also accompanied by sentimental numbers from the First and Second World War such as *Keep the Home Fires Burning*, as well as Monty Python's wry *Always Look on the Bright Side of Life*. War-ready passengers alternated The Beatles' cheery *Here Comes the Sun* with invented anti-Argentinean pastiches of the main song from the contemporary musical *Evita*. The Fleet Air Arm's version was:
"Don't cry for me, Argentina
The truth is, we will defeat you.

And with our Sea Harrier
We'll zap your [aircraft] carrier."[12]

Three decades later, significantly, this *mélange* of tourism and combat, and femininities' temporary connections with masculinities continues to be occluded by several discourses. Macho glory is, as in the 30th anniversary of those war voyages in summer 2012, still celebrated by many combatants and armchair combatants. Naval and military historians continue enduring debates about naval strategy. Political historians and pub customers discuss of the moral correctness of the war, especially as substantial oil deposits have recently been uncovered.[13] Hugh Bicheno, the revisionist historian of the conflict, jokes that "Never in the field of human conflict has so much been written by so many about so few."[14] And never, too, in recent conflict, have so many women and camp gay men (meaning male homosexuals who perform an overtly hyper-feminine, ironic social role) among the participants in war been so omitted by so many writers.[15] The role and practices of these overlooked seafarers and the shifts of femininities and masculinities on merchant ships were not discussed at the time and they

---

[12] Rick Jolly, *The Red and Green Life Machine*, Liskeard 2007, p. 59.

[13] Some critics charged that access to mineral reserves was actually the main but secret reason for the war. See http://www.guardian.co.uk/theguardian/2010/feb/27/falklands-oil-dispute-ian-jack, accessed 23 May 2012.

[14] Hugh Bicheno, *Razor's Edge: The Unofficial History of the Falklands War*, London 2007, p. 330.

[15] There are only two books on British women in the conflict. Journalist Jean Carr tellingly entitled her book *Another Story: Women and the Falklands War*, London 1984, when she wrote about the land-based wives and widows of combatants. It is indeed a very different story, not about ships. Nursing Sister Nicci Pugh's recent book, *White Ship, Red Crosses*, Ely 2010, is as the writer says, a 'simple story' about nurses on the *Uganda*, rather than a gender-aware analysis. War artist Linda Kitson wrote some autobiographical text in her *The Falklands War: A visual diary*, London 1982. The main place where the deaths of three Falklands women, victims of friendly fire, is recorded is in Lucy Beck's blog: http://www.ppu.org.uk/falklands/falklands 3.html, accessed 13 Mar 2012. Googling produces just two references to homosexuality in the Falklands conflict, both fictional, apart from the soldiers' accounts included here. Mel Keegan's thriller, *Ice, Wind and Fire,* 1999, features stable gay partners Alex and Greg (a photojournalist and a war-reporter) whose history is that they had met in the Falklands. The book is mainly set in Jamaica. *Hellblazer*, the Vertigo comic, featured camp shopkeeper Ray Monde, who never had a relationship again after his monogamous but AIDS-carrying lover of 20 years, 'Sergeant Bill', was burned to death aboard his ship, R.F.A. *Sir Galahad* in the Falklands War (Issue 7, 1988 and Issue 120, 1997).

continue to be overlooked. But they are now, for the first time, revealed in this chapter, which uses unique testimony from women and from gay, bisexual and transgender seafaring men.

Gender and Sexual Orientation

The aim of this article is to explore the occluded presence of women and camp gay male seafarers working on these South Atlantic war-time trips. Without their stories, accounts of the conflict are skewed and incomplete. That impoverishes all human beings. The narratives are presented here because the author concurs with sociologist Michael S Kimmel that it is a tragedy that hegemonic masculinity constitutes itself by excluding Otherness and thereby fails to embrace the impressive diversity of human potential. In particular, such a pursuit of such masculinity means that those who promote it are struggling to live "up to impossible ideals of success leading to chronic terrors of emasculation, emotional emptiness and a gendered rage that leaves a wide swath of destruction in its wake."[16]

'Femininity' within the hegemonic masculinity of 'war' is an inconvenient topic and full of contradictions and fuzziness, which therefore deserves attention. To understand the maritime element of the Falklands/Malvinas conflict in all its dimensions means acknowledging the convenient myth of wall-to-wall masculinity (meaning that all the men involved were nothing but ruggedly brave all the time), and going beyond it to see that there was no simple binary polarity between 'soft' civilian crew serving sissy canapés to rufty-tufty marines who were gearing up for war, fighting bravely on land and then coming back as heroes. There was no simple divide: "women and poufs were scared/ troops were tough." Many were tough. Many were frightened. All wrote their wills and goodbye letters, just in case. Highly camp men volunteered to work on ships' guns. Women who were only going to make the beds braved aerial attacks. Homophobic troops didn't have the courage to express their bigotry but only muttered. Senior merchant navy officers shook with fear.

To give this remarkable phenomenon the attention it deserves is to make the crucial point that war is a complex business that can embrace the domestic, the

---

[16] Michael S. Kimmel, "Introduction," in: Michael S. Kimmel and Thomas E. Mosmiller (Eds.), *Against the Tide: Pro-Feminist Men in the U.S., 1776-1990, A Documentary History*, Boston 1992, p.1-51: 45. Othering refers to the practice of classifying someone as 'not one of us', and excluding them as different from the norm, for example, some white people othering black people would be an example of this practice.

joyful, the unexpected and the 'transgressive'. It is important to this chapter that we see ships in general as heterotopias, Othered spaces.[17] Michel Foucault uses the term heterotopia (its etymology is Other place) to mean a situation where spatial arrangements may seem normal. But in social meaning this is an Other world, full of disturbing 'oddness'.[18] Examples for heterotopias include Alice's Wonderland, cemeteries, ships, and musicals. In addition, heterotopias are mental and physical; there is duality and contradiction, reality and unreality at the same time. It is particularly useful to see a ship as a heterotopia, in order to understand how additionally heterotopic a passenger ship is when used as a war vessel. Conversion to military use both enhances the 'peculiarity' of the ship at sea and upends its inhabitants' predictable expectations. Alice could never have imagined her tea party would be so odd, so unlike the normal; but maybe veteran merchant seafarers could because they already knew that "Everything's queer once you've left that pier."

Using the concept of heterotopia helps us re-see the traffic on the South Atlantic in 1982 as an exceptional phenomenon that produced complex subjective effects on its 'citizens'. Such an approach is consistent with modern historiographical practices that understand human subjects as people with fluid, provisional identities that are produced in relation to circumstances, and who can behave in contradictory and ambiguous ways. It is important to remember no unitary 'I' exists. This means narratives composed by these Falklands interviewees and writers are a reflection of only one aspect of themselves, revealed in particular circumstances.

It could be argued that women and camp gay men were not numerically significant (0.3 per cent and circa 10-20 per cent respectively) and that the 'femininity' (or not) of a ship is irrelevant. The point, rather, is the ships' victories. But actually, their exclusion from the record is significant of enduring gendered homophobic and misogynist attitudes to war, and indeed to valorized hyper-masculine activities. Similarly, Larry Tye's history of black Pullman porters and

---

[17] For fuller discussion see Jo Stanley, "Queered seafarers in heterotopic spaces", in: Richard Gorki and Britta Söderqvist (Eds.), *The Parallel Worlds of the seafarer: Ashore, Afloat and Abroad, Papers from the 10th North Sea History Conference*, Gothenburg 2012, p. 179-200.

[18] Michel Foucault, "Of Other Spaces", in: *Diacritics,* 16 (1986), p. 22-27 or "Other Spaces: The Principles of Heterotopias", in: *Lotus* 48 (1986), p. 9-17; "Space, Knowledge and Power" in: Paul Rainbow (Ed.), *The Foucault Reader*, Harmondsworth 1986, p. 239-256. For an interesting critique of this use of heterotopia see Benjamin Genocchio, "Discourse, Discontinuity, Difference: The Question of "Other" Spaces", in: Sophie Watson and Katherine Gibson (Eds.), *Post-Modern Cities and Spaces,* Oxford 1995, p. 35-46.

Julie Wheelwright's investigation of women cross-dressers in armies and navies enable a greater understanding of macro-situations by revealing the micro-stories of these geographically-mobile minorities and their practices.[19]

Why are women and lesbian, gay, bisexual and transgender (LGBT) people so absent from the record? It's partly a product of conventional focus on the Royal, not Merchant Navy (apart from histories by Roger Villar and John Johnson-Allen).[20] And it's partly an indication of unconscious needs to perpetuate myths that war is exclusively a masculine endeavor and thereby ignore domestic, fragile and frivolous aspects. Such omissions are not new or singular phenomena. Cynthia Enloe, the major writer on gendered war, discerns a pattern in conventional historical approaches that "underestimate [...] the extent to which states militaries have relied on women to conduct military operations."[21] Similarly, Allan Bérubé, the principal historian of LGBT service personnel's invisibilized and marginalized lives during the Second World War, made the point that he used both his library ticket *and* his tape recorder, "to *create* as well uncover documents to tell this story".[22]

These pages too involved creating sound documents by interviewing the marginalized women seafarers and camp merchant seafaring men who sailed in that conflict, as well as reading existing accounts against the grain for evidence of gender's role. Collecting oral testimony was the only way such information could be gleaned, as it was not in the public domain. Such a method reveals the presence of femininity; intimate, sometimes sexual connections between troops and ships' personnel; the merging of the boundaries between civilian and military; and above all a new non-naval, non-military, non-male and non-heterosexual version of that ostensibly hyper-masculine South Atlantic battle.

The numbers of camp gay men who worked aboard these heterotopic merchant ships are not known (nor, of course, are the numbers of other, closeted, LGBT service personnel known.) Together with men who were available for contingent

---

[19] Larry Tye, *Rising from the Rails: Pullman porters and the making of the black middle class*, New York 2004; Julie Wheelwright, *Amazons and Military Maids*, London 1994.

[20] Roger Villar, *Merchant Ships at War: The Falklands Experience*, Annapolis 1984; Johnson-Allen, *They Couldn't Have.*

[21] Cynthia Enloe, *Maneuvers: The international politics of militarizing women's lives*, Berkeley, 2000, p. 36.

[22] Italics added. Allan Bérubé, *Coming Out Under Fire: The history of gay men and women in world war two*, New York, 1992, p. 281. See also John D'Emilio and Estelle B. Freedman (Eds.), Allan Bérubé, My Desire for History: Essays in gay, community and labor history, Chapel Hill/NC 2011.

sex with men the number is certainly in the hundreds,[23] although evidence of only a dozen has been found in this research process. Not all were camp. Homosexuality was still illegal at sea until 1999, seventeen years after the Malvinas/Falklands Conflict. And it was still a stigmatized identity in Britain although it had been partially legalized fifteen years earlier in 1967. But recent research by Baker and Stanley has shown that late twentieth-century British passenger ships were the main place where men could be out and camp.[24] Campery was a major feature of the subculture gay men built on ships. Such 'Gay Heavens' were crewed by catering departments that could comprise 95 per cent queered men. They were valued by employers and passengers and accepted by straight crew.

---

[23]   This is the absolute minimum number possible, in my opinion. Standard estimates for the percentage of 'homosexuals' in the whole population vary between 3 per cent and 28 per cent. In view of the gay culture at sea and the prevalence of homosexuality in single-sex organizations, the figure has to be far higher. Of course, there is vast range of queer identities including MSM (Men who have Sex with Men) and married men who are contingently 'married' to a man at sea.

[24]   Paul Baker and Jo Stanley, *Hello Sailor! The Hidden History of Homosexuality at Sea*, Harlow 2003. See also information about the related exhibition, *Hello Sailor! Gay Life on the Ocean Wave*, http://www.liverpoolmuseums.org.uk/maritime/visit/floor-plan/life-at-sea/gaylife/, accessed 13 Aug 2017. My blog on gender, sex and the sea (http://genderedseas.blogspot.com) carries information about new developments and my latest papers on the subject. For the US story of queer seafarers see chapters in Bérubé, *My Desire*. For the Swedish story see Arne Nilsson, *'Såna' på Amerikabåtarna* (*'Those Ones' on the American Boats*), Stockholm, 2006.

SHIP	WOMEN CREW	WOMEN PASSENGERS
SS *Canberra*	15	0
RMS *QE2*	34[25]	1
SS *Uganda*	10[26]	40
MV *Norland*	3	0
St Helena	2	0
British Tamar	1	0
British Dart	1	0
TOTAL	**66**	**41**

Table 1: Women on ships to the Falklands conflict.[27]

Women staff's presence in Falklands/Malvinas Conflict has been overlooked too, yet at least 66 were there. Indeed, the existence of four stewardesses and a woman in a 'man's job' on a BP tanker only came to attention as this chapter was being

---

[25] 33 women were among the 650 *QE2* volunteers according to *QE2/Discuss*, http://www.flickr.com/groups/qe2/discuss/72157624625701724/, accessed 3.11.2009. However, the senior nurse on the ship, Jane Yelland, believes women numbered only 16. She remembers four ship's nurses; one senior hotel officer, Frances Milroy; two bar stewardesses (officers); and nine steam queens (laundresses) in their 40s or 50s. Interview with author, 21.7.2009. There were also dancers at one point, who usually are seen as freelances not company employees, which may explain the numerical discrepancy. Public Rooms Hostess Lesley Barnes firmly believes the total was 34 (Briefing with author, 17.5.2012.).

[26] Women on the *Uganda* include two registered general nurses, a civilian doctor and about six administration staff, but no stewardesses (Approximate figures from author's interview with a purser.) I have been unable to ascertain precisely how many women were on these ships because of administrative difficulties at the shipping line headquarters, the legal restrictions on revealing information about personnel, and some crews' reticence about speaking to me, as 'an outsider'.

[27] Sources include interviews; multiple anecdotal sources; Johnson-Allen, *They Couldn't Have;* Muxworthy, *The Great White Whale*; Villar, *Merchant Ships*.

finally edited.[28] Table 1 indicates the likely numbers of women, who worked as stewardesses, ship's nurses, telephonists, public room attendants, pursers, laundresses, plus a Second Officer and two doctors. (The passengers referred to are war artist Linda Kitson on the *QE2*[29] and on the *Uganda*, which became a hospital ship, and the fifteen Nursing Officers and 26 female nurses in Queen Alexandra's Royal Naval Nursing Service (QARNNS). They were not civilians but under Royal Navy discipline.[30])

The presence of women, and of queered men, is of course only one (problematic) indicator of 'femininity' on these wartime ships to the Falklands, or indeed in any conflict. Now is the time to discuss the concepts of femininity and masculinity in this example before moving on to applying these gendered notions to ships and their occupants. It is normal academic practice to use the terms 'femininities' and 'masculinities' in the plural to indicate the range involved.[31] (For example 'masculinity' can include toughness or, say, tender paternalism). But in this case the singular is used to refer to hegemonic masculinity and femininity, meaning behavior, traits and attributes, which are related to gender. They are politically determined but culturally represented as natural and desirable, and came to the fore in popular discussions of this war. Judith Butler argues that gender is inscribed by repeated performances of behavior deemed gender-appropriate, such

---

[28] Evidence about the three stewardesses on the *Norland* emerged with the article "Bombs hits ships either side of us," *Hull Daily Mail*, 19 April 2012, http://www.thisishullandeastriding.co.uk/Bombs-hit-ships/story-15857858-detail/ story.html, accessed 19 Apr 2012. The presence of a stewardess and a Second Officer on B.P. ships was 'tripped over' by B.P. expert Graham Wallace, who I thank for his thorough support. Two other women's stories emerged into the public domain only in 2010. Sally Children, the Assistant Purser on the *Canberra*, tells her story at http://www.jamescusick.co.uk/2011/02/sallys-story.html, accessed 20 Apr 2012. And *Canberra*'s acting deputy purser Lauraine Mulberry's diary extracts appear in Johnson-Allen, *They Couldn't Have*. I subsequently interviewed her, 7 May 2012.

[29] Linda Kitson's outward voyage was on the *QE2*, then *Canberra*, and on the MV *Edmund* going home.

[30] In addition, three additional female QARNNS nurses flew out from Britain, and then sailed out to Falklands in mid-July after hostilities ended. Unusually they sailed on Royal Navy ships: HMS *Hecla*, *Herald* and *Hydra*. Making up 'the Fearless Forty' they worked on *Uganda*. Later they stayed and relieved nurses at King Edward civilian hospital in Stanley. Pugh, *White Ship*. The wider story of women's history as merchant seafarers appears in my book, *From Cabin 'Boys' to Captains: 250 Years of Women at Sea*, Stroud 2016.

[31] See, for example, Becky Francis, "The Nature of Gender", in: Christine Skelton *et al*, (Eds.), *The Sage Handbook of Gender and Education*, London 2006, p. 12.

as women smiling 'agreeably', and men carrying heavy bags for women.[32] 'Femininity' is classically associated with gentleness, domesticity, reproduction, empathy, sensitivity, tolerance, nurturance, and even deference and self-abasement. A 'feminine' woman is sometimes seen as one whom men see as an attractive and compliant sexual object. By contrast 'masculinity' is understood to be about bravery, public life, domination, physical toughness and so on. In 1982 popular discourse, particularly in the tabloids where the Falklands/Malvinas Conflict was reported in a traditionally gendered way, such macho masculinity was still represented as the norm, and women were represented as lesser, Other, and of course unsuited to war except as exceptionalized angels (nurses). In fact gender was and is complex, ambiguous and shifting.

In Britain the Women's Liberation Movement had been challenging such reductive polarities for around fifteen years. A decade before the Falklands/Malvinas Conflict women had started being allowed to do 'men's jobs' on ship, such as engineer, navigator and deck officer, although they were still rare. Similarly, the Gay Liberation Movement had been asserting LGBT rights for several years, although the recent emergence of HIV/AIDS had worsened homophobia. But British Merchant Navy ships were remarkably tolerant of camp ratings (but not of non-camp gay officers). Cabin steward Tony Wall, who was on *Canberra* in the war, says "The women and gay crew members served alongside us, performed their duties well. And, to be honest, sex or sexual preference was never an issue."[33] In the patchy 'anything goes' atmosphere on heterotopic British merchant ships at that time it was absolutely normal for bedroom and dining room stewards to be effeminate, even camp. Gays not only performed regular drag shows for all on board, in crew shows, but minced and flirted through the working day. The high campery performed by some men was generally welcomed on ships because it provided entertainment and diversion from the relentless work, boredom, and necessarily imprisoning nature of the ship.

By contrast in the Falklands/Malvinas Conflict the 'guests' from the armed forces who were 'hosted' by these gay-friendly crew members belonged to a culture where hyper-masculinity was prized and homophobic bullying occurred. Femiphobia (fear-based hostility to feminine traits in men, a relatively common feature in armed forces) was of course associated with hegemonic masculinity, which is constructed to coincide completely with heterosexuality. As Kimmel argues, femiphobia functions as a kind of homophobia. Just as hegemonic

---

[32] Judith Butler, *Gender Trouble: Feminism and the subversion of identity*, New York 1990.
[33] Email to author, 21 Oct 2011.

masculinity allows real women only certain positions such as nurturing mother or object of sexual desire, so too it necessitates the subordination of 'female' traits' in men.[34] Such a military culture meant women and effeminate men on these ships were likely to be discursively positioned as of lesser value than battle-ready macho men.

And indeed the ships themselves could in some ways been seen as 'feminine'. It's a hoary chestnut that ships are female. Deeply-held attitudes are expressed in silly jokes, such as those found on tea towels in seaport knick-knack shops. They claim a ship is like a woman because she/it "has a waist and stays [corsets] [...]. It takes an experienced man to handle her correctly; and without a man at the helm, she is absolutely uncontrollable."[35] Women, like ships, it used to be claimed, were at their best when made fast to a sturdy b(u)oy.[36] It wasn't until 20 years after the conflict in the South Atlantic that *Lloyds List*, the major ship insurers, broke 268 years of sentimental tradition by controversially declaring these "pieces of maritime real estate" 'it' not 'she'.[37]

In fact, ships could actually be viewed as hyper-masculine in the sense that they are large powerful vehicles managed through difficult situations by the highly-skilled male technocratic successors of rugged sailors. But, like mothers, ships offer domestic space and ease to the 'children' within their 'wombs.' Passenger ships in particular could be seen as places where soft-living, lounging, self-indulgence and decorative inactivity were normal, by contrast to the highly-disciplined and righteous civic institution style of the warship.

The presence of female and effeminate male crew on passenger liners, amongst all the evidences of the easy-going peacetime shipboard culture, would tend to reinforce the discursive reproduction of the ship as largely 'feminine', indeed sissy. Applying the concepts of masculinity and femininity to ships taking troops to battle we can imagine that the professional soldiers, Royal Navy sailors, and Marines on board ships could symbolically be seen as the hyper-masculine within the somewhat feminine. However this over-simplified binary will now be problematized, as we explore how masculinities and femininities affected what occurred on ships in the South Atlantic going to and from the Falklands/ Malvinas

---

[34] Kimmel, "Introduction".
[35] http://forum.wordreference.com/showthread.php?t=425232, accessed 6 May 2007.
[36] 'Why a ship is "she",' *Ditty Box*, Dec 1944, p. 6.
[37] Andrew Hibberd and Nicola Woolcock, "Lloyd's List sinks the tradition of calling ships 'she'" in the *Telegraph,* 21 Mar 2002. http://www.telegraph.co.uk/news/ uknews/1388373/Lloyds-List-sinks-the-tradition-of-calling-ships-she.html, accessed 6 Jan 2012.

Conflict and indeed moored in the war zone that the South Atlantic temporarily became.

'Girlie' Ships get 'butch'?[38]

Let us turn initially to the ships, then to the people on them, and examine how the wartime situation in the South Atlantic shifted those reductive gendered polarities. In other words, let us see how the conventional 'masculine' became 'feminine' and vice versa, as well as how those binaries became irrelevant at times: transcended, refuted and made far more nuanced by the real situation.

Of the approximately 52 merchant vessels sailing in that war, three huge liners were disproportionate in carrying a high number of troops, the usual gay crew, and women: *Canberra*, *Uganda*, and the *QE2*. Small numbers of women also sailed on the *Norland*, *St Helena*, *British Tamar* and *British Dart*. GBT men (not necessarily camp) were presumably on all ships. But the most publicized camp gay man of the war, Roy 'Wendy' Gibson, was on the *Norland*.[39] The big three vessels, amounting together to 129,000 tons, represented roughly a third of the total 500,000 tonnage of all the STUFT ships. P&O's *Canberra* and Cunard's *QE2* were acting as troop transports. The *Uganda* was a hospital ship. All three were very grand liners that were associated with comfortableness and style (which could be seen as archetypically feminine), although the *Uganda* had recently been used for school cruises.

Were ships so sissy? Is it appropriate to equate luxury travel with girlie-ness? On the *QE2*, (tellingly styled not 'the king', but the 'Queen of the Ocean') Gurkha officer Mike Seer spoke as someone using the tourist gaze[40] as he gleefully described the breathtaking décor. He had an outside room on the boat deck, which "boasted a terrace with a panoramic sea view [...] full-length floral curtains

---

[38] Butch is the commonly used term for hyper-masculine. Some gay men, of course, can be 'butch', as can some lesbians. The term tends to refers to tough self-presentation, e.g. black leather clothing, moustaches.

[39] The presence of camp men was more publicized later, not at the time, see Warren Fitzgerald, *All in the Same Boat: The Untold Story of the British Ferry Crew who helped win the Falklands War*, London 2016.

[40] Tourism is now seen not so much as an *activity* in which individuals explore a culture and Otherness, but an attitude. It is a state of mind whereby the foreign – which can include the ship as "resort" – is scrutinized with a socially organized and systematized "tourist gaze". Tourism sociologist John Urry argues that "what makes a particular tourist gaze depends on what it is contrasted with." John Urry, *The Tourist Gaze*, London, Thousand Oaks and New Delhi 2002, p. 1.

framing the large windows, fitted carpet, large table lamps [...] comfortable sofa and armchair [...] and even [...] a bidet."[41]

Clearly such stylish personal space was not militarily 'masculine.' Indeed, it made the journey to war into, to some degree, a (sissy?) holiday-style pleasure that would never normally be affordable; it normally cost £600-a-day (now the equivalent of 2,000 Euros). Lower down the scale, rifleman Baliprasad Raj was thrilled at the social mobility his surroundings seemed to confer.

> "I never dreamt of being on a ship, much less the world's greatest liner. Where before only millionaires and men of means had wined and dined, strolled and played, there I was, a boy from Bagsila, Nepal, savouring the same air of opulence. My shoes may not have been made by Gucci, but at least they were tramping the same corridors!"

But, he tellingly added, "Life on the *Queen Elizabeth 2* was much the same as in *Queen Elizabeth* barracks."[42] *Habitus* transformed subjective experience of habitat.

Ships should be understood as complex 'total institutions'[43] that were suddenly the habitat for two sets of people with largely opposing *habituses*. In social anthropologist Marcel Mauss's usage, *habitus* means that people had a shared unspoken and embodied sense of their own – and others' – place and role in the world.[44] They operate with socially-learned structures of the mind, upon ideas that 'go without saying'. Post-structuralist philosopher Pierre Bourdieu elaborated Mauss's concept to show how *habitus* is dependent on our histories and memories. As their interpreters Hillier and Rooksby clarify, people play the game with both external limits on available resources and opportunities (to which they don't have necessarily equality of access and agency) and with their own ideas of what is possible and right.[45] So these wartime ships were institutions

---

[41] Mike Seer, *With the Gurkhas in the Falklands,* Barnsley 2003, p. 84.

[42] Seer, *With the Gurkhas,* p. 99, quoting from Baliprasad Raj's *From Bagsila to Bluff Cove – a soldier's story of the Falkland's war,* as told to Jasbahadur Gurung, June 1982, no publisher traceable.

[43] Sociologist Erving Goffman uses the term "total institution" for ships, prisons etc. For further discussion on how this term is applicable to ships see Heide Gerstenberger (1996) "Men Apart: The Concept of 'Total Institution' and the Analysis of Seafaring", *International Journal of Maritime History,* Vol. VIII, no. 1, June, p. 173-182.

[44] Mauss originally expressed these ideas in "Les Techniques du corps", *Journal de Psychologie,* No 32, 1934, p. 3-4.

[45] Pierre Bourdieu, *Outline of a Theory of Practice,* Cambridge 1977. Pierre

where seafarers and military guests negotiated complex new rules of gendered behavior but also interacted on the basis of old understandings.

Figure 16: Merchant seafarers had to be dressed for trouble; Kevin Smith poses in his gas mask on *Canberra*.

Different vessels had different identities. Seminally, people on those ships deep in the war zone mocked the *QE2* (which was too large and felt to be too significant a target to be allowed too close) with the competitively macho slogan "*Canberra* cruises where the *QE2* refuses." But in general, the ships could be said to be de-feminized – and made more like barracks – in the following ways: they were sailing with a new rationale; their spaces were transformed; they were carrying very untouristic provisions; their personnel were prepared for trouble and offered the opportunity to learn to fire guns; and they were in a war zone. And of course, ships varied. When Mike Seer moved from the luxurious *QE2* to the North Sea

---

Bourdieu and Wacquant Loïc, *An Invitation to Reflexive Sociology*, Chicago 1992. Jean Hillier and Emma Rooksby, *Habitus: A Sense of Place,* Aldershot 2002, p. 26.

ferry *Norland*, it was like "the difference between night and day. Her Spartan accommodation had a homely feel with its permanent blackout created by black plastic [domestic rubbish] bags stuck over portholes and windows" [with gaffer tape].[46]

Figure 17: Gurkhas practice aboard *QE2* by the world map usually used by passengers to revel in their distance from home.

Canberra Chief officer Martin Reed summed up the changes as he saw them. First, he wrote "The usual aim of any cruise liner is to lead a planned, settled and orderly life for the enjoyment and pleasure of her passengers." This included getting the ship from A to B safely and exactly on time. Instead they were obliged

---

[46] Seer, *With the Gurkhas,* p. 120.

to zigzag as an evasive tactic, stay in a 'box' of sea, an area that covered only a few square miles, and "generally expect the unexpected at every turn."[47] Second,

> "the Bosun and his deck crew have to keep the ship gleaming white; then maintain the safety gear; to moor and unmoor the ship; and to ensure the safe passage, by boat and gangway, of all the passengers off the ship [...] [instead] they had to watch, helplessly, as the ship's immaculate side slowly rusted until she looked like a weather and battle-scarred veteran."[48]

Circumstances now forced crew to cope with preparations for being hit by the enemy, which was "far from normal cruise ships' activity". Rather than stopping at a port a day, as on cruises, *Canberra* only moored twice during the entire trip. Instead of sending launches to ferry groups of tourists to and from quayside consumer opportunities, such as postcard vendors, liners ran the small boats that transported troops and garrison supplies to the war zone and took Argentinean prisoners-of-war from the war zone. And "just as a sideline, the deck crew volunteered to help as stretcher bearers, hospital auxiliaries and – as part of the ship's air defense teams, as machine gunners'"[49] Third, the carpenter and plumbers usually maintained the ships' internal fabric and domestic piping to the "very high standard expected by passengers and P&O." Instead, on this trip, they ripped out the luxury fittings, tore up carpets instead of laying them, as well as blacking out

> "the best-lit ship in the word, [and] fight[ing] a continuous battle against cigarette butts in lavatories [...] the deck department in particular got used to the cry 'stay flexible', so much so that he suggested the ship's motto should be changed from its established one, *Orbem Cingit* (We circle the world), to *Non audiaviste, omnia mutatis est*! (Haven't you heard, it's all been changed?)."[50]

So the changed rationale – meaning the ship's duty was to take soldiers to war, not to take holidaymakers to desirable resorts – altered culture and practices, and of course affected the ship's spaces. The main physical changes were internal de-beautifying, the addition of helicopter pads, and the intensified use of sleeping space. Because the numbers aboard were doubled in many cases, new needs emerged such as additional desalination plants. Cleanliness and potable water were not seen as luxurious extras but essential. Non-essentials such as curtains and candelabra were stripped out and stored in warehouses. Hard-wearing

---

[47] Muxworthy, *The Great White Whale*, p. 157.
[48] Ibid.
[49] Ibid.
[50] Ibid.

chipboard was laid over monogrammed deep-pile carpet. And, old spaces were put to new uses. Public rooms where holidaymakers reveled were converted into austerely functional spaces: lounges became hospital wards. On ferries the car deck became the area where troops exercised. Artillery was mounted in the *QE2*'s shopping arcade. In the mauve and flowery Steiner hairdressing salon the intelligence team sat under the pink hairdryers to plan operations, to the delight of photographers.[51] In this way, the 'feminine' ship became more 'masculine' in its physical state, but also really feminine places were appropriated for 'masculine' purposes.

Likewise, some of the provisions that came aboard were unlike those of any normal, 'feminine' tourist trip. Apart from military equipment such as ammunition, the most jarringly un-holiday-like items were empty coffins which really underlined the surreal and heterotopic nature of the voyage for those who witnessed the loading. Beer was brought on board in great quantities. Conversely wine and champagne were taken off. And there were odd items, such as 50 ironing boards (presumably to enable troops to keep their trousers pressed). On *Canberra* 5,000 condoms were ordered. Captain Scott-Masson said laconically "In view of our ultimate destination I queried the need." He was told they would be inflated and then released for use as targets.[52] In fact they could be seen as a macho monochrome version of the colored balloons that cruise ship so often used for parties.

Above all, the ships were in a new place, a war zone. This meant not only that they were at risk of being destroyed or sunk by enemy action. But having machine guns mounted on decks meant the floating hotels were a target. So far from home, fueling needs meant they had to replenish at sea: RAS. RAS-ing is a tricky operation, especially in storms, involving dangerous proximity with the refueling vessel. In peacetime it was normally done by Royal Fleet Auxiliary ships servicing naval vessels, not passenger ships as it was now. Further, although merchant ships were kept out of dangerous waters if possible, they had to be there at times to disembark the troops. The hotel became, in effect, another war vehicle, as well as a barracks, parade ground and heliport floating on the South Atlantic.

---

[51] Kitson, *Falklands War*, p. 30, 41. See the photo in Muxworthy, *The Great White Whale*, p. 20.
[52] Johnson-Allen, *They Couldn't Have*, p. 48, citing Scott-Masson, no source given but extract refers to mid-April.

Masculinized and Feminized People and their Practices

Being in this war situation on a transformed ship meant that the people on board were both 'hardened' and 'softened.' War made situations and practices less gender-polarized, in some degree. Merchant Navy personnel were affected in the following ways. For the male deck officers it had become a more hyper-masculine situation as they tried to deliver service as usual. *Canberra*'s captain Scott-Masson summed it up as having "to get used to throwing 45,000 tons of ocean splendor around like a destroyer" without flinching.[53] In the *QE2*'s case the ship had to sail without radar, to avoid detection. But a number of Merchant Navy officers on liners were actually familiar with Royal Navy methods of operating (though usually not in wartime conditions) because they were members of the Royal Naval Reserve. And personnel on the *Norland* were used to transporting British troops traveling to and from German bases, albeit on leave. To them the new practices were not so anomalously 'masculine.'

But very senior Merchant Navy men could be seen to have their masculinity reduced by having to accept the Royal Navy's authority on their ships, a delicate situation which has yet to be fully explored. Although the official version is that the two captains on each bridge collaborated cheerfully, the reality was that the Merchant Navy commanders' usual authority over their kingdom was assailed; at times they had to defer. Also, attack makes everyone feel that 'feminine' emotion, fear. As *Canberra* was attacked in San Carlos Water on May 21 and fired back its machine guns and blowpipe missiles, Chief Officer Martin Reed found his hands were shaking, as too were those of his First Officer.[54]

---

[53] "Cruising as it never was before," in: *P&O Wavelength* 120, Aug/Sept (1982) Falklands Special, p. 4.
[54] John Johnson-Allen, *They Couldn't Have,* p. 30.

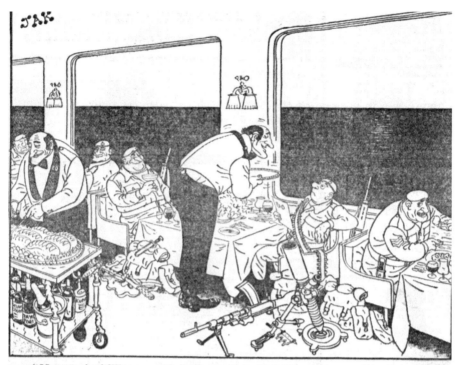

Figure 18: Stewards looking after passengers in new ways: "More caviar! Where would sir like it, down his flak jacket, or up his nose?"

If the ship is seen as one of Goffman's total institutions, then the hotel-side staff were warders who had authority over the inmates. This is a dominant masculine position, whether or not that is consciously articulated. But it is mitigated by stewards' view of themselves as 'looking after' passengers (a motherly position), and contact workers' dependence on passengers tipping them. In this war situation, the hotel-side merchant seafarers looked after; and they didn't expect (or get) tips.

Those lower down the social scale had to do their usual work, such as wait tables, despite the attacks looming. They were often able to hear but not see the danger (a position of impotence that some thought was worse than witnessing battle) because they were ordered below decks when Argentinean forces were attacking. Take a key day. On 21 May, at dawn Captain Burne, the Senior (Royal) Naval Officer and Captain Scott-Masson, the ship's senior Merchant Navy officer, were in San Carlos Water side by side on *Canberra*'s bridge awaiting the next event, before they landed the troops. By 8.45 a.m. they were diving for cover as

Argentinean aircraft attacked the ships in the bay. At 11.45 a.m. there was a lull and then waiters served lunch in the Pacific restaurant, as usual, but "dressed in a variety of warm combat rigs […][with] one ear cocked listening for the latest warning broadcast."[55] This illustrates the way both civilian and military practices and people were often co-present and interlinked with each other, so that there was almost an interleaving of "now it's a military situation, now it's a civilian situation" and boundaries were blurred.

Women at Sea

Like male seafarers, the 66-odd women in the crews of the various ships were similarly working as normally as they could despite the attacks. They had volunteered. Some had been determined to be part of the voyage despite the Royal Navy initially opposing women's presence (successfully in the case of the Navy anesthetist who was barred from participating, to her colleagues' regret[56]). And none wanted to turn back. The only one who did so was Carol, an elderly *Norland* stewardess who became ill – and took much persuading to leave her comrades. But contemporary attitudes towards femininity meant their bravery was seen as remarkable. Captain Scott-Masson's diary for 22 May reports that he found the women in *Canberra*'s Purser's Bureau, on hearing the repeated call over the Tannoy, 'Take cover, take cover!' "took up their lifejackets again and calmly placed themselves in the kneeholes of the desks […] like rabbits each in their own hutch."[57] Their cheerfulness under fire was noted. For example on D-day

> "two of the cabin staff, Jan and Paula, carried on bustling from cabin to cabin changing bedding. During air raids they would retreat inboard a little and make themselves comfortable on the floor of one of the pantries. The Supply Officer passing hastily by on one such occasion quizzed them for looking so comfortable. They grinned back and complained about the frequency of the raids, which were interfering with their work, they said!" [58]

Like male crew, women also donated as much blood as they were allowed to the ships' blood transfusion banks. Many, too, were ready to go ashore and help if needs be.

---

[55] Muxworthy, *The Great White Whale*, p. 68.
[56] Linda Kitson, interview with author, 11 June 2009. The lack of sufficient naval anesthetists proved crucial in the conflict, because it meant there were too many surgeons waiting for them, in order to perform urgently-needed operations.
[57] Johnson-Allen, *They Couldn't Have*, citing Scott-Masson, 22 May 1982, p. 52.
[58] Muxworthy, *The Great White Whale,* p. 68.

But because the military was so used to women not being in positions of power, it was sometimes difficult for women to be as respected by passengers as they usually were. Jayne Simpson found on *Uganda* that their male military guests mistook the women pursers' high status. "It had to be made clear that we were officers and not crew."[59] Such were the entrenched patterns and so unusual were high-status women in the army that military people didn't know how to address women officers. When ship's nursing Sister Diane McLean was moving about the *QE2*, the troops – particularly Gurkhas – said "Good Morning, Sir."[60] They had had no experience of using the word for female officers: Ma'am.

On normal voyages women officers are not usually the focus of massive men's attention. But such was the female-to-male ratio on Falklands trips that many female crew felt they had to organize their own 'de-feminisation' in some ways, such as reducing obvious sexual allure, and only sunbathing in places where men couldn't see them. *Norland* stewardess Carol told Frank Green, a camp steward "I haven't put no perfume on [because of] all these men here." He jokingly replied "Ooh, right, I think I'll put extra on".[61] On the *QE2* Jane Yelland and her colleagues used the distant penthouses for sunbathing. They tucked themselves away partly out of respect for the troops, so as not to excite them, and partly "to protect ourselves from prying eyes."[62] The voyeuristic caption of a photograph of a helicopter hovering over their bit of deck, where women lie around in bikinis, underlines this: "Being a helicopter pilot has its compensations."[63] But the point was all the crew realized that they had to adjust their behavior because their cooped-up young male passengers were sexually frustrated and mainly unable to relieve that frustration. The negotiation was complex. *QE2* senior nurse Jane Yelland found "You had to be one of the lads – but on the other hand you want to keep your femininity too. You tried to be neutral but feminine."[64]

Often the women found themselves in situations where these combatants focused on their femininity, and indeed attributed hyper-femininity to them. Men opened doors, offered their helmets, and would clearly attempt to rescue women in times of trouble. Women were embarrassed that they were treated so exceptionally that gallant troops would have put their own lives at risk in order to look after women. Such privilege was not what most women there wanted, as Linda Kitson articulated. After all, as feminists since the First World War had argued, gendered

---

[59] Jayne Simpson, interview with author, 19 July 2009.
[60] Diane McLean, interview with author, 20 July 2009.
[61] Frank Green, interview with author, 2 May 2012.
[62] Jane Yelland, interview with author, 21 July 2009.
[63] Muxworthy, *The Great White Whale*, p. 47.
[64] Yelland, interview.

chivalry is predicated upon the protector's idea that the protectee is unable to look after themselves; that she is not really an equal and competent adult. As Charlotte Despard argued after the Titanic's sinking, "We want a new conception of chivalry. We want it to go outside the shell of conventional manners [...] a chivalry, the reigning principle of which will be reverence for every honest worker, with special regard for the weaker amongst their number."[65]

Although the "Women-and-Children-First" practice in abandoning ship had waned somewhat by the 1980s, entrenched gender patterns meant women continued to play their usual archetypically feminine roles in on-board entertainment as late as this trip. For example, at the *QE2*'s Crossing the Line (Equator) ceremony two nurses, Jane Levine and Wendy Marshall, accepted the usual women's role of mermaid. Their legs bound so tightly in pink frilly plastic that they had to be carried to the makeshift canvas pool, this time with a huge male audience.[66] (By contrast, no women took on male roles such as King Neptune, although men appropriated the opportunity to cross-dress.)

Women seafarers, whether ratings or officers, mixed socially with military officers rather than men in the lower ranks. They drank and dined with them in messes at night. Nursing Sister Diane McLean enjoyed a very busy social life in the wardroom, both in the Cunard officers' mess and with the army and naval groups most evenings, where she recalls that women were treated "with respect and kindness."[67] And it seems that the wartime situation temporarily meant the rare women were treated at times as a status-neutral category; there was not the usual prohibition on fraternization between the ranks. Some had loving relationships, mainly with officers rather than other ranks because they were nearer in age (thirties) and similarly well-travelled. The numerical imbalance certainly meant women were in demand. They could afford to be choosy, and at least one woman rating on the *Canberra* had multiple lovers. But when it came to courageousness, another *Canberra* rating was shocked to find her lover was too scared to go ashore; she had to give him a pep talk and marshal his friends into persuading him of his duty.

Camp Male Crew

Male stewards may have been implicitly positioned as the ladies of the ship because they did 'feminine' work, i.e. low-status tasks connected to personal service, an almost 'motherly' role. But it is unlikely that there was any top-level

---

[65] Charlotte Despard, *Women's Franchise and Industry*, London 1913, p. 7.
[66] Yelland, interview.
[67] McLean, interview.

discussion about whether homosexual civilian crew should be allowed to sail to war with the troops (and thereby exacerbate the moral and security risks then associated with homosexuality). The reasons for not excluding them, as some women were, are that gay stewards are seen as so sensitive to passenger needs that they are valuable workers; that GBT men were so numerous that any such move would have added organizational problems as well as inflamed an anti-discrimination reaction; and that the union's closed shop would have meant that such exclusion was impossible anyway. Long experience with camp stewards had shown employers that homosexuality by no means meant that these seafarers would be a liability, rather the opposite. But for army and naval officers it was a culture shock to find 'minions' larking about with impunity, being so familiar with 'superiors' and even urging mighty commanding officers to "Eat up your greens, dear."[68]

Like women, camp gay men (and of course there were many GBT men who were not out and camp) did their usual job and more. The most lauded camp man of the war, Roy 'Wendy' Gibson on the *Norland*, was one of many doing in effect a double shift. When he finished his own stewarding work for the day he'd sprinkle glitter in his hair, put on his sparkly waistcoat and wear his fingers to the bone playing his pink piano in the various ships' bars, keeping up troops' morale with sing-along numbers. Others helped the sick – talking, writing letters, offering cigarettes. Some volunteered to learn how to fire their ships' new machine guns.

The differences that military and naval passengers made to gay men's voyages were several. Hyper-masculinity goes with homophobia and so some camp men were wary about being too outrageous in case they were attacked by homophobes. Others were so used to being accepted on ship that they simply didn't care if the troops saw it as "a freak show"; they carried on camping. In some cases this brought muttered insults such as "dirty queer". One man was even gay-bashed. But soldiers also learned from the tolerance that was so normal aboard; they saw that gay men could be respected. This was not least because GBT men proved themselves brave. They had volunteered to go to the Falklands/Malvinas; they stayed with their ships despite being given the chance to fly home at Ascension Island; and they didn't complain about being civilians suddenly being placed in a war zone, despite the danger from Argentinean planes and the horrors of burning ships sinking all around them.

When paratroopers such as Ken Lukowiak and his colleagues now reminisce, "it is true to say that he [Wendy] now gets more of a mention than the likes of Colonel Jones, VC [...]. And no longer is Wendy referred to as [...] an arse-

---

68   Kevin, interview.

bandit […] "Gay boy" is about the worst you will hear and it's always […] said with affection. You see, we do live – and we can learn."[69]

The 2 Para Battalion made Wendy their first gay 'mascot'. They awarded him with their official red beret. He attended their 25th anniversary celebrations at Aldershot in 1997. And some journeyed many miles to join with him and others from the *Nor-land* in the 2012 celebrations in Hull's camp seafarers' pub, Frankie's Vauxhall Tavern.

For some gay men, the troops had been eye candy to be enjoyed as they exercised in shorts, pounding round and round the deck. Paratrooper Vince Bramley noted

> "The queers from the Merchant Navy, the stewards, always came on deck to watch. It was not uncommon to see [our] lads blowing sarcastic kisses at them, or dropping their trousers, to flash at them in passing. It was all in good humor and the queers would shout back, 'Oh, you naughty boys', or 'My, my, aren't we a big boy then.' Obviously, some stewards liked living dangerously and would try to score. The lucky ones got the good news, 'Like a beating?'"[70]

Aside from the homophobia, some gay men did have relationships with some soldiers. This wasn't as extensive as others fantasized. No squaddies[71] could afford to be seen as having gay sex, even as a one-off act of domination or a way of getting contingent 'relief'. In that nosey community their mates would have jeered. Worse, servicemen at that time could have been court-martialed, imprisoned and dishonorably discharged. But officers managed it more easily. An unanticipated phenomenon occurred: some military men felt they didn't want to die without having tried intercourse with a man. Stewards – being characteristically helpful enablers – obliged in some cases. Also, as Bernie L, the Captain's Steward on the *Canberra* explained, many formed affectionate bonds with their passengers, including Argentinean prisoners.[72]

Many crew, whatever their sexual orientation, began to feel at one with the troops as they drew closer to war. They started saying 'we' and identifying with the troops. Indeed, some felt so much like part of the war team that they tried to assist. A senior NCO of 2 Para recorded that amidst the hell of war when the *Norland* had been hit twice,

---

[69] Ken Lukowiak, *A Soldier's Song: True Stories from the Falklands*, London 1993, p. 174.
[70] Vincent Bramley, *Excursion to Hell: The battle for Mount Longdon*, London 1992, p. 26.
[71] This is the common, but not derogatory, word for soldier of a low rank.
[72] Bernie L, interview with author, 28 Dec 2011.

"we're all working like slaves to load a landing craft and I've got fucking Wendy beasting me to get a move on. Fifteen fucking years I've waited for this, and when it does finally happen I've got some gay boy leaning over me telling ME to fucking hurry up because HIS boys are running out of fucking ammo."[73]

In the troops' quests for additional beer and entertainment and off-limits pleasure, mutual friendships grew. Camp guys and homophobes could find that 'the enemy' was not a member of such a distinctly Other tribe. Much of this focused round alcohol; troops wanted more than the military allowed. In the crew bar and in their cabins seafarers – both gay and straight – tried to give the passengers what they wanted. In one case, on the *QE2* going home, this actually brought a remarkable phenomenon: butch troops exchanging clothes with gay stewards so that they could use the crew bar. Camp steward Terry (Tracey) H and his friends Minger and K had made the exchange. But then the military police patrolling the ship burst into the bar. They spotted Minger, a small bald man with a limp from when he had polio and dragged him out, imagining he was a soldier because of his clothes. "We were on the floor laughing because of all the people less military was [Minger] […]. But he got back in[to the bar later] and they never caught any of the soldiers who came in with us. And that's where K got the soldier he had sex with that night, all for a pint […] in his cabin."[74]

Unremittingly Hyper-Masculine Soldiers?

What role did hyper-masculinity play for the soldiers on board these ships, by contrast? Unexpectedly, macho soldiers did not reject the 'femininity' of the ships as despicably sissy. Rather it was the valued – though exaggeratedly over-reverenced – counterpart of military hyper-masculinity. The *Uganda*'s usual nickname 'UgTug' tellingly became 'Mother Hen.' And military men appreciated the ship's civilized qualities after they came from the battlefields stinking of peat, blood, sweat and shit. Naval doctor Rick Jolly drew this out when describing the difference between the muddy cold battle zone ashore where he had worked for a week and the *Uganda*:

"What a cool beautiful haven this lovely ship is – the wards are spotless, the staff wear white plimsolls [gym shoes] as they pad silently along the carpeted decks, and best of all, there are female nurses!

---

[73] Un-named NCO quoted in Lukowiak, *A Soldier's Song*, p. 173.
[74] Terry H, interview with author, 2 Feb 2006.

> The girls [the professional naval nurses] look divine and smell impossibly fragrant as they tend our customers of the previous week."[75]

The most striking, indeed notorious, stories of interpersonal behavior are told in paratrooper Vince Bramley's notorious memoirs. He describes his colleagues' response to the full sacks of mail that arrived from enthusiastic unknown women back in Britain. Men selected the most obviously beautiful women from the accompanying photographs. But the rejects were referred to in cruel terms. "Platoons took to keeping their personal 'grot boards' [noticeboards, and ran] 'Ugly Pig contests' [...] [comments were made such as] 'Fuck me, who'd love that beast?' or, 'Pig in Knickers.'"[76]

At Freetown on the outward voyage they were not allowed to disembark and so some Paratroopers on board screamed sexist abuse at an English family who stood at the dock to wave a Union Jack at the ship. Bramley recalled that:

> "the flag and their good wishes were the last thing we were interested in, once we spotted the daughter. She was dressed in a flimsy dress and her large breasts were more than noticeable. From us, looking down her cleavage, the general scream was 'Get yer tits out, love' or, 'Sit on my face, while I wave a different flag for yer.' They [the family] tried to smile and pretend they hadn't heard us, but you can't ignore hundreds of sex-starved men, shouting for nookie." [77]

In contrast, such attitudes were not openly expressed towards women seafarers, probably because they were older (twenties and thirties) than the girl in the quotation.

War prowess appears to be linked to hyper-masculinity. At their South Georgian destination one officer got out of bed and declared robustly, "Right, girls! The party's over. It's from here that the real fun's about to begin." That is, he addressed his male cabin-mates as what they were not, and described the voyage as a non-work prelude.[78] Similarly, another officer referred to his exercise program as "a Jane Fonda work-out", in a jokey attempt to highlight how much the men were not female, and not movie stars who could choose to be lithe or slothful. But the troops seemed able to shift from imagining 'feminine' behavior was impossible to accepting a more sensible position. Troops on the *Norland* were taught field medicine including how to give intravenous fluid through the anus. "Most of the Toms joked they'd rather bleed to death than drop their

---

[75] Jolly, *The Red*, p. 91.
[76] Bramley, *Excursion*, p. 11.
[77] Bramley, *Excursion*, p. 14. Nookie is a colloquial term for casual sexual intercourse.
[78] Seer, *With the Gurkhas*, p. 118.

trousers and have [Doctor] Steve's tube rammed up their arse in the freezing Falkland's wind." But they learned to do it and see the value of it, Mike Seer reported.[79] Similarly, on the *QE2* sensible troops expecting cold conditions bought up all City Queen seamless ladies tights from the ship's shop. It's likely that those confident about their masculinity could afford to allow in 'the feminine.'

Figure 19: Shopping in the ship's shop on *QE2*.

---

[79] John Geddes, *Spearhead Assault: Guts and Glory on the Falklands Frontlines*, London 2008, p. 59.

Figure 20: home wounded on *QE2*.

By the time they were on their return trip, victoriously, the combatants seem to have further eased up on maintaining hyper-masculine appearances. The ships were allowed to become holiday spaces where hard men sunbathed – and of course where some mourned their lost comrades, reappraised their values and the worth of the battle, and faced their own fragility: some were wounded and some had combat-related Post Traumatic Stress Disorder.

On *Canberra*, sailing north towards Ascension Island on June 28, the playful atmosphere was such that troops posted spoof memos concerning ice-cream consumption and sunbathing positions. The memos emphasized the choice that was normal in tourism, while acknowledging the enduring hierarchal distinctions. The jokey Officers' Mess notice 32/82 re ice creams stipulated that Lieutenant Colonels and above were allowed "Caviar Crunch […] served with hall-marked solid sterling silver spoon." Majors and Lieutenant Commanders were entitled to "Devon Country with crustation of clotted cream supplied with a plastic spoon." Lower down the hierarchy Special Duties Officers were to be allowed Mr. Whippy cornets. Captains were "also entitled to a [chocolate] flake." Engineering Officers' rations were "Strawberry Bombino Cornetto[s] with intricate fiddly wrapping paper." [80]

Homeward bound, there appears to have been more cross-dressing than on the outward voyage. Even the hyper-masculine Gurkhas on the *Norland* organized a

---

[80] Muxworthy, *The Great White Whale*, p. 116-118.

tamang dance where one man dresses as a female, supplementing the absence of real women but also, maybe, edging closer to smudging boundaries around sexual orientation.[81] Terry H, a *QE2* steward, found that the Navy could put on Sod's Operas (camp revue shows similar to crew shows that were staged on passenger vessels) that were just as good as theirs.

> "It was announced that each ship would do a bit in a Sod's Opera [...] They offered the crew 'Did you want to join in?', and the crew said, No, there were no gay guys who would want to do anything. We hadn't seen a Royal Navy Sod's Opera beforehand [...] [so didn't want to risk taking part in it]. We all went up [to see it] that evening [...] the language was very blue [...] [The performers announced] 'If any woman would like to leave now [please do so] because we are not going to change our script. We normally do this [show] on a ship where there are no women and if you want to leave, leave now.' Nobody got up to leave [...] [Royal Navy] sailors, three or four of them were in suspenders [...] the one [number performed] in underwear was done behind a silhouette-type thing [...] it was done very cleverly as well." [82]

They too learned that the 'enemy' was not so other. Para Ken Lukowiak, one of the many military men who shifted to respecting Wendy after beginning to see him as a participant, not an outsider, affirmed this temporary coming-together. He recorded that Paras came to regard Wendy as "One of our war's leading characters." On the voyage back Lukowiak was playing cards with some paratroopers when Wendy waved as he walked past.

> "One of the 3 Para soldiers asked who the fuck the dirty little queer was. I think he wished he hadn't. The whole table turned on him. He was told that Wendy might be queer but he was our fucking queer, and unless he wanted his fucking teeth pushed down his fucking throat he should shut the fuck up. The soldier apologized."[83]

Thus crew and passengers shifted in gendered attitudes. Intense proximity forced knowledge and tolerance upon people. Their common cause united them. Victory, and having evaded death, relaxed them.

---

[81] The 'girl' is a *maruni*, a role which originates in nineteenth century *kaids*, entertainments designed to boost flagging morale when men were at outposts far from Nepal and women. Seer, *With the Gurkhas,* p. 310.
[82] Terry H, interview with author, 2 Feb 2006.
[83] Lukowiak, *A Soldier's*, p. 171.

Figure 21: Wendy Gibson and Frankie Green welcome home their shipmates who went again to the Falklands, February 2,1983.

Conclusion

The available evidence from merchant personnel going to the Falklands/Malvinas Conflict makes three key things clear. Women seafarers were present in this war situation, and negotiated complex shipboard relations with their male military guests. The usual campery continued, but more cautiously. Performative hyper-femininity was never in any way of proof that men weren't men; in fact it helped some see how much stereotypes about sexual orientation had been limiting them. And military men with a felt obligation to be hyper-masculine managed to cope with the presence both of women and camp men: indeed, some used the situation for homosexual experimentation and heterosexual romance. These were extraordinary voyages. They were dictated by habitus, and enabled by the voyage's heterotopic nature, but changed again by the impressive adaptations that human beings make as they cope with war.

Absences of popular cultural recognition of merchant personnel going to the Falklands/Malvinas, especially of marginalized crew such as women and camp men, reflects a preferred version of the conflict where hegemonic masculinity and femininity dominate and non-heterosexuality has no place. This article's examination of the role gender played for people sailing to the Falklands/Malvinas Conflict has found only piecemeal evidence. There is much complexity that needs more disentangling than is possible here. Certainly it requires that maritime historiographers begin to recognize gender and sexual orientation as a valid category of analysis, not an irrelevance or something distasteful.

This unique oral testimony, as well as written memoirs and the few available documents show that voyages were deeply un-touristic in that they were not focused on pleasurable consumption, not done with free will, and so deeply imbricated with death and destruction. And yet there was that surreal holiday atmosphere, that ludic delight in ice cream, sunbathing and sexual liaison. New understandings of seafarers and warriors as voyagers in their own right are needed, so that comparisons across time, space and situations can be made. For example, how do these patterns connect with troops' use of airplanes to go to new wars such as Afghanistan?

In analyzing the Falklands/Malvinas Conflict it is clear that in a reversal of the usual host/ guest positions on ships, the hosts had a somewhat happier time than the guests, because they were civilians, not warriors. But the merchant seafarers were deeply implicated in war-making. For example, their interest in victory, and in illegally acquiring Argentinean weapons and helmets as souvenirs, was as avid as that of troops. Death, Post-Traumatic Stress Disorder and suicide were sad consequences for some. A far higher percentage of seafarers than soldiers came back alive. Nine Merchant Navy men were lost (0.2 per cent) in contrast to 247 of the 30,000-plus armed forces (0.8 per cent). Combat-related Post-Traumatic Stress Disorder is so severe that at least 20 per cent of military veterans are thought to have it. And at the last count 264 military veterans had committed suicide.[84] There are no formal studies of PTSD incidence in merchant seafarers, but informal evidence from counselor's reports that it exists.

Gender relations certainly ran on familiar lines that related to habitat-specific habitus, as well as on unfamiliar tracks caused by the disruption of war. That is, camp stewards carried on camping, women carried on being treated like desirable ladies, male merchant personnel carried on being gay-friendly. It appears that the polarization of hegemonic femininity and masculinity was to some extent exacerbated by war, as well as lessened. Real women were excluded, or faced with relegation, if not exclusion. Correspondingly, 'femininity' in male troops had long been seen to be inimical to pursuing a war.

---

[84] Information from the South Atlantic Medal Association and http://www.dailymail.co.uk/news/article-94492/Suicide-Falklands-veterans.html#ixzz1bRczN9NU, accessed 21 Oct 2011. Nine Merchant Navy people died, none of them women. The three civilian casualties in the Falklands were all women and all victims of 'friendly fire'.

Homosexuality on the Falklands/Malvinas Conflict ships appears to have been a situation of some conflict and denial caused by the guests' focus on war and the consequent pressure to perform in a very robustly masculine style. Their habitus appears to have led many warriors to initially and formally rebuff civilian homosexual hosts, especially camp men, on the outward voyage, although some who were not feeling bereaved were able to ease up on the trip home.

For this writer, the significance of what occurred is a heartening sign of human potential to change and to accept the Othered. If gendered norms could sometimes be overlooked in the shared pursuits of the greater goal – military victory in this case – then where else might such beneficial change occur? Transcendence of norms was temporarily enabled by the focus on being in a crisis, close encounters with the Othered, and serving a common purpose within a heterotopia. If the real civilian Wendy/ Roy Gibson could be accepted by Royal Marines and paratroopers, those acmes of robust masculinity, then how many other Wendys could be more quietly accepted into the hearts and arms of men who had imagined they were safely straight?

The South Atlantic was the site of these extraordinary experiences, and perhaps the geographical far-awayness of that sea exacerbated the heterotopic nature of the ship. Never before in war have frocks and guns been as close as on these passenger ships temporarily taken out of their usual pattern. And probably never has a war been so like a cruise holiday – in external appearances. Never before have men so flagrantly camped their way to and from war. That makes these voyages the most extraordinary in naval, military and maritime history.

5. "Even being idle has to be learned" – Overcoming Liminality on Atlantic Passenger Ships, 1840-1920s

Dagmar Bellmann

Introduction

Can travelling across the high seas be seen as pleasure trip? The answer to this question seems to be self-evident from today's perspective: pleasure cruises are supposed to be fun. Nothing is better suited to illustrate this point than the advertisement of a big cruising company in 2012: "Carnival is so sure that passengers will be satisfied with their cruise experience that they are the only cruise line to offer a Vacation Guarantee. You just have to notify them before your first port of call if you are unhappy for any reason."[1]
However, there do not need to be accidents like the shipwrecking of the cruise liner *Costa Concordia* in the Mediterranean in January 2012 or the famous sinking of the *Titanic* to arouse ambivalent feelings about sea voyages. In the course of the 19th century, practices were developed to keep these ambivalences at bay, which were taken to the extreme in the late 20th century. This essay intends to uncover this important precondition for modern cruise tourism.
Positive attitudes towards sea travelling are relatively recent in the long history of sea voyages. Even with the advent of steamships on the Atlantic Ocean in the 1840s, travelling by ship was still seen as a life-threatening experience. An example for this opinion is the *Guidebook for travelling ladies* from the American Catherine R. Ledoux, who wrote in 1878:

> "Some advise wearing old worthless clothing at sea [...]. To this I cannot wholly agree. You might be very ill, requiring strangers to be about you. Accidents, too, and loss of life are possible at sea, and I have always felt that a body washed ashore clad in good clothes, would receive more respect and kinder care than if dressed in those only fit for the rag bag."[2]

Sea voyages were only gradually becoming pleasure trips in the 1880s. In this period, passengers began to use ships not just for mere transportation.

---

[1] Carnival Line http://www.cruisesfun.com/carnivalcruiseline.html, accessed 17 Jan 2012.
[2] Kate Reid Ledoux, *Ocean Notes and Foreign Travel for Ladies,* New York 1878, Reprint 2009, p. 10.

Nevertheless, the rate of ship accidents was still relatively high at that time. The German newspaper *Hamburgischer Correspondent. Morgen-Zeitung der Börsen-Halle* published the number of ships that were lost worldwide only in the month of August 1882: 74 sailing ships and 16 steamships.[3] So technology obviously was not the only factor in transforming the image of passenger shipping. Other factors were also necessary in order to reduce ambivalent feelings in favour of positive feelings about sea voyages.

Travelling is not only exciting, inspiring or amusing, but it can also turn into a frightful experience if the passenger is not familiar with the area he or she is visiting. This is especially true for a voyage on the ocean. It was an experience that could cause alternately fear, boredom or a sense of being lost, of feeling 'in-between' and of passing a "threshold"[4] in this alien and uncanny space of the sea. One way of overcoming these negative feelings were games and playful rituals. The voyagers thus sought to transform their undefined situation between land and sea, between technology and nature, between security and danger, into a clear and orderly situation.

This paper will concentrate on means – and limits – of converting ambivalent feelings of the passengers into an understanding of Atlantic travel as pleasure by creating rituals on board ships such as farewell ceremonies, Captain's dinners, games and sports. These activities played not the only, but certainly a major role in soothing and comforting the passengers, helping them to push aside the knowledge of the inherent dangers of ocean travel and to create a positive image instead. I will analyze these activities with the concept of *liminality* by Victor Turner. With this approach, not only rituals and games on board ships can be analyzed, but also the ambivalent potential of sea voyages allowing for both negative and positive conceptions. The focus lies on the period between 1880 and the 1930s with regard to Atlantic passenger transportation with a side-glance to pleasure trips to other destinations.

This article is divided into four parts: First, I will give a brief overview of steamship travelling across the Atlantic in the 19th century. As there is a wide range of literature about the technical development of steamships available[5], I

---

[3] *Hamburger Correspondent*, 3 Oct 1882. The journal derived these numbers from the Bureau Veritas, an internationally renowned classification and certification society for ships.

[4] Walter Benjamin, *Gesammelte Schriften V.1 - Das Passagen-Werk*, Frankfurt am Main 1982, p. 618.

[5] See for example Denis Griffiths, *Power of the great liners – A history of Atlantic marine engineering,* Sparkford 1990; Denis Griffiths, *Steam at sea – Two*

will focus on aspects that were important for the perception of ocean voyages. Second, I will explain Victor Turner's theory of liminality and its application to steamship travel. Third, liminal experiences on board ships causing fear, distress or ambivalent feelings of the in-between are presented. Afterwards, means on board ship to overcome these liminal experiences will be analyzed, followed by a brief discussion of their limitations. The article closes with a summary and outlook on future research.

Travelling across the Atlantic

With the advent of steam shipping across the Atlantic, a new era of passenger transportation began. With steamships, faster voyages with reliable timetables were possible. The first steamship that crossed the Atlantic was the *Savannah* in 1819, though the ship used sails most of the time during the passage.[6] Nevertheless, it was not until 1838 that regular trips across the Atlantic started with the two ships *Sirius* and *Great Western*.[7] Steamship travelling across the Atlantic from its beginnings up to the Second World War can basically be divided into three phases: the first lasted from 1840 to the late 1870s, the second from the 1880s to the First World War, and the third from 1918 until the Second World War.

---

centuries of steam-powered ships, London 1997; Denis Griffiths, Lambert Andrew and Walker Fred, *Brunel's ships,* London 1999; Lars U. Scholl (Ed.), *Technikgeschichte des industriellen Schiffbaus in Deutschland Bd. 1: Handelsschiffe, Marine-Überwasserschiffe, U-Boote,* Hamburg 1994; and Lars U. Scholl (Ed.), *Technikgeschichte des industriellen Schiffbaus in Deutschland Bd. 2: Hauptantriebe, Schiffspropulsion, Elektrotechnik,* Hamburg 1996.

[6] Denis Griffiths estimates that the journey took 27 ½ days, see *Griffiths, Steam at sea,* p. 8. Some sources claim 22 or even 20 days, see the journal *Leisure Hour,* Oct 1885 and Christoph Bernoulli, *Handbuch der Dampfmaschinen-Lehre für Techniker und Freunde der Mechanik,* Stuttgart and Tübingen 1833. For an account of this first trip see J. Elfreth Watkins, "The log of the Savannah", in: *Report of the United States National Museum* 1890, p. 611–639.

[7] See Tjard Schwarz and Ernst von Halle, *Die Schiffbauindustrie in Deutschland und im Auslande: Erster Theil: Der Weltschiffbau. Unter Benutzung amtlichen Materials,* Berlin 1902.

During the first phase, internationally operating steamship companies were formed, such as the Cunard Line in 1840[8], the Hamburg-America Line in 1847, the Inman Line in 1850, the Norddeutscher Lloyd in 1856 and the White Star Line in 1869.[9] The first steamships on the Atlantic were technically similar to steamboats on rivers, aside from the fact that they were larger and carried sailing rigs with them. These were partly used in turn with steam power, partly to counterbalance the movement of the ships.[10] The first ocean-going ship hulls were of wood, from the late 1840s of iron; paddle wheels were used until 1866.[11] In the 1850s and 1860s, some significant innovations were introduced such as screw propulsion instead of wheel propulsion and condenser and compound engines. In the 1870s steel replaced the iron hulls of the ships. Only then, it was possible to enlarge the size of the ships. In 1897 the steam turbine was introduced and replaced the old compound system. The introduction of electricity on board ships was also important; in 1879 the company Siemens & Halske installed the first electrical lights on board steamships.[12]

Technological developments also brought considerable changes with regard to passenger accommodations. Most important was the introduction of screw propulsion in turn for wheel propulsion. Before, all machinery had to be placed in the middle of the ship and thus all passenger rooms had to be placed in the aft and in the front of the ships. Now, amidships became the center of passenger accommodation for first class passengers (whereas steerage passengers were still placed in other sections of the ship). The space in the middle of the ship had two

---

[8] This shipping company was founded by the Canadian Samuel Cunard in 1840 and was first named British and North American Royal Mail Steam Packet Co. This name was changed to Cunard Steam Ship Company Limited in 1878. In 1934 the Cunard Company bought the White Star Line and formed the Cunard-White Star Limited.

[9] This company was founded by T. H. Ismay in 1867. For further information see Robin Gardiner, *The history of the White Star Line,* Hersham 2001. For all the other references see N. R. P. Bonsor, *North Atlantic Seaway – An illustrated history of the passengers services linking the old world with the new*, Lancashire 1955.

[10] Arnold Kludas and Dietmar Borchert, *Das Blaue Band des Nordatlantiks - Der Mythos eines legendären Wettbewerbs,* Hamburg 1999.

[11] Bonsor, *North Atlantic*, p. 596.

[12] According to a brochure of the Siemens company Siemens AG: Industrial Solutions and Services Marine Solutions (2007), *125 Jahre Innovationen im Schiffbau,* https://www.industry.siemens.com/verticals/global/de/marine/Documents/ 125-Jahre-Schiffbau-de.pdf, accessed 13 Aug 2017.

advantages: first, ships' movements were considerably attenuated, and second, much more space for public rooms was available.

The space on board the first steamships was narrow and passenger accommodations extremely plain. Charles Dickens voyage in the *Britannia* in 1842 is famous in this respect for humoristic passages such as:

> "[...] that this utterly impracticable, thoroughly hopeless, and profoundly preposterous box, had the remotest reference to, or connection with, those chaste and pretty, not to say gorgeous little bowers, sketched by a masterly hand, in the highly varnished lithographic plan hanging up in the agent's counting-house in the city of London: that this room of state, in short, could be anything but a pleasant fiction [...] – these were truths which I really could not, for the moment, bring my mind at all to bear upon or comprehend."[13]

An example for a typical ship's arrangement during this first period is the *Bremen* of the Norddeutscher Lloyd in 1857. As Germany's shipbuilding industry lagged behind the British industry, which was leading in the world, German ships were ordered in Great Britain until the 1880s.[14] The *Bremen* was built by Caird & Co. in Greenock.[15] Behind the machine room was a long saloon with doors leading directly to the sleeping cabins. In the middle of the saloon tables and benches with foldable backs were installed so that they could be either used as sitting chairs or sofas. Illumination was provided by the side windows and a few roof lights. At night, oil lamps illuminated the saloon. The cabins were intended for two, three or four persons with bunk beds, a small washing table, a sofa and a

---

[13] Charles Dickens, *The Complete Works of Charles Dickens (in 30 volumes, illustrated): American Notes and Pictures from Italy,* New York 2009.

[14] Only then, German shipbuilders started to become competitive. This can largely be contributed to the fact that the building of steamers was supported by the German government by a law from 6th April 1885, the so-called "Dampfersubventionsgesetz". According to this law, only shipping companies that ordered German-built steamships could apply for German post line contracts, see Tjard Schwarz and Ernst von Halle, *Die Schiffbauindustrie in Deutschland und im Auslande: Zweiter Theil: Der deutsche Schiffbau. Unter Benutzung amtlichen Materials,* Berlin 1902. Great Britain started to subsidize post line companies in a similar way in 1838, the United States in 1849/50 and France in 1851, see *Schwarz et al. 1902,* p. 113.

[15] For the following description see Rudolf Haack and Carl Busley, *Die technische Entwicklung des Norddeutschen Lloyds und der HAPAG). Erstmaliger Reprint d. Sonderdr. aus d. Zeitschrift des Vereins Deutscher Ingenieure, Jg. 1890 – 1892, erschienen im Jahre 1893, neu hrsg. u. eingeleitet von Lars U. Scholl,* Düsseldorf 1986.

window. From the saloon another door lead to the saloon for the ladies that also offered access to a small bathroom area. There were no upper decks besides staircases that led downstairs and to the wheelhouses.

In this first phase of steamship travelling across the Atlantic, not only emigrants – who remained by large the most important customer group until the First World War – but also an international rich clientele was targeted for the upper cabin classes. Especially rich Americans became more and more important as is described in an article published in the *Milwaukee Sentinel* in 1872:

> "The steamships leaving New York and Boston are crowded with passengers, and all the best stateroom accommodations are engaged ahead into midsummer. [...] We are known to the world as a nation of travelers, [...] we think little of crossing the sea, or of exploring Europe from end to end. [...] But as time goes on, those who have already crossed the ocean are repeating the trip, many of them very frequently. [...] On one of the crack Cunarders not long since, on her way to Liverpool, crowded with first-class passengers, more than half the number had previously been in Europe, [...] English travel to the United States is increasing, but not so rapidly". [16]

But it was not until the second phase of steamship voyages that excursion trips for touristic purposes on the high seas were explicitly offered.[17] Albert Ballin, the director of the Hamburg-America Line, is usually said to have been the inventor of excursion trips on a regular basis, with a trip offered by his line in 1891 on board the *Augusta Victoria*.[18] In the decades before, only a handful of pleasure trips were made as for example the trip of the P&O Company 1844 to the Mediterranean Sea, which W.M. Thackeray attended; the voyage of the *Quaker City* to the Holy Land in 1867, where Mark Twain was on board[19]; or the world cruise of the SS Ceylon in 1881/82.[20] The most cherished routes were trips to the

---

[16] "Transatlantic Travel", in: *The Milwaukee Sentinel*, 17 May 1872.

[17] Pleasure trips on rivers and on smaller lakes were already offered in the 1820s, see John Armstrong and David M. Williams, "The steamboat and popular tourism", in: *The Journal of transport history* 26: 1 (2005), p. 61-77; John Armstrong and David M. Williams, "The Thames and Recreation, 1815 – 1840", in: *London Journal* 30:2 (2005), p. 25-39 and Benedikt Bock, *Baedeker und Cook – Tourismus am Mittelrhein 1756 bis ca. 1914,* Frankfurt am Main 2010.

[18] Arnold Kludas, *Vergnügungsreisen zur See. Eine Geschichte der deutschen Kreuzfahrt: Bd. 1: 1889 – 1939*, Hamburg 2002.

[19] See Ibid., p. 14-16.

[20] David M. Williams, "The Extent of Transport Services' Integration: SS Ceylon and the First 'Round the World' Cruise, 1881– 1882", in: *International Journal of Maritime History*, XV: 2 (2003), p. 135-146.

North Cape, to the Mediterranean Sea and to the Caribbean Islands. The ships used for such trips were rarely built expressly for this purpose, but were regular liners used in low seasons (so-called "Dual Purpose-ships") or ships that were altered into pleasure cruisers.[21] The term "cruise" was not used until the 20th century[22]; instead, expressions like "excursion" or "pleasure trip" were employed. At the end of this second phase of Atlantic steamship travelling, shipping companies tried to win a new clientele other than first and second-class cabins on the one hand and the steerage class on the other hand by creating third-class cabins. For example, around the turn of the century, the Norddeutscher Lloyd offered third-class cabins for all people who could not afford second-class cabins, but nevertheless wished to distinguish themselves from "South-East European steerage class passengers".[23] In this second phase of steamship travelling, steamships increasingly became a matter of national pride. To a great degree, this development was due to the fact that national armament programs were launched, especially by Great Britain and Germany.[24] The enthusiasm for naval issues was enormous in both countries.[25] Not only launches of naval vessels and naval reviews turned into national events but also the building and launching of the

---

[21] See Kludas *Vergnügungsreisen,* p. 178-181; and Philip Dawson, *Cruise ships: An evolution in design,* London 2000.

[22] A German dictionary for tourism even claims that – at least in Germany – the term "cruise trip" [„Kreuzfahrt"] was not used until the year 1960, when the Hamburg America Line introduced this term to promote its ship *Hanseatic,* see Günter Schroeder, *Lexikon der Tourismuswirtschaft,* Hamburg 1995, p. 151.

[23] Own translation of: "von dem Gros der südosteuropäischen Auswanderer getrennt befördert" (Archive of the Deutsche Schifffahrtsmuseum, NDL 1900 – 1905 [false dating, *own comment*], *Reisen in der III. Klasse nach New York,* around 1909, p. 1–8: 2).

[24] For Great Britain, this was the *Naval Defence Act* from 1889, see Sidney Pollard and Paul Robertson, *The British shipbuilding industry, 1870 – 1914,* Cambridge/Mass, 1979. In Germany the armament program started with the first law for the building of a naval fleet from 1898. Further amendments followed in the years 1906, 1908 and 1912, see Heinrich Walle, "Schlachtflottenbau und Flottenenthusiasmus", in: Volker Plagemann (Ed.), *Übersee: Seefahrt und Seemacht im deutschen Kaiserreich,* München 1988, p. 211-215.

[25] See Jürgen Osterhammel, *Die Verwandlung der Welt: Eine Geschichte des 19. Jahrhunderts,* München 2011; and Rolf Hobson, *Maritimer Imperialismus: Seemachtideologie, seestrategisches Denken und der Tirpitzplan, 1875 – 1914,* München 2004.

newest ships destined for the use on the Atlantic.²⁶ An important factor in this nationalization of civil shipping was the race for the so-called "Blue Riband", the record for the fastest tour westbound to the United States.²⁷ Much has been written about this legendary honorary title.²⁸ The "Blue Riband" has never been officially awarded, but was proclaimed by journalists. In 1890, the term "Blue Riband" was first mentioned and was then borrowed from horseracing.²⁹ The "Blue Riband" was closely connected to national pride and the fight for supremacy on the Atlantic, and there was fierce competition mainly between British, German and US-American shipping lines to beat the latest record.

During the third phase after the First World War, more and more people travelled across the Atlantic. The search for a new clientele for third-class cabins, which had already started before the First World War, was present in every company. The most important reason was the decreasing number of emigrants crossing the Atlantic due to the restrictive immigration policy of the United States.³⁰ In this phase, conceptions about "filthy lower classes" could no longer be openly pronounced, as had been the case in the first period of steamship travel. Instead, the shipping companies targeted different customer groups and stressed the recreational and beneficial effects of ocean travelling.

This is the context of passenger transportation across the Atlantic during the 19th century and until the 1930s. But this so-called 'objective' history of facts does not take into account the passengers themselves.³¹ Nothing is said about how they felt on board ships, what their pastimes were and how these developed during the

---

26 See Jan Rüger, *The great naval game: Britain and Germany in the age of Empire*, Cambridge 2007; Mark A. Russell, "Picturing the Imperator: Passenger Shipping as Art and National Symbol in the German Empire", in: *Central European History*, 44 (2011), p. 227-256.
27 For a list of record passages for westbound as well as eastbound trips across the Atlantic from 1838 to 1952, see Bonsor, *North Atlantic*, p. 591-593.
28 For a thorough critical bibliography, see Kludas and Borchert, *Das Blaue Band*, p. 19-26.
29 Ibid., p. 10.
30 In 1924, United States' Congress approved a law stipulating the yearly numbers of immigrants to 164,000 a year based on quotas on nationality based on the census of 1890, the "National Origins Act", see Volker Depkat, *Geschichte Nordamerikas: Eine Einführung*, Köln 2008.
31 One exception is the monograph of Markus Günther, *Auf dem Weg in die Neue Welt: Die Atlantiküberquerung im Zeitalter der Massenauswanderung; 1818 – 1914*, Augsburg 2005. The author herein analyses travel accounts of emigrants with regard to their experiences of the Atlantic passage, but concentrates on the individual experiences.

period covered in this article. My basic argument is that social practices such as games and rituals were intended to reduce ambiguities and fears about travelling on sea in order to create an explicitly positive image of about crossing the ocean. This was partly undertaken by passengers themselves, partly promoted by shipping companies. During this process, three distinctive characteristics of pastimes on board can be observed: First, pastimes that used to be self-organized increasingly became the crew's responsibility, which also meant that these pastimes lost their spontaneity and flexibility. Second, after some time passengers came to expect and anticipate certain travel experiences and emotions. Last, pastimes on board became important in order to gain social prestige.

The Liminal and the Liminoid

In order to understand the content and meaning of pastime on board ships, the theory of *liminality* by the anthropologist Victor Turner is used. Turner based his ideas on Arnold van Gennep's *Rites de passage*. The word *liminal* was derived from the Latin *limen* for "threshold". According to van Gennep, "rites de passage" in tribal cultures can be divided into three different phases: separation, transition and incorporation. It is during the transition that the phenomenon of the *liminal* appears.[32] It is this phase of transition that Turner concentrated on in his anthropological studies. But his ideas can be transposed to other fields of research, as Turner himself did when he broadened his theory from tribal cultures to cultures driven by industrialization and individualization, like the so-called modern Western societies.

For Turner, the *liminal* denotes a phase which has a potential for change, as people who are transgressing the phase of the *liminal* are passing a threshold separating them from their previous lives.[33] This potential change is due to the fact that during the *liminal* phase, people have to follow rituals which give them new social roles before returning or reintegrating into their community. According to Turner, innovation can take place in liminal phases, which later on become "legitimated in central sectors".[34] But as the *liminal* indicates the new and the unknown, it can also engender ambiguity and fearful feelings. This

---

[32] Arnold van Gennep, *Les rites de passage: Étude systématique des rites de la porte et du seuil, de l'hospitalité, de l'adoption, de la grossesse et de l'accouchement, de la naissance, de l'enfance,* Paris DL 2011.

[33] Victor Turner, "Liminal to Liminoid, in Play, Flow, and Ritual. An Essay in Comparative Symbology", in: Victor Turner (Ed.), *From ritual to theatre: The human seriousness of play,* New York 1982, p. 20-60: 24-25.

[34] Ibid., p. 45.

correlates with the fact that people often have to enter a special place while going through the phase of transition. This 'other' place has the double-effect of placing people physically and socially in the in-between. The problem of the in-between is its uncertainty and unstableness, but at the same time, its virtue is its openness for experimenting with new social forms of living together. Thus, there are multiple potential outcomes of the *liminal* state.

Turner's concept can be applied to the study of sea voyages on modern passenger liners with one exception: in Turner's view, the transformative *liminal* phase is supposed to change the participants for good. This is not the case for a normal sea voyage. Rather, a sea voyage is a temporary suspension of normal life which is resumed once the voyage ends. Besides this exemption, a ship is a *liminal* space as well as others: it provides a temporary home for people of both sexes and of all classes who are transgressing national borders and find themselves on the water in the middle of nowhere. They live in a place strictly separated from normal social life. But not only a ship is a *liminal* space; this is also true for the sea itself. The sea is an alien space which seems to be infinitely wide and deep and adverse to human habitation. In the Christian tradition, the Sea was a refuge for the Leviathan[35] and has often been associated with trouble, disaster and madness.[36] Sea travelling was considered life threatening and extremely uncomfortable. To go on board a ship "just for the fun of it" was unthinkable still in the 1870s. Voyaging by ship meant potential danger, which could give rise to "social dramas", as Victor Turner puts it. For him, "social dramas" have four stages: breach, crisis, redress, and either reintegration or recognition of schism.[37] He claims that these social dramas have a "universal processual form"[38] and find their expression in the stage of redress in cultural performances.[39] These are needed in order to give "the appearance of sense and order to the events leading up to and constituting the crisis." In other words: the state of the *liminal* or crisis is transcended by cultural performances and practices.[40]

These forms of cultural practices often find their way in *liminoid* elements. In difference to the *liminal* which comprises compulsory practices in tribal cultures, Turner stresses the element of play free from external constraints. In his view, only the division between work and leisure, which modern western society had

---

[35] See Old Testament, The Book of Job, 41:1-34.
[36] Alain Corbin, Meereslust. Das Abendland und die Entdeckung der Küste, Berlin 1990, p. 20.
[37] Turner, *ritual to theatre*, p. 69.
[38] Ibid., p. 71.
[39] Ibid., p. 74.
[40] Ibid., p. 75.

engendered, can provide this opportunity for play.[41] Leisure does not only set people free from constraints, but in addition gives "freedom to transcend social structural limitations, freedom to play [...] with ideas, with fantasies, with words [...], with paint [...], and with social relationships."[42] Of course, Turner's strict distinction between 'tribal cultures' and 'industrialized cultures' can be challenged, but nevertheless his argumentation is helpful in finding the common roots of art performances, entertainment and leisure activities in spite of all their differences: they are all means of coping with the *liminal*.

Before the age of mass emigration[43] to North America during the 19th century – and to a smaller extent to South America – there were practically no tourists on board ships alongside seamen, explorers and a few businessmen and adventurers. Sea life was restricted to a very small group. When passengers began to cross the Atlantic, they developed new specific rules and rituals for the departure, the crossing and the landing. In this *liminal* state of being, new rituals were created to develop a new lifestyle on board which had the potential to form a *communitas;* that means the forming of a spontaneous community of all passengers taking part in the state of the *liminal*. Turner defines *communitas* as "society as an unstructured or rudimentarily structured and relatively undifferentiated comitatus, community, or even communion of equal individuals who submit together to the general authority of the ritual elders."[44] In the period studied in this article, the community on board the first and second classes can basically be divided into a leading group and another group submitting to their rules. The leading group plays the role of the "ritual elders" who, according to Turner, lead and advise the *communitas* of passengers. These elders are often experienced travelers imposing their way of seeing things on newcomers by giving normative advice and judgements.

There are three principal modes of developing a new lifestyle on board a passenger ship: presentations acted out for the passengers; rules for the passengers; rituals and games performed by the passengers themselves. Presentations are events like listening to concerts or watching a movie. Rules are formally established regulations by the passenger line and the captain which must be observed. Such regulations comprise a multitude of domains: regulations which provide order on board, rules which divide the day in times for eating and times for sleeping and which prescribe the demarcation between the different

---

[41] See ibid., p. 35.
[42] Ibid., p. 37.
[43] Apart from the mass transportation of slaves as history of its own right.
[44] Victor Turner, *The ritual process – Structure and anti-structure,* New York 1995, p. 96.

passenger classes. Presentations and rules are passively experienced, observed and sometimes challenged by passengers whereas rituals and games are actively performed by them.

Rituals can be defined as symbolic *mis-en-scènes* with performative character[45] and some main characteristics: they follow formal rules and have a normative function as they reflect and consolidate power structures; they have a certain dramatic structure; they are performed in public[46] and they create a community by inviting everybody to participate. It is characteristic for rituals that they stand outside of everyday life, but nevertheless recall the mundane social order.[47] Rituals and games on board ships are closely linked, even if rituals belong more to the *liminal* and games more to the *liminoid*. They both give a 'storyboard' of social practices to the participants, which helps them deal with the in-between, with the situation of being on a ship. There are a multitude of social practices: balls and diners, dress codes, the outstanding role of the captain for the social fabric on board, the Captain's Dinner, games typical for sea voyages such as *shuffleboard*, farewell and welcoming rituals etc. As sea voyages became more popular, such games and rituals were diffused in guidebooks, narratives from other passengers, articles and literature. Sea voyages thus turned from threatening experiences into something that could be mastered before even setting foot on board a ship.

Liminal Experiences

Liminal experiences in the sense of Turner can take many forms on a passenger ship. A sea voyage generates experiences that evoke both positive and negative feelings. Life on board away from every-day life can be regenerating, but it can also evoke boredom and disorientation with regard to time and space. The awe and beauty of the sea can entail sublime feelings, but also fears of shipwrecking

---

[45] This definition is given by Christoph Wulf and Jörg Zirfas, "Performativität, Ritual und Gemeinschaft - Ein Beitrag aus erziehungswissenschaftlicher Sicht", in: Dietrich S. Harth and Gerrit Jasper (Eds.), *Ritualdynamik. Kulturübergreifende Studien zur Theorie und Geschichte rituellen Handelns*, Heidelberg 2004, p. 73-93: 74.

[46] This means that a ritual creates reality and does not only imitate it, see ibid., p. 86.

[47] This – not exhaustive – list of attributes for rituals is compiled from Burckhard Dücker, *Rituale, Formen – Funktionen – Geschichte; eine Einführung in die Ritualwissenschaft*, Stuttgart, Weimar 2007, p. 29-30; and Wulf and Zirfas, Performativität, p. 73-93.

and a sense of the loneliness of human life. Society on board can have a lively and stimulating effect but can also lead to annoyance and oppressing constraints from fellow-passengers. These experiences and their perception do not remain the same in the course of time but tend to change in accordance with broader cultural and technological developments.

In this chapter I will concentrate on the more negative aspects of *liminal* experiences. A lot of these were first experienced on sailing vessels. Travel reports of sailing vessels were well known among the public, especially since the advent of mass emigration to America. The bad image of sea voyages was based on accounts like this one:

> "I feel circumscribed in limit above deck; but, in the steerage cabin below, my feeling is simply suffocation, [...] I turn, [...] to the doctor's cabin. To denote its size by a pleasant word, it is snug; scarcely large enough to swing a cat in, [...] If we weep here, it may be from fatigue, hunger, or exhaustion; but we cannot cherish sentiment".[48]

Whoever might think that all these inconveniences and fears must have passed away as soon as steamships replaced sailing ships is wrong – even if we take into account the increased speed of steamships, which reduced the travelling time considerably. The inter-relation between technological changes and changes in the perception of sea travelling is in fact much more complicated and cannot be reduced to in a one-way relationship towards perpetual progress. Fear could last during the age of steamship, and ambivalent feelings still remained, but they could take new shapes and interpretations.

A good example for a change in perception is seasickness. This overall topic across all centuries underwent an important change: when it was first associated with dangerous gales and thus potentially life threatening, it was considered very dangerous for the health. But at the end of the 19th century it became more and more a favorite topic of amusement and laughter. Better technological equipment alone did not automatically enhance improvements in ship movements, which could have directly resulted in a corresponding change in the feeling of being seasick. The reason for this is that in the beginning of machine propulsion steamships were even more prone to waves than sailing ships. The sensation of seasickness itself basically remained the same until the introduction of anti-rolling tanks in the first decades of the 20th century. In my view it was moreover due to the facts that sea travelling in general became less dangerous combined with the reduced travelling time and the overall feeling of general comfort that

---

[48] *All the Year Round*, 12 Apr 1862, p. 113, 115.

entailed a certain feeling of security among the passengers. It was the feeling of security that changed the notion of seasickness and not the sensation of feeling seasick itself.

Another problem that was already known in the age of travelling by sail, especially in times of calms at sea, was boredom. This problem remained on board steamships but underwent important changes in interpretation: although boredom was still considered a nuisance, it paled in comparison to other dangers at sea, and in addition, it seemed to be easily cured. We can read this line of interpretation in a marketing brochure of the *Cunard Line* of 1876, written by the journalist George Augustus Sala: "Ennui is the Real Flying Dutchman. Clap on all sail; get up steam at its highest; and let us get away from that awfullest of all bores, Captain Vanderdecken, late of the Dutch Merchant Navy".[49]

Boredom is associated here with the legend of the Flying Dutchman van der Decken who was restlessly sailing on the seas without ever finding salvation. By exaggerating the pains of boredom, the author ironically assures his readers that the only dangerous thing on a steam voyage nowadays is boredom, but that even this could be tackled on board a modern steamship. Here, we can find a similar line of argumentation as in the case of seasickness: compared with real physical dangers and inconveniences of sea voyages in the past, seasickness and boredom became minor problems.

A real concern associated with boredom was less openly admitted by steamship companies: they feared that boredom could lead to agitation among the passengers and disturb the established order on board. It was considered a necessity to entertain the passengers with all kinds of amusements. Everything had to be done by the personnel to "ban" and to "fight" boredom on board a ship.[50] As for the passengers, the more their attention drifted away from inconveniences and dangers of sea travelling, the more another danger came to the fore: boredom and monotony could lead to a confrontation with oneself, with one's own situation. As a German doctor on service on a German passenger ship to South America noted in a letter to his wife on 30th June 1923: "One could almost say that even being idle has to be learned."[51] Boredom was also closely associated

---

[49] George Augustus Sala, "Transatlantic Trips", in: *Official Guide & Album of the Cunard Steamship Service*, 1876, p. 79-95: 81.

[50] Ulrich Myers, "Wie man sich an Bord vergnügt – Eine Skizze aus dem modernen Reiseleben", in: Bibliothek der Unterhaltung und des Wissens (around 1890), Archive des Deutschen Schiffahrtsmuseum II B 77-4182.

[51] *Own translation of:* "Selbst das Faulenzen will gelernt sein." (Alfred Engler, *Briefe an seine Frau*, 1923, Archive des Deutschen Tagebucharchiv Emmendingen (DTA), Reg.No. 279, transcript)

with idleness, a vice that was seriously condemned in the Protestant tradition. This is the reason why most distractions had to be given justifications such as being sociable, sportive or healthy. Activities focusing on health and sports were intended for individual improvement of the body and spirit and thus socially accepted.

Another problem was disorientation with regard to time and space. The passengers lost any feeling for times of the day if they weren't instructed by watches or the ship's crews. Even worse was their feeling of being lost in space. Nothing but water – this was the only view they had. Even the sky sometimes blended with the water in bad weather and storm. Orientation with one's own senses was thus impossible on the high seas. One voyager put this feeling into these words:

> "The infinite volume of the ocean would, I fear, mentally drown us. […] voyaging in this boundless space, where clouds only are formed and rain made, there is nothing to catch the wandering eye or fix and occupy the vacant mind. There are no objects, no distinctions, no limits, no standards, no contrasts."[52]

The sea could arouse notions of the vastness, brutality and depth of the ocean in contrast to one's own little and fragile existence. Closely linked to these feelings were fears of shipwrecking as was lively described by a German musician travelling to the United States in 1909: "At sea! On the Atlantic Ocean for a long, long time. Not everyone is able to walk on water. Exactly at 11 o'clock we went on board the huge and stately English vessel Majestic, which was to carry us, dead or alive, to the New World."[53]

Even the society on board could cause considerable distress. The passenger was not able to escape his or her fellow passengers; they usually even had to share their cabins with strangers. Accounts of annoying fellow passengers were already known in travel reports about journeys by coaches and trains. The situation on board ship was even worse as people were forced to live together for days or even weeks. As early as 1859 this problem was addressed in a satire written by Thomas Chandler Haliburton. In this book, the author assembles types of persons by letting them write letters. For example, in a "Letter from one of the Society of

---

[52] Martin Morris, "At Sea", in: *The Nineteenth century: a monthly review*, Sept 1896, p. 412-421.

[53] *Own translation of:* "Auf See!! den Atlantischen Ocean, welcher keine Balken in sich birgt; auf lange, lange Zeit. Punkt 11 Uhr bestiegen wir den großen stattlichen engl. Dampfer 'Majestic', welcher uns, ob tot oder lebendig, nach der neuen Welt America bringen sollte." (Arthur Wunderwald, *Reisebericht,* 1907, DTA, Reg.No. 883).

Friends to her kinswoman" he describes a pious old maid dedicated to the uplifting of the poor, who writes: "And how often amid the vain and frivolous scenes that I have daily mingled in on board this ship, have I wished for thy conversation, thy companionship, and support. Strange sensations have affected me by such associations as I have had here."[54]

In this passage, "frivolous scenes" on board a ship are insinuated. This refers to the mingling of the sexes. The fact that men and women, who were strangers to each other, found themselves together in the confined space of the ship was considered quite indecent in the 19th century. Even worse was the fact that all social classes were on board a passenger ship. Besides their servants, people of the upper and higher middle classes usually had no contact to lower social classes. They were separated from each other by spaces allocated to different social classes like different urban districts. This separation was also set up on board: Steerage passengers were accommodated in the lower decks and in the front and aft of the ships whereas the other classes occupied a much larger portion of the ships' spaces in the center and the upper decks. Nevertheless, it could not be denied that all these different classes had to share the same enclosed space of the ship. When talking about the steerage class, the public had in mind all the frightening and scandalizing reports about the conditions on emigrant sailing ships, so the steamship lines had to set themselves as much apart from these accounts as possible. Remarks about the accommodation in the steerage were always addressed to potential customers for the cabin and second classes, as the expensive brochures were exclusively made for this clientele. Thus, a careful balance was maintained between the need to put the upper classes "out of danger", and the stress on a human and decent accommodation for the lower classes.

The remarks in a *Guide* from the Inman Line of 1878 are typical in this respect:
> "All the sleeping bunks are more or less private, and except in the case of families as just mentioned the sexes are divided. The hospital regulations and provisions are on a broad and liberal scale. [....] Ventilation, light, plenty of water, comfortable berths, and a generous supply of wholesome food, make the steerage a world of luxury and cleanliness to many of the poor passengers, who often learn their first lessons of order on board the steamer [...]."[55]

Dangers which were closely connected to the lower classes were contagious maladies and sexual relationships between unmarried people. In this example, the

---

[54] Thomas C. Haliburton, *Life in a Steamer or the Letter-Bag of the Great Western*, 1859, Reprint 2006, p. 51.
[55] Inman Line: "Official Guide", 1878, MMM MAL, DX/934, p. 19.

Inman Line took these fears into consideration and, at the same time, managed to highlight the educational and uplifting effect of such 'generous' attendance for the poor.

The Liminoid – a Solution for Reducing Ambivalences

One way to reduce ambivalent feelings was the element of the *liminoid* in the form of pastimes undertaken together. These playful and amusing pastimes often served as rituals as well. Rituals got passengers acquainted with life on board, placed them in the internal social ranking (for example as to the sitting order at table), distracted them from the dangers, boredom or void of the sea, and created a *communitas* among the inhabitants of the same class on board. While analyzing some of these occupations, I will refer to the ambivalent feelings mentioned in the previous section: disorientation, boredom and monotony, the danger and vastness of the sea and the society on board.

Popular bets on the ships' runs every 24 hours can be interpreted as means to solve feelings of disorientation with regard to time and distance on the high seas. These bets have to be distinguished from bets on ships' records for the whole travelling distance across the Atlantic which were closely linked to the Blue Riband since the 1890s. The latter were betting games played on land covering the whole length of a journey. To the contrary, the ships' runs were published on a black board by the ship's command on a daily basis. The only means for orientation and location for passengers in the space of the ocean was information about the distance covered by the ship since its departure and the remaining distance until the port of destination. Bets on the daily ships' runs played with this need for orientation and had the potential of forming a community consisting of passionate betters. The practice of daily bets basically remained the same from the late 19th century until the late 1920s, only the money at stake increased. Usually, each participant paid a certain amount in an auction pool and received a lot with a number in turn. The person who retained the nearest number to the actual daily run, which was posted the next day, received the whole amount of the lottery. In 1893, a voyager on the *Majestic* described these bets as follows:

> "Our first day's log [...] announced 480 miles, and these figures, posted at noon on the following day, were the foundation of a very lively competition for the possession of the numbers immediately approaching or exceeding 500, [...] The sequel proved the

prognostications of those who pinned their faith to daily runs of about 500 miles to be correct, [...]"[56]

In German, this daily distance was called "Etmal". In a German book of 1902 with the title *How to entertain oneself on board* ["Wie man sich an Bord vergnügt"], the betting on the "Etmal" is described in detail.[57] This tradition did not change as two travel descriptions of 1922 and 1930 prove. In 1922, the author describes the pool as "hat pool" and writes about his bets on a daily basis; apparently, this game runs as a continuous *leitmotiv* throughout his whole journey around the world on board the Cunard liner *Laconia*.[58] In 1930 on board the liner *Bremen* of the Norddeutscher Lloyd, the female narrator describes the passionate gamblers and even claims that a passenger won the fabulous sum of 25,000 Dollar.[59]

Another means of placing oneself in relationship to geographical points, which also served as integration into the ship's community and marked the entrance into a new life on the other side of the world, was the Crossing-the-Line ceremony. This ceremony is one of the few customs directly derived from sailor's customs. As this ritual comes very close to the *liminal* state as is described for tribal cultures in Turner work, I will quote a longer description of the Crossing-the-Line ceremony:[60] In the late Middle Ages, this ceremony was generally held on ships "that crossed the border between two shipping districts". But on French ships "sailor's baptisms on the Equator took place in 1529 and in 1577", and were later adopted on ships of other European nations. Around the 17th and 18th century the ritual was as follows:

> "The experienced sailors got the newcomers on deck, where the old hands jumped around in disguise, playing kettle drums. In most cases, the candidates for baptism encountered a mock judge before the great mast, before whom they had to stand at attention. In order to show his respect, the sailor who was to be baptized sometimes had to endure the judge's foot on his neck, or kiss the foot. All of this created feelings of humiliation, alienation, and detachment in the candidate.

---

[56] *Strand Magazine*, July 1893, p. 204-205.
[57] Myers, possibly 1890, p. 219-220.
[58] Joel W. Burdick, *Our World Tour 1922 – 1923 – An account of the first ever World Cruise by a passenger line,* London 1990.
[59] Ann T. Leitich, *An Bord der "Europa": Radiobericht von der ersten Amerikareise. Sonderdruck aus dem Juniheft 1930 überreicht vom Norddeutschen Lloyd,* 1930.
[60] The following quotations are taken from Herman Ketting, "Crossing the Line", in: John B. Hattendorf (Ed.), *The Oxford encyclopedia of maritime history: Volume 1,* Oxford 2007, p. 517-518.

> The break with his social past and his admission into the ship's community was ultimately symbolized by the actual sailors' baptism. The candidates were hoisted up to the end of the yard and plunged into the water below the deepest point of the keel three times. Halfway through the eighteenth century, the practice began of having some playing the role of Neptune, [...] In this role playing, Neptune generally took over the role of the mock judge. With the advent of Neptune, ducking from the yard disappeared as well. Its place was taken by the shaving ceremony, in which the experienced sailors smeared the naked or very scantily dressed newcomer with oil, tar, or other filth [...] and he [the candidate] was submerged in the barrel of seawater or wastewater. Those who found the whole ritual offensive could buy their way out of the baptism."[61]

The practices were very rough and had to be considerably attenuated for passengers. Nevertheless, the basic ritual remained the same: the baptism with water, the mock trials, the disguise of the protagonists and the possibility to buy oneself out of the ceremony. But in the course of the time, the efforts spent by the ships' personnel on this ceremony increased considerably.

The Crossing-the-Line-ceremonies on trips to South America on smaller steamships transporting only a few passengers seems to have been relatively plain. A female passenger wrote in her diary on the 20th December 1891:

> "During the whole day, we were teased and we were made to believe that we would be baptised; everyone had his own account of it. After dinner there was a performance and afterwards we were all sitting on deck. We were singing a lot and drinking punch. I was baptised as well for the new world, by the captain pouring a glass of water over me."[62]

---

[61] Ibid., p. 518. The expression 'old hands' means the experienced workers on board a ship.

[62] *Own translation of:* " Schon den ganzen Tag über hatte man uns gefoppt u. wollte uns weißmachen, daß wir getauft würden, was ein jeder uns auf eine andere Weise schilderte. Nach Tisch war Theateraufführung u. nachher saßen wir all alle zusammen auf dem oberen Deck. Es wurde viel gesungen u. Bowle getrunken. Auch ich wurde getauft, für die neue Welt. Es geschah dieß indem der Kapitän von hinten ein Glas Wasser über mich ergoß." (Emma Hochstetter, *Tagebuch. Reise nach Amerika,* 1891, transcript, DTA, Reg.Nr. 890/I, transcript, p.26-48: 32). The name of the ship is not mentioned. It might have been a ship of the Hamburg-Südamerikanische Dampfschifffahrts-Gesellschaft because the port of departure was Hamburg and this line exclusively served South-American destinations in Germany.

The difference between this modest ritual and the sophisticated ritual accomplished on board the passenger liner *Monte Oliva* of the Hamburg-Südamerikanische Dampfschifffahrtsgesellschaft in 1925, as described in the diary of the German professor of Romance languages, Victor Klemperer, is obvious. Here, the ritual served to amuse the passengers and give them an enduring touristic impression. Klemperer depicts the disguise of the ship's personnel as Neptune and his followers. A big box full of water is set up on deck and the passengers are plunged in it, shaved with knives, scissors and brushes while a man disguised as priest is preaching a satiric variation of the biblical quotation 'Come unto me, all ye that labour and are heavy laden' as 'Come to me, all ye that are coming from Europe'. Even the women are treated in this way, though less roughly.[63]

Apparently, passengers crossing the equator were so used to rituals associated with crossing this line that a passenger of the world tour on board the *Laconia* writes:

> "After crossing the equator this morning, Father Neptune came over the bow and held a megaphone conversation with the captain, as to the ship's right to be in sub-equatorial waters, etc. [...] There were the usual indignities perpetrated on the so-called tenderfeet and landlubbers. The more elderly folk were spared the duckings and barbering which almost all of the younger ones had to endure, and we all received our diplomas certifying that we were thereafter immune from further trial for encroaching on Neptune's domain."[64]

The Crossing-the-Line ceremony served here as initiation rite separating the experienced travelers from the newcomers while making them undergo degrading and comic trials. Not only the passengers, but also the entire ship was involved in the ceremony and had to ask permission to enter the 'alien' space of the equator. The whole was embedded in a performance with disguised protagonists. The travelers expected this ceremony as necessary part of their travel event and already knew the ingredients of the spectacle in advance. In addition, a certificate was handed out serving as touristic souvenir.

The mock trial mentioned in the Oxford Encyclopedia of Maritime History as forming part of the Crossing-the-Line ceremony can also be found in other circumstances, which had nothing to do with crossing the equator. Mock trials are mentioned in the article "From London to Chicago" from 1893 as well as in

---

[63] Victor Klemperer, *Leben sammeln, nicht fragen wozu und warum - Tagebücher 1925 – 1932,* Berlin 1996.

[64] Burdick, *Our World Tour,* p. 81.

the world tour description of 1922. I will quote both here in order to illustrate the changing concept of these mock trials:

> "The only approach to a *contretemps* during entire trip occurred one evening in mid-Atlantic, in the heat of the auction sale [...] The proceedings on this occasion were partially interrupted by a somewhat hilarious young gentleman, who donned a false nose and proceeded to treat the company to a song, not having been invited to contribute to the general entertainment by any vocal effort whatever. [...] In fact, later unanimously [the auction pool committee on the ship's daily run, *editorial comment*] adjuged that the offending vocalist should be immediately thrown overboard. [...] the court graciously reconsidered its decision, and magnanimously proclaimed a general amnesty.[65]
> As an incident of shipboard life, there was a mock trial of the Purser, [...], on the charge that he clandestinely went to a Hula Hula performance at Honolulu. The farce was well done and funny."[66]

By looking at these two accounts from 1893 and 1922, the same phenomenon as in Crossing-the-line ceremonies can be observed, that means a considerable shift from more or less spontaneously organized mock trials by passengers to a performance acted out by the personnel for the passengers.

The fear of shipwrecking was one of the most apparent negative feelings. It was often associated with seasickness as this evil usually occurred during bad or even stormy weather. Seasickness was thus strongly connected to danger. But as already mentioned, by the end of the 19th century the perception of seasickness underwent a considerable change. It became a topic for laughter and was considered a kind of initiation rite for every real sea voyager. At the same time, by concentrating on the inconveniences of seasickness, passengers were detracted from other dangers of the sea. There are several arguments to be made for interpreting seasickness as initiation rite: first, new voyagers expected it in advance as inevitable experience. In almost every account of an Atlantic crossing, there was at least one passage mentioning seasickness – whether by narrating one's own experience or whether by expressly noting that it has not affected oneself. For example, the famous author and journalist Mark Twain ironically noted on his way to Europe: "By some happy fortune I was not seasick. – That was a thing to be proud of. [...] If there is one thing in the world that will make a

---

[65] *Strand Magazine*, p. 209-210.
[66] Burdick, *Our World Tour*, p. 47.

man peculiarly and insufferably self-conceited, it is to have his stomach behave himself, the first day at sea, when nearly all his comrades are seasick."[67]

A young German crossing for the first time the Atlantic, was writing in his diary pretending to know already all about seasickness:

> "Unfortunately, the allocated space on deck and the increasing wind were the reasons that the first signs of the well-known seasickness showed up. Probably the fear of becoming seasick was playing a role. The sea became rough and the ship started to toss around, so that the well-known feeling started soon."[68]

Second, being seasick was sometimes described as "making a sacrifice" – and here the comical touch becomes obvious – "to Neptune"[69]. Third, a clear demarcation between the newcomers who made their first trip, and the experienced travelers was set up by the latter, who by preference gave all kinds of advice to newcomers: "Everyone who ventures on a voyage will, before sailing, and even after leaving the land, be bountifully supplied with any number of what they will be assured are 'sure preventives.'"[70] Last, seasickness caused a spontaneous *communitas* of all people enduring seasickness.

As to ambivalent feelings about the constraints of society on board, there were numerous games and rituals concentrating on the social fabric. The most important ones are evening galas and masquerades, the Captain's dinner, flirts, deck games such as shuffleboard and mock trials. On the one hand, as social events were strictly separated between different passenger classes, they created a *communitas* among people who had booked the same passenger class. On the other hand, these events served as criteria for distinction and for gaining social

---

[67] Mark Twain, *The Innocents Abroad, or, The New Pilgrims' Progress* [1869], New York 2003, p. 16.

[68] *Own translation of:* "Leider war der Platz in Bezug auf die Seekrankheit so daß zusammen, mit dem einsetzenden stärkeren Wind der erste Anstoß der bekannten Seekrankheit einsetzen konnte. Vielleicht spielte die Angst davor eine nicht kleine Rolle. Der Seegang nahm zu und das Schiff begann allmählich zu schwanken, so daß das bekannte Gefühl bald einsetzte." (Kuno Burkhard, *Reise nach den USA*, 1927, DTA, Reg.Nr. 1341, p. 17).

[69] „Nothing of them doth fade / But doth suffer a sea-change / at the first touch of Neptune's hand." (J. Street, *Ship-Bored: Illustrated Edition,* 1912, Facsimile); "And so, on the last day of our voyage, we were in a state which brings a sacrifice to Neptune." *[own translation]* . In the Original: "[…] so gerieten wir am letzten Tage unserer Fahrt in die Verfassung, die Neptun ihr Opfer bringt." (Clara Plassmann, *Nordkapfahrt 1928. Ein Reisetagebuch,* DTA, Reg.Nr. 809/IV, p. 39).

[70] *Bow Bells*, 13 July 1888.

prestige among the *communitas* itself. This could contribute to a splitting up of the *communitas* for the benefit of smaller parties. But even here, a potential for a reversal of 'normal' social rules remained or was at least attempted. This is shown in a satire *Ship-Bored* from 1912, written by an American:

> "As to ourselves, we were not even up there [on deck], but were sitting in the lounge, trying, as I recollect, to match passengers with names upon the sailing list, and failing very badly. The woman whom we picked for Mrs. H. Van Rensselaer Somebody (travelling with two maids, two valets, one Pomerian, one husband, and no children) proves to be a Broadway showgirl; [...]."[71]

As already mentioned in the German book *How to entertain oneself on board* ["Wie man sich an Bord vergnügt"] from 1912, this playing with mutual attraction is alluded to several times. The author even assigns the personnel the duty to flirt with the ladies: "The officers and the ship's doctor even have the duty to pay honourably court to the ladies who like this."[72] Flirts between the sexes were explicitly allowed and supposed to distract the passengers from the daily routine. They became an integrative part of life on a passenger ship. This is not only testified by numerous penny novels in general interest magazines[73], but also by diaries and travel reports. In the satire from 1912 already mentioned, the author makes fun of flirts:

> "Ah, confidences besides a life-boat on the upper deck! [...] "And I was taken with you from the second that I saw you!" – "And I with you – –!" [...] Of course we didn't overhear them; it was the third life-boat on the port side of the ship that overheard, as it has overheard so many other times on other voyages."[74]

In 1930, a German traveler in the third class even felt obliged to reassure his girlfriend in a letter: "I haven't noticed any of those disreputable dalliances on board, because you are never alone even for a second. I guarantee that in the third class no dalliance arose."[75]

---

[71] Street, *Ship-Bored*, p. 7.
[72] *Own translation of:* "Selbst die Pflicht, gewissen Damen, die dies gern haben, in allen Ehren den Hof zu machen, haben die Offiziere und der Arzt." (Ibid., p. 212-213).
[73] For example: By the author of "Lord Lynn's Wife", "Lady Flavia, & c.", "The wrong boat; or, Dropped among Diamonds", in: *Temple Bar, A London magazine for town and country readers* 33 (Oct 1871), p. 348-384.
[74] Street, *Ship-Bored*, p. 6-7.
[75] *Own translation of:* "Auch die verrufenen Bordliebschaften, ich hab' da nichts

In the same context of sexual attraction a game can be placed which was called "threading game" ["Einfädelspiel"]: the lady held a twine, the gentleman a sewing needle. Both had to approach each other and try to thread the twine through the needle. This game with its undeniable sexual allusion was played on deck and gained its attraction by the ship's movements, which made the exercise difficult.

In summary, the practice of flirting on board ships shows the potentiality of the *liminoid* to introduce new rules of social interaction between men and women that were not possible on land: The flirts between strangers lasted only for the duration of the voyage. In addition, their visibility made them on the one hand socially acceptable, and on the other hand could form a spontaneous *communitas* of all people witnessing and gossiping about these flirts. Both these aspects are clearly demonstrated in the passage from Julian Street quoted above.

Pastimes to gain social prestige were closely connected with evening balls and Captain's dinners. Captains on modern passenger liners became more and more a part of the social fabric and functioned as a sort of Master of Ceremonies. It was an honor to be allowed at the Captain's table, and people attached great importance to being singled out by the captain. Numerous entries in guestbooks that were collected from the Commodore Leopold Ziegenbein, a famous ship's commander of the Norddeutscher Lloyd in the 1920s, confirm this. In his guestbooks, everybody who claimed to be someone important, made an enthusiastic entry in order to profit from the captain's grandeur. Some even tried a poem, interpreting the captain as modern chivalrous hero:

---

von gemerkt, weil Du nicht eine Sekunde allein sein kannst. Ich garantiere in der III. Klasse ist keine Liebschaft zustande gekommen." (Passenger "Theo", DSM, III/A/2683/13, letter of 31 Dec 1930, last page).

To Captain Ziegenbein
>   On all the seas the Lloyd is known
> For men of courage, strength & Skill!
> They steer their ships through fog & storm
> In safety to what ports they will.
>   Among these heroes there is one
> We love as well as venerate,
> As Captain he is unsurpassed:
> To him all gladly trust their fate.
>   But when this duty's fully done
> He sometimes condescends to play,
> And then that man is grand at fun!
> So we are safe & also gay.
>   As now alas! Our course is run,
> And halc into New York we slip,
> We wish him scores of years to come
> Upon some stalwart German ship![76]

But not only the captain, but also his officers were supposed to attend to the passengers. In *How to entertain*, the author stressed the point that the captain and his officers had to encourage the passengers to build pleasure committees which should organize the various pastimes such as balls, concerts, games and even ships' journals.[77] That passengers formed organizing committees was common practice. They organized auction pools, masquerade balls, charity concerts for the families of deceased sailors, they worked as editors for journals produced by the passengers and they organized competitive games such as shuffleboard, which was exclusively played on board ships. The committees can be described as a form of "ritual elders" who, according to Turner, lead the persons involved in a *communitas*. The members of organizing committees were partly chosen by the captain of the ship, partly by passengers in accordance to their social rank on land. But from the late 19th century to the 1920s, a shift from pastimes organized by passengers and their committees to activities channeled by the ship's personnel can be observed. This development can be exemplarily shown in the ship's journals which were common on all passenger liners since the last quarter of the

---

[76] Commodore Ziegenbein, *Gästebücher,* DSM III/A/1755, I, here: entry from 16 June 1928.
[77] Myers, possibly 1890, p. 214-215.

19th century.[78] Ship's journals were even produced on emigrant ships.[79] In the beginning, they were mostly hand-written and sometimes printed afterwards on arrival in the port. In the course of time, they became more and more sophisticated and organized from above. The journal printed on board the German *Augusta Victoria* of the Hamburg-America Line in 1894 on a trip to the North Cape is a good example. This journal was written by the ship's personnel, and the passengers were invited by the editors to produce articles themselves. But the editors set up the humorous style of the proposed articles – namely, by stressing the atmosphere of playful flirting between the sexes:

> "To our Readers: The Augusta Victoria journal, the only newspaper in the world, which doesn't possess paper baskets or scissors, asks for contributions from the passengers. [...] *Local news*: Theft: Strange women are supposed to have stolen a lot of hearts. The guilty parties are zealously searched for. – Arson: Dark and blue eyes have ignited and caused considerable damage. The affected [gentlemen] weren't insured."[80]

This journal even served as advertisement material for the Hamburg-America Line later on.[81]

After all, the various activities on Atlantic passenger liners such as Crossing-the-Line ceremonies, balls, dinners and games on deck which had been more or less conducted by the passengers themselves during the 19th century, were bundled together, professionalized and diversified in the 20th century. Nothing was left to chance, and the opportunities for free play and experimentation were reduced to a considerable degree. The narrative of a young German woman travelling with her friends on a tour to the North Cape in 1928, serves as good indicator for this

---

[78] About the origin of ship's journals see Vanessa H. Roberts, "Publishing and Printing on Board Ship", in: *The Mariner's Mirror*, 74:4 (1988), p. 329-334.

[79] An example is the *Netherby Gazette* of 1866 on board an emigration ship to Australia, MMM MAL, SAS/33E/1/4.

[80] *Own translation of:* "Die 'Augusta Victoria-Zeitung', die einzige Zeitung der Welt, die keinen Papierkorb und keine Scheeren besitzt, bittet um Beiträge aus ihrem Leserkreis. / Locales. Diebstähle. Fremde Damen sollen zahlreiche Herzen gestohlen haben. Auf die Schuldigen wird eifrig gefahndet. / Brandstiftung. Dunkle und blaue Augen haben vielfach gezündet und grossen Schaden angerichtet. Die Betroffenen waren nicht versichert." ("Bordzeitungen Nordlandfahrt Augusta Victoria 1894", Staatsarchiv Hamburg, 621-1/95 Sign. 4283).

[81] See H. Weth, *Die Orient-Reise der "Augusta Victoria" vom Januar bis März 1891: Nach den Berichten in den Feuilletons des "Hamburger Fremdenblatt" und des "Berliner Börsen-Courier"*, Hamburg 1891.

professionalization: in her travel report she writes about a public memorial act to dead German Marines; dancing on the promenade deck; a Crossing-the-Arctic-Circle ceremony performed by the ship's personnel and a baptism document handed out to the passengers; she describes a "Bavarian evening" for the passengers as well as a wake-up song for the passengers every morning; she describes the farewell ceremony of the ship's orchestra as well as the salutation between encountering pleasure ships in the North Cape by tooting and fireworks.[82] With this ceremony, the cruising industry not only celebrated itself, but created another event for the passengers that was similar to farewell and welcome ceremonies and had a sublime effect on them as the mountains resounded the echoes.[83]

This densely organized ship life is certainly a result of the increasing professionalization of the tourism business as a whole, offering more and more services. But I would also presume that self-entertainment on an experimental basis as means of coping with the 'new experience' of travelling on the ocean was no longer needed. After the First World War, people were becoming accustomed to travelling across the Atlantic, whether by own experiences or whether by the countless travel reports, movies and marketing brochures of shipping companies.

The Limits of Reducing Ambivalences

There are limits to the force of shaping perceptions through rituals and games. There are three main reasons responsible for this: frst, as already mentioned, the more these rituals and games become regulated and professionalized, the more they lose their flexibility and in consequence run the risk of losing their creative power as the passengers engage less in performances and rituals and are confined to the role of spectators. At the same time, the *communitas* tends to become structured – as Turner himself has noticed: "Communitas itself soon develops a structure, in which free relationships between individuals become converted into norm-governed relationships between social personae."[84] Second, it seems highly plausible that not everyone wanted to be involved in rituals and games or did not feel emotionally affected. Third, tendencies to distinguish oneself from other passengers, for example by being cherished by the captain, could have counterproductive effects for maintaining the *communitas*.

---

[82] Plassmann, *Nordkapfahrt 1928,* p. 1-3, 5-6, 8, 16-17, 28, 30, 37.
[83] See Plassmann, *Nordkapfahrt 1928,* p. 8.
[84] Turner, *The Ritual Process*, p. 132.

Victor Klemperer offers an example for the back and forth between wanting to take part in the *communitas* and his wish to keep some distance to his fellow passengers: he writes in his diary how he was first amused by watching the Crossing-the-Line ceremony but got bored later on. He managed to be spared of taking part in the ritual by buying himself out of it[85], which may be one of the reasons why he did not feel emotionally involved. But on the other hand, even if Klemperer did not take an active part in the event, he felt flattered when the organizing team asked him to become a member of the honorary committee of the ceremony, because they needed "prominent names," such as the captain and passengers like him.[86] So even if the ritual of the Crossing-the-Line ceremony did not lead to an emotional involvement for Klemperer, it did in fact contribute to him gaining social prestige on board.

Even if fear and boredom could be eliminated by liminoid games and rituals, feelings of ambivalence towards one's own situation could come in "through the back door". In his diary, Victor Klemperer found a poetic expression for this state of being:

"No land in sight, a rarity since Buenos Aires, because we keep close to the coast. Unlike our outward voyage to South America, the sea is calm and the morning air is refreshing and mild. But I am very depressed. One is so alone with oneself, exactly like a ship at sea, but one is not even swimming in solid water, but in a void. It is horrible to stay awake during the night."[87]

The weather is mild and the sea calm and peaceful, but this situation seems to remind Klemperer even more of the wideness of the sea and in consequence of the loneliness of human existence. This entry exemplarily shows the difficulty of reaching a balance between the inner self and the outside world. To cite a recent example: The American author David Foster Wallace, on a cruising tour on board an American luxury ship in 1995 for coverage for an American journal, put his ambivalent feelings in these lines:

"And the ocean […] turns out to be basically one enormous engine of decay. Seawater corrodes vessels with amazing speed […] Not so the Megalines' ships. It's not an accident they're all so white and clean,

---

[85] Klemperer, *Leben sammeln, nicht fragen wozu und warum*, p. 91.
[86] Ibid., p. 89.
[87] *Own translation of:* "Nirgends Land, eine Seltenheit seit B.A., da wir dicht der Küste folgen, anders als beim Hinfahren, stille See, erfrischend laue Morgenluft. Aber sehr bedrückte Stimmung. Man ist mit seinem Ich so gänzlich allein wie ein Schiff auf See, aber man schwimmt nicht einmal im festen Wasser, sondern im Nichts. Scheußlich ist es, in der Nacht eine Zeitlang wachzuliegen. –" (Klemperer, *Leben sammeln, nicht fragen wozu und warum*, p. 130).

for they're clearly meant to represent the Calvinist triumph of capital and industry over the primal decay-action of the sea. [...] But on a 7NC Luxury Cruise, we are skilfully enabled in the construction of various fantasies of triumph over just this death and decay. [...] The 7NC's constant activities, parties, festivities, gaiety and song; the adrenaline, the excitement, the stimulation. It makes you feel vibrant, alive."[88]

In this passage, Wallace confronts the professional entertainment machinery and the destructive capacities of the sea which have to be hidden at all costs from the passengers. He also alludes to the ultimate goal of festivities and games: suppressing fears of death and destruction. Here, the ambivalent potential of a sea voyage becomes obvious once the mechanisms of pastimes are revealed, and all efforts to keep fear of mortality at bay seem to be useless.

Summary and Outlook

Travelling across the high seas can in fact be regarded as enjoyable and pleasurable. Sea cruising nowadays means fun, luxury and comfort. For the passengers, life on board a cruising ship functions as a self-sufficient microcosm, offering everything they could possibly wish for. But this has not always been self-evident in the long history of travelling across the seas. Seasickness, boredom, disorientation, dangers arising from the sea or from other passengers were always impending. Only by changing these feelings and experiences, steamship travel could turn into what it seems to be now: luxury, comfort and pleasure. One cause for this change in the attitude towards the sea were games and rituals developed by passengers, as for example betting on distances, Crossing-the-Line ceremonies, mock trials, jokes about seasickness, flirts and Captain's dinners. Passengers could thus turn their attention away from the sea and its potential dangers or from the sense of boredom and disorientation when confronted with the monotony of the sea. Victor Turner's concept is a useful approach for understanding the ambivalent potential of sea voyaging which enables both negative and positive interpretations and feelings. It also provides a means of analyzing the practices of changing these ambivalent feelings into positive ones. Playful pastimes and rituals not only offered orientation to passengers but also served as diversion from dangers and created a *communitas* on board ship. A lot of these practices also helped to gain social prestige among

---

[88] David F. Wallace, "A supposedly fun thing I'll never do again", in: Ibid., *A supposedly fun thing I'll never do again: Essays and arguments,* London 1998, p. 256-353: 263-264. The expression "7NC" is an abbreviation for "7-Night Caribbean Cruise", see ibid., p. 256.

fellow passengers. They could even turn uncomfortable experiences such as seasickness into a humorous initiation sacrifice to 'Father Neptune'. But in the course of time, pastimes were organized by the ships' personnel instead of being organized as self-entertaining amusements by the passengers so that it became a normative part of sea travelling that voyagers expected in advance. On the one hand, it helped them to prepare mentally for their voyage, but on the other hand, it lost some of its creative potential.

The other side of the coin of reducing fear and dullness is presumably the confrontation with oneself as there was nothing substantial anymore to worry about. Ambivalent feelings about sea travelling could thus persist, even if they had considerably changed their content. For the future, there remains a lot of research to do, namely investigating this new ambivalence and examining further factors also contributing to changes of attitude towards sea travelling since the beginning of steamship travel on the Atlantic in the 1840s.[89]

---

[89] Besides *liminality*, there are factors such as providing comfort, procuring a sense of security and creating positive images of sea travelling from the part of the press and shipping company. These topics are dealt with in my on-going dissertation.

6. War Crossings: The American GI as Transatlantic Traveler during the Second World War

Mark D. Van Ells

Introduction

Military personnel are seldom viewed as travelers, but they should be. Travel is an integral part of martial life. Duty often takes soldiers and sailors far from home, and brings them into contact with distant lands and different cultures. When not on duty, they often act like tourists and "see the sights." Servicemen and women must also be transported from one place to another. During the Second World War, the GI – as the American service member was known – crossed the Atlantic Ocean to serve and fight in North Africa and Europe.[1] Before the war few Americans had ever crossed the Atlantic, and those who did tended to be the wealthy and educated. But between 1941 and 1945, mass numbers of everyday Americans – in uniform – made the crossing too.

In his memoir of the Second World War, J.J. Kuhn wrote that crossing the Atlantic as a soldier was "far from a summer pleasure cruise."[2] Kuhn was not alone in using the language of peacetime tourism to describe his transportation to the war zone. For the typical American GI, the Atlantic war crossing involved a series of bewildering juxtapositions pitting the popular imagery of transoceanic travel against the hard realities of war. Many troops sailed on opulent luxury liners, for example, but lived in cramped quarters that some compared to slave ships. Many became desperately homesick and seasick, but were still awed by the majesty of the ocean. Surrounded by the trappings of pleasure travel, the GIs went off to the serious business of war. The unusual hybrid world of the troopship accentuated the soldier's feelings of disconnection from home, family, and the peacetime world. In their letters, diaries, and memoirs, American troops described their conflicted feelings about crossing the Atlantic. Their accounts leave us with an unusual and seldom examined record of the transatlantic travel experience.

---

[1] For an excellent introduction to the American GI in World War II, see Lee Kennett, *GI: The American Soldier in World War II*, New York 1987.

[2] J.J. Kuhn, *I Was Baker 2: Memoirs of a World War II Platoon Sergeant*, West Bend, WI 1994, p. 63.

Boarding

The soldier-passenger arrived at the docks by train or truck. Like conventional travelers they had luggage, though it was far different than that of the peacetime tourist. Soldiers began their journey with a rifle, a helmet, a gas mask, two barracks bags, and a field pack strapped to their backs. The ordinary GI was his own baggage handler. "Our bodies carried all the burden," wrote Leo Bogart, and the "aggregate weight [of the equipment] fell cruelly in awkward and tender places."[3] The boarding process often took hours, and the troops had to lug all of their baggage with them across the docks and waiting areas, whether in the searing summer heat or the icy winds of winter. While they waited, a band played patriotic tunes to cheer them up, and Red Cross volunteers passed out coffee and doughnuts. "My aches subsided as I devoured those delicious Red Cross donuts and felt rejuvenated," recalled Marvin Bertelson.[4] "If the 'girls' passing out the refreshments hadn't all been past sixty," claimed Robert Chapman, "I think I would have kissed every one of them right then and there."[5] Others were less enamored. Boarding on a hot day, Jack Sheridan thought it odd that the Red Cross passed out hot coffee when "all [we] wanted so devoutly was a glass of cold water!"[6]

At the foot of the gangplank, passengers were checked in as they boarded. Each soldier's surname was read aloud, and they would respond with their first name and middle initial. "Our line moved and our own names began to be read out," wrote Robert Welker. "Suddenly there seemed to be a kind of finality about the scene."[7] After having their name called, the GIs stepped off the terra firma of their native land and onto the ship that would transport them to a distant one. "Up the gangplank they go," claimed the official history of the Hampton Roads Port

---

[3] Leo Bogart, *How I Earned the Ruptured Duck: From Brooklyn to Berchtesgaden in World War II*, College Station/TX 2004, p. 46.

[4] Marvin Bertelson, *From A Halftrack and A Piano Bench*, privately published, n.d., p. 135.

[5] Robert B. Chapman, *Tell It To the Chaplain*, New York 1952, p. 64.

[6] Jack W. Sheridan, *They Never Had It So Good: The Personal, Unofficial Story of the 350th Bombardment Squadron (H), 100th Bombardment Group (H), USAAF, 1942 – 1945*, San Francisco 1946, p. 40.

[7] Robert Welker, *A Different Drummer: The Odyssey of a Home-Grown Rebel*, Boston 1958, p. 127.

of Embarkation, "with their packs on their backs, ready for the great adventure."[8] A few did indeed feel adventurous. Robert Kotlowitz was an ardent Francophile, and as an infantryman sailing from New York in August 1944, he was sure he would end up in France. "My teeth were grinding together from the excitement," he recalled.[9] Paul Fussell remembered that he "simply radiated college-boy optimism."[10] "We're sailing to fire and mutilation and death with idiot grins," claimed Brendan Phibbs. "What has the army done to us?"[11]

Others were less enthusiastic. "I don't think 1 percent of the men on board feel as if they are going off on a great mission," Herman Obermayer told his family. "They're just a lot of poor bastards who got caught in the draft."[12] Indeed, many dreaded getting on the boat. "Regardless of how much I had wanted to go," wrote Robert Chapman, "when I came to the point where I was actually to board a ship, my knees felt weak and I wasn't at all sure just where my stomach was."[13] "I dared not stop," wrote Avis Shorer, "despite the burden of loneliness, fear, and equipment I carried."[14] Kenneth Gowen remembered that as he walked across the gangplank, "I felt as though I had crossed a continent. I felt suddenly so desperately alone."[15] Some suffering from "gangplank fever" even tried to desert. "On the pier a strange thing happened," Marshall Hardy reported in a letter home, "one of our men disappeared." Hardy and his men "searched the area to no avail," and speculated that perhaps the soldier "fell off the pier and drowned."[16] Once in Europe, Hardy received "official notice of his apprehension as a deserter." The young man had dived into the water "with his full field equipment," he later learned. "How he managed to swim ashore, I'll never know."[17] Military officials took measures to keep such episodes to a minimum. Carl Lyons remembered that

---

[8] Reginald W. Wheeler, *The Road to Victory: A History of the Hampton Roads Port of Embarkation in World War II*, New Haven/Conn. 1946, p. 38.

[9] Robert Kotlowitz, *Before Their Time: A Memoir*, New York 1997, p. 50.

[10] Paul Fussell, *Doing Battle: The Making of a Skeptic*, Boston 1996, p. 101.

[11] Brendan Phibbs, *The Other Side of Time: A Combat Surgeon in World War II*, New York 1987, p. 44.

[12] Herman Obermayer, *Soldiering for Freedom: A GI's Account of World War II*, College Station/TX 2005, p. 91.

[13] Chapman, *Tell It To the Chaplain*, p. 62.

[14] Avis Schorer, *A Half Acre of Hell: A Combat Nurse in World War II*, Lakeville/MN 2000, p. 56.

[15] Kenneth K. Gowen, *Granddaddy, Tell Us About the War: A Southern GI's Experiences in World War II*, Oxford 1998, p. 33.

[16] Marshall B. Hardy to Sis, 27 June 1942, Marshall B. Hardy Papers, Filson Historical Society, Louisville, Kentucky.

[17] Marshall B. Hardy, "Ligamentary Narrative," Hardy Papers.

at the docks military police "stood with tommy guns making sure we were all willing to go overseas."[18] "I was afraid of the water," remembered Joe Dixon, "but I was more angry than I was afraid. If I could have escaped I would have."[19]

The GI usually went to war on a civilian passenger ship that was – like himself – drafted into military service. As in the First World War, the United States brought its merchant fleet under government control, including passenger liners. The *S.S. America* of the United States Lines, for example, was renamed the *U.S.S. West Point*. Army troopships often had an eclectic range of personnel. The captain and crew were typically U.S. Merchant Marine. The army assigned a permanent staff of about 50 to 100 per ship to handle such issues as medical care, morale activities, and security. The U.S. Navy usually provided the gun crews. Great Britain also took control of its merchant fleet and passenger ships, and many Americans made the crossing on British boats. In addition to their own ships, the U.S. and Britain commandeered those of Allied nations under German occupation whenever they could; these included the French liner *Ile de France* and the Dutch ship *Nieuw Amsterdam*.[20]

Among the ocean liners pressed into service were the world's largest and most famous ships, the *Queen Mary* and the *Queen Elizabeth*. Owned and operated by Britain's Cunard White Star Line, "the Queens" were essentially floating five-star hotels – the epitome of luxury travel in their day. Completed in 1936, the *Queen Mary* was not just elegant, but fast. In 1938, she captured the record for the shortest transatlantic crossing, making it from Britain to New York in less than four days. When war came, the *Queen Mary* was repainted grey for camouflage and outfitted with guns, her luxury furnishings removed and put into storage. Swimming pools were converted into sleeping quarters, and luxury shops turned into offices. The *Queen Elizabeth* was still under construction when the war began, but became the largest ship afloat in 1940 when she sneaked out of a Scottish shipyard and raced to New York to avoid Nazi attack.

---

[18] Carl J. Lyons, *World War II Experiences of Carl J. Lyons*, privately published, n.d., p. 7.

[19] Joe Robert Dixon, *Hard Times: Memoirs of a Southern Black Boy Raised during the Depression*, Indianapolis 1996, p. 28.

[20] James Bykofsky and Harold Larson, *The Transportation Corps: Overseas Operations*, Washington/DC 1990; David H. Grover, *U.S. Army Ships and Watercraft of World War II*, Annapolis 1987; Benjamin King, Richard C. Briggs, and Eric R. Criner, *Spearhead of Logistics: A History of the United States Army Transportation Corps*, Washington/DC 2001; and Chester Wardlow, *The Transportation Corps: Movements, Training, and Supply*, Washington/DC 1956, p. 145-148.

Britain initially used the Queens to bring troops from Australia to Europe and the Middle East, but after U.S. entry into the war they were transferred to North Atlantic duty. With their size and speed, they made excellent troop transports. At peak capacity, each could carry more than 15,000 soldiers – an entire infantry division. [21]

The GI passengers were often thrilled at the prospect of crossing over on these famous luxury vessels. The first thing that impressed them was their sheer size. "To someone who'd never been on anything larger than a rowboat," Norman Bussel wrote, the "Queen Liz looked like a tall building, floating horizontally on the water." Once inside, Bussel saw "evidence of her former splendor ... everywhere."[22] Others saw it too. Morton Elevitch wrote that in the dining room of the *Queen Elizabeth* "the ceiling was high – decorated with stars concealing tiny sprinkling systems. Soft light, elaborate trimmings and mirrors produced a startling effect, giving one the feeling of being in the dining room of a large hotel."[23] Bill Etheridge wrote that the interior of the *Queen Elizabeth* was "bathed in soft light that illuminated carpeted corridors and wide stairways, spacious dining rooms with handsome murals and modernistic columns."[24] Some noticed only hints of the ships' former opulence. Richard Letsinger recalled that "all the elegant parts" of the *Queen Elizabeth* were "covered with plywood."[25] Others were struck by the contrast between peacetime stylishness and the practical demands of troop transport. "Fourteen thousand men and women were jammed into every crevice and corner of the rolling, reeking stripped-down grand hotel," Tracy Sugarman wrote of the *Queen Mary*. "The once-elegant salons were bedlam."[26]

Most troop transports were not nearly as famous as the Queens. Marshall Hardy sailed on the *U.S.A.T. Thomas H. Barry*, formerly the *S.S. Oriente*, which he

---

[21] Daniel Allen Butler, *Warrior Queens: The Queen Mary and Queen Elizabeth in World War II*, Mechanicsburg/Penn. 2002; William H. Miller and David F. Hutchings, *Transatlantic Liners at War: The Story of the Queens*, New York 1985; Alister Satchell, *Running the Gauntlet: How Three Giant Liners Carried A Million Men to War*, Annapolis 2001.

[22] Norman Bussel, *My Private War: Liberated Body, Captive Mind: A World War II POW's Journey*, New York 2008, p. 81-82.

[23] M.D. Elevitch, *Dog Tags Yapping: The World War II Letters of a Combat GI*, Carbondale/Ill. 2003, p. 69.

[24] Bill Etheridge, *ETO Diary*, privately published, 1945, p. 3.

[25] Richard Letsinger, "And How Was Your Trip Abroad?," Richard Letsinger Papers, Indiana Historical Society, Indianapolis, Indiana.

[26] Tracy Sugarman, *My War: A Love Story in Letters and Drawings*, New York 2000, p. 18.

recalled had been a "$49.50 week-end cruise ship to Havana."[27] Indeed, many soldiers noted that their ships seemed a bit careworn. "The Samaria had been one of the Cunard White Star Line's finest ships," wrote Ted Hartman, but "there was no question ... that it had seen better days." He noted "large areas on the bulkheads where the paint was chipped off" and that the "air-handling system was pretty inadequate."[28] Roscoe Blunt sailed on the Edmund B. Alexander. Originally built in 1905, Blunt believed she looked every bit her age. "Expansive steel plates, mostly buckled and dented and in need of repair or replacement, formed the ship's hull," he recalled. "Looking at the rusted corrosion, I wondered about the ship's seaworthiness."[29] For some, even a decrepit passenger ship would have been a luxury compared to the converted freighters that also became troopships. More than 500 Liberty Ships – the mass-produced cargo vessels that were miracles of American wartime industrial genius – were configured to carry anywhere from 300 to 500 troops.

Departure

When the departure time arrived, the soldier-passengers sought one last look at America – fearing it would be their last. For those leaving New York, the Statue of Liberty took on immense significance. "Nine thousand men stood on deck that morning when the [ship] passed the Statue of Liberty," recalled Ty Carpenter, and "the silence penetrated the soul. You could read the prayers in men's eyes."[30] Soldiers were sometimes kept below decks for departure, and were forced to sneak whatever surreptitious views they could. "Through the porthole I could see the Statue of Liberty as we sailed past," recalled David Rothbart. "After nearly two years of soldiering in anticipation of shipping overseas, it was difficult to realize that this was now taking place."[31] As their ships sailed eastward into the Atlantic, the GIs watched the land they had sworn to defend slowly dissolve into the horizon. "I went to the rear of the vessel," recalled Leon Edel, "and looked for a long time at New York's obtrusive and arrogant skyline, fading into a sad

---

27 Hardy, "Ligamentary Narrative," Hardy Papers.
28 J. Ted Hartman, *Tank Driver: With the 11th Armored from the Battle of the Bulge to VE Day*, Bloomington/IN 2003, p. 39.
29 Roscoe Blunt, *Foot Soldier: A Combat Infantryman's War in Europe*, New York 2001, p. 4.
30 C. Tyler Carpenter and Edward H. Yeatts, *Stars Without Garters!: The Memoirs of Two Gay GIs in World War II*, San Francisco 1996, p. 83.
31 David Rothbart, *A Soldier's Journal: With the 22nd Infantry Regiment in World War II*, New York 2003, p. 149.

grey sky."[32] It was the same leaving other ports. "Fading behind us in the neutral afternoon lay the elbow of Cape Cod," wrote James Lord of his leaving Boston. "I hung on to the rail and gazed back at the blue silhouette of home."[33] Mel TenHaken departed from Hampton Roads. We "stood against the railings to strain our eyesight," he remembered, "and questioned whether that line on the horizon was the last view of our homeland – or was now just part of our imagination."[34] Troops left not knowing their destination. "Woke up this morning on the Atlantic," James Cole wrote in his diary. "Don't know where I'm going."[35] The most likely destination was Great Britain, but troopships leaving the East Coast of the United States could end up anywhere. Many went to Africa or the Mediterranean. After D-Day, some went directly to France. Still others headed for the Middle East or South Asia, rounding the Cape of Good Hope into the Indian Ocean. A few even veered southwest into the Caribbean toward the Panama Canal, destined for the vast Pacific. Rumors abounded. "At various times we were supposed to be off the coast of Spain, Greenland, Iceland, and God knows where else," recalled James Knox. "Somebody even started one that we had turned around and headed back toward the states." [36] A few managed to learn their destination ahead of time. "It was general knowledge that we were headed to Casablanca," recalled Benedict Alper, citing "local barmaids" as his source.[37] The length of voyage varied. Big ocean liners like the Queens could make it to Britain in less than a week. Voyages to the Indian Ocean could last three weeks, and Pacific journeys even longer. Most took from ten to fourteen days.

The destination was revealed after a few days at sea. Herman Obermayer learned that he was headed to France. "Fear naturally ratcheted up several notches when our destination was announced" he wrote. "For many of us that meant our rendezvous with death was near at hand."[38] After the announcement, passengers were issued a guidebook, prepared by the army, describing the peoples, cultures, and history of their destination country. After these pamphlets had been issued on his ship, James May noticed "many are standing around in groups reading

---

[32] Leon Edel, *A Visitable Past: A Wartime Memoir*, Honolulu 2000, p. 29.
[33] James Lord, *My Queer War*, New York 2010, p. 145.
[34] Mel TenHaken, *Bail-Out!: POW, 1944 – 1945*, Manhattan, Kansas 1990, p. 22.
[35] Diary of James Cole, 17 July 1943, James Cole Papers, Wisconsin Veterans Museum, Madison, Wisconsin.
[36] James M. Knox, "The Bluffers at Home and Abroad", p. 14, in Ellis Waldron Papers, Wisconsin Veterans Museum, Madison, Wisconsin.
[37] Benedict Solomon Alper, *Love and Politics in Wartime: Letters to My Wife, 1943 – 45*, Urbana/Ill. 1992, p. 3.
[38] Obermayer, *Soldiering for Freedom*, p. 88.

them."[39] If headed to a non-English-speaking country, they also received a language phrasebook. "We spend many hours the next few days practicing our French and Arabic phrases," wrote Avis Shorer, who was bound for North Africa.[40] Soldiers also received lectures on the customs and cultures of their destination. "Indoctrination on the British is intense," wrote Robert Peters. "They are a proud people," he was told, "so don't act superior – although we are again forced to save them from the Germans." The lecturer advised them on such topics as "tea time," their "quirky" monetary system and "queues." He also reminded the GIs that "we are allies, not an occupation force," and warned that they would likely encounter "English cities blitzed to smithereens from German bombs."[41]

All voyages have their hazards, and the GI faced the same perils as other transatlantic travelers. In the North Atlantic, there could be dense fog, wind-whipped rain, and icebergs. Farther south, there was the possibility of tropical storms and hurricanes. Many crossings occurred without major incident, but others experienced rough weather. Writing his wife, James May told of hanging on to the handrail and looking out over the side during a storm. "One minute you'd be looking in the water," he wrote, "and the next at the sky."[42] On another occasion, May watched a St. Christopher medal on a hook in his sleeping quarters "swing back and forth until [it] would almost touch the wall."[43] "On the roughest day you could feel the whole ship vibrate," wrote Herman Obermayer, "and the prow lurched forward and the propeller came out of the water."[44] "Some of the waves came over the bow," Robert Kenney wrote home, "and sometimes she rocked under water from guard rail to guard rail on each side."[45]

Even in relatively calm seas the troopships rose and fell with the ocean swells, promoting the bane of many ocean travelers – seasickness. "For American troops, the first unpleasant act in their active and dangerous participation in [the war]," claimed Paul Fussell, "was throwing up in the transports."[46] For some,

---

[39] James W. May to Mrs. James W. May, 2 Dec 1944, James W. May Papers, Emory University Archives, Atlanta, Georgia.
[40] Shorer, *Half Acre of Hell*, p. 61.
[41] Robert Peters, *For You, Lili Marlene: A Memoir of World War II*, Madison 1995, p. 33.
[42] James W. May to Mrs. James W. May, 4 Dec 1944, May Papers.
[43] James W. May to Mrs. James W. May, 11 Dec 1944, May Papers.
[44] Obermayer, *Soldiering for Freedom*, p. 96.
[45] Robert L. Kinney to parents, 31 Jan 1943, Robert L. Kinney Papers, California State Library, Sacramento, California.
[46] Paul Fussell, *The Boy's Crusade: The American Infantry in Northwestern Europe, 1944 – 1945*, New York 2003, p. 15.

seasickness began immediately. Alton Carpenter was puzzled that a fellow officer complained of seasickness while still at the dock. "I had to admit that he looked ill," he recorded in his diary, but what really struck him as odd was the fact that "he's the psychiatrist!"[47] Others witnessed the same phenomenon. "Some of the men became violently ill while we were still tied up at the pier," wrote Henry Heyburn to his parents, "and have gotten progressively worse since then."[48]

In their wartime accounts, countless GIs tell of vomiting in the ships' latrines or hanging their heads over the side rail to "feed the fish." "The decks were thick with people trying to get air," wrote James Knox, "and you had to be careful where you stepped because some guys hadn't quite made the rail."[49] Robert Kotlowitz watched one soldier "throw up into the wind."[50] Alan Cope remembered that on the deck of his ship "there were 55-gallon drums everywhere to throw up in."[51] There were also vomit receptacles below decks. "We've even got Merry Christmas written on the puke bucket," James May wrote his wife during his December 1944 crossing.[52] Lawrence Collins noted that "a good eighty-five percent" of his fellow passengers became seasick soon after leaving Hampton Roads. He had managed to keep the contents of his stomach down, but claimed that "when the ship rolls I never know whether I'll make it for another minute or not." Despite his queasiness, Collins – a physician – recorded some observations on seasickness in his letters home. He noted, for example, that "the green color that you've heard about actually exists on those afflicted. Their faces turn the most nauseating aquamarine you ever saw." He also found "something very funny about the poor devil who is seasick. Miserable as they are, they all laugh at whoever is heaving when they are not."[53]

For most, seasickness was temporary, lasting just a day or so. Some took a little longer to adjust. By "the third & fourth day out," explained Robert Kinney, "I was a pretty good sailor."[54] But for some, the mal de mer was unrelenting. Roscoe Blunt spent most of his voyage immobilized on his bunk. He sometimes went on

---

[47] Alton Earl Carpenter, *Chappie: World War II Diary of A Combat Chaplain*, Mesa, Arizona 2007, p. 32.
[48] Henry Heyburn to parents, 31 Oct 1944, Henry Heyburn Papers, Filson Historical Society, Louisville, Kentucky.
[49] Knox, "The Bluffers at Home and Abroad", p. 13.
[50] Kotlowitz, *Before Their Time*, p. 51.
[51] Emmanuel Guibert, *Alan's War: The Memories of GI Alan Cope*, New York 2008, p. 83.
[52] James W. May to Mrs. James May, 6 Dec 1944, May Papers.
[53] Lawrence Collins, *The 56th Evac Hospital: Letters of a WWII Army Doctor*, Denton/TX 2005, p. 4.
[54] Robert L. Kinney to parents, 31 Jan 1943, Kinney Papers.

deck hoping fresh air might help, but found that "the debilitating nausea intensified and left me barely able to stand up, much less walk." After nearly two weeks at sea, he claimed to be "even too weak to make it unassisted to the galley." Blunt saw heavy combat in Europe, but after the war he counted the Atlantic crossing was one of his most terrible wartime memories. "To this day, half a century later, I vividly remember the two weeks of constant seasickness," he wrote. "It is a tortuous experience that no one should have to endure." Blunt claimed that "real seasickness ... is one of the few times in life when you actually hope that you will die."[55] Others agreed. "The one advantage to seasickness is that you don't have to worry about the boat sinking," wrote Frances DeBra, "you actually hope that it will sink and put you out of your misery."[56] "Don't care if we get torpedoed," June Wandrey recorded in her diary, "would almost welcome it."[57]

And getting torpedoed was a possibility. German submarines, known as U-boats, prowled the Atlantic in search of Allied vessels. For most, it was their first exposure to enemy guns. To protect their shipping, the Allies sent their boats across the Atlantic in convoys, and troopships were placed in the center of the convoys for maximum safety. The GIs were often awed by the sight of these massive naval formations. "By evening I could count sixty vessels," recalled Robert Kotlowitz, "naval, cargo, troop transport, even a couple of aircraft carriers – spread in a stupendous 360-degree sweep that extended across the horizon."[58] Large passenger liners could outrun U-boats and usually went unescorted. Allied ships also made frequent course changes in order to confuse the U-boats tracking them. Robert Welker remembered that "every few minutes, by some signal as hidden as that which seems to control a wheeling flock of sandpipers, the convoy swung uniformly left or right, each ship remaining as separate yet as integrated as a minnow in a school."[59] "One night the Big Dipper was at the stern," wrote Charles Dryden, "the next night at the bow, the next at port, and the next on the starboard side."[60] "There were thirty five Air Force navigators among the air crew personnel on our ship," recalled Mel TenHaken. "Curiosity, practice, and

---

[55] Blunt, *Foot Soldier*, p. 6-8.
[56] Frances DeBra Brown, *An Army in Skirts: The World War II Letters of Frances DeBra*, Indianapolis 2008, p. 70.
[57] June Wandrey, *Bedpan Commando: The Story of A Combat Nurse during World War II*, Elmore/OH 1989, p. 11.
[58] Kotlowitz, *Before Their Time*, p. 52.
[59] Welker, *Different Drummer*, p. 130.
[60] Charles W. Dryden, *A-Train: The Memoirs of a Tuskegee Airman*, Tuscaloosa 1997, p. 113.

boredom were the reasons given for many of them to bring out their sextants and confirm our location. Destination remained a military secret, but we always knew our position and direction."[61] Crossing in this zigzag pattern usually added about 10 percent to the length of the voyage.[62]

There were other precautions. At night, the convoys were blacked out. "Men of the ship's company went around, covering the holes and the windows, locking in the lights of the ship," wrote Jack Sheridan, "and she became a part of the night around her."[63] Smoking on deck after dusk was strictly forbidden. "We were cautioned that on a clear night a flame lighting a cigarette might be seen by a plane 50 miles away," Edward Reep recalled.[64] Gun crews practiced, but passengers were seldom informed beforehand, sometimes causing alarm. Lloyd Wells remembered hearing the "dull booms of their depth charges[65] and sometimes the sharper crack of their surface weapons" from ships in his convoy. "At first we assumed that our friends in the navy were waging a heroic struggle against enemy submarines," but later learned that "it was just an exercise."[66] "Three times our escort ships dropped depth charges," reported Marshall Hardy, "whether in practice or action against the enemy we never knew, but one bombing was very extensive."[67]

Not all the gunfire was practice. One afternoon Ruth Haskell noticed "a couple of corvettes … chasing around in circles at the edge of the convoy firing off depth bombs." A crew member later told her that they had "made a hit on a submarine, for an oil slick and some wreckage were floating about."[68] U-boats staged many deadly attacks on the convoys. Nearing the British coast one night, Robert Peters spotted "smoke and flames on the horizon." A ship in his convoy had been sunk. Not long afterward he noted "a massive oil slick … blackening our ship" and

---

[61] TenHaken, *Bail-Out!*, p. 22.
[62] For more on convoys and other U.S. naval operations in the Atlantic during World War II, see Samuel Eliot Morison, *History of United States Naval Operations in World War II, Vol. 1: The Battle of the Atlantic, September 1939 – May 1943*, Boston 1947; and Samuel Eliot Morison, *History of United States Naval Operations in World War II, Vol. 10: The Atlantic Battle Won, May 1943 – May 1945*, Boston 1956.
[63] Sheridan, *They Never Had It So Good*, p. 41.
[64] Edward Reep, *A Combat Artist in World War II*, Lexington 1987, p. 20.
[65] A depth charge is an underwater explosive used to combat U-Boats.
[66] Lloyd Wells, *From Anzio to the Alps: An American Soldier's Story*, Columbia 2004, p. 25.
[67] Marshall B. Hardy to Sis, 27 June 1942, Hardy Papers.
[68] Ruth Haskell, *Helmets and Lipstick*, New York 1944, p. 37-38.

"bits of flotsam slue and slide, washing past us."[69] On his crossing, Emiel Owens saw duffel bags floating in the ocean. He then saw bodies – victims of a ship sunk ahead of his own. "The cold, salty ocean water had washed their faces and army uniforms sparkling clean," he wrote of the incident. "It was very strange, but they looked alive just floating in the ice-cold ocean water." Owens found it a sobering experience. "This scene was my first full awakening to the meaning of life and death," he wrote, "that death could overtake you right out here in the middle of the ocean."[70] All told, U-boats managed to sink a mere handful of troopships, but there were other dangers. Gordon King remembered a near collision with another ship in a dense fogbank. "Hundreds of us on deck amidship could only gasp in alarm," he wrote, "as the gray wall of vapor turned to black wall of ship in an instant. Fortunately, within moments courses had been corrected."[71]

Passengers had to be prepared in case of attack or accident. Each was issued an orange life vest, and was expected to wear it whenever on deck. Lifeboat drills were also mandatory. "These drills can hardly become a laughing matter," claimed James May, "for each time you have a little of the feeling, 'Well, this could be it.'" [72] Many others were less concerned. "You could feel the tension in the crew," claimed William Dreux, "but I hardly ever thought of a torpedo slamming into the ship and myself floundering in cold waters."[73] "There was a sense of danger about our journey but no sense of fear," claimed Robert Welker. "Death waited not here, but in that corner of a foreign field."[74]

Accommodations

The quality of sleeping quarters depended on one's rank. For the enlisted soldier, they were invariably cramped and uncomfortable, whether on a Liberty Ship or the *Queen Mary*. Cargo holds and other large rooms located deep in the bowels of ships were devoted to warehousing the troops. There were often no windows or any source of natural light, and ventilation was poor. Every square inch was utilized. "Our quarters were in an old dining room in the center of the ship," remembered Ted Hartman. "We settled ourselves (about seventy men in a 20 ×

---

[69] Peters, *For You, Lili Marlene*, p. 33.
[70] Emiel W. Owens, *Blood on the German Snow: An African American Artilleryman in World War II and Beyond*, College Station/TX 2006, p. 39.
[71] Gordon King, "A Small Place in History: Remembering D-Day Fifty Years Later," in *Wisconsin Academy Review* 40 (Summer 1994), p. 11.
[72] James W. May to Mrs. James W. May, 2 Dec 1944, May papers.
[73] William B. Dreux, *No Bridges Blown*, Notre Dame, Indiana 1971, p. 21.
[74] Welker, *Different Drummer*, p. 130.

30 – foot room) as comfortably as possible."[75] Even those fortunate enough to get a stateroom on a luxury liner were squeezed into every conceivable space. On the *Queen Elizabeth*, Norman Bussel was housed in a room "intended for two" but which "now slept eighteen men."[76] The common soldier found that his sleeping berth was typically located below the waterline. "The image in my mind was a torrent of water pouring into the hold," wrote Leon Edel, "and I knew it would take a miracle to survive."[77]

Soldiers usually slept on canvas bunks six feet long by two feet wide, and stacked from floor to ceiling – in some cases six levels high. James Lord thought them "designed for discomfort."[78] With only about two feet of space between each bunk, soldiers found it challenging even to get in them. One did so "by edging yourself sideways," according to Jack Sheridan, "finishing the process with a giant thrust that lands you in the middle of the sagging bunk."[79] Once in, other problems became evident. If the bunk above was occupied, according to Bill Mauldin, "there were about fifteen inches of headroom before you encountered the sagging butt of the man above."[80] "The guy in the berth above mine must have weighed 300 pounds," remembered Alan Cope. "His weight forced the bunk's canvas down and bent the support bars."[81] On some ships soldiers slept on hammocks, which had the advantage of swaying with the movement of the ship, but offered little else in the way of improvement. "Our sleeping accommodations consisted of canvas hammocks suspended one above another from the floor to the ceiling," recalled Lloyd Wells. "They hung so close you couldn't raise your knees without bumping the rump of the guy above."[82]

To make matters worse, passengers were expected to stow their gear with them on their bunks. Accomplishing this required creativity. "You pile some of your equipment at the head of the bunk," according to Jack Sheridan, and "hunch around, to try and make yourself comfortable."[83] Bill Mauldin claimed that "the only way to stretch out" was to "kick your barracks bag [...] onto a neighbor's territory. If he was asleep, he wouldn't kick back."[84] The lack of storage space made for a chaotic appearance in the enlisted quarters. "Everywhere there is

---

[75] Hartman, *Tank Driver*, p. 38-39.
[76] Bussel, *My Private War*, p. 82.
[77] Edel, *Visitable Past*, p. 29.
[78] Lord, *My Queer War*, p. 145.
[79] Sheridan, *They Never Had It So Good*, p. 40-41.
[80] Bill Mauldin, *The Brass Ring*, New York 1971, p. 156.
[81] Guibert, *Alan's War*, p. 84-85.
[82] Wells, *From Anzio to the Alps*, p. 25
[83] Sheridan, *They Never Had It So Good*, p. 40-41.
[84] Mauldin, *Brass Ring*, p. 156.

equipment," claimed Jack Sheridan, and the passengers would constantly "trip over rifles [and] stagger over blanket rolls."[85] "You can't move without bumping into another soldier," complained Keith Winston.[86]

Hygiene was difficult to maintain while aboard ship. Because fresh water was in short supply, GIs had to take baths or showers in salt water. Few found them satisfying. "At one time I was running more salt into my pores than was coming out," claimed Morton Elevitch.[87] According to Lloyd Wells, the showers emitted "cold, brackish, salt water [that] came in irregular and unpredictable bursts."[88] The army developed a special soap to lather in salt water, but "all it did was curdle up on our bodies," complained Charles Wise.[89] Such conditions "discouraged many of us from taking frequent showers," claimed Ted Hartman.[90] In addition, troopships did not have laundry facilities for passengers. "We didn't change our clothes the entire time," wrote Richard Letsinger. "We had on wool uniforms and the collar bands became black, slick, and greasy."[91] Latrine facilities were also lacking. Dean Joy remembered "a long, narrow compartment in the very bow of the ship" where "a dozen or so toilet seats were bolted to the sloping steel hull," offering little privacy.[92] "Urinals were improvised in dead-end corridors with a drain along the bottom of a slate-covered wall," wrote Herman Obermayer, and "choppy seas made these corridors into slippery 'slop alleys.'"[93] J.J. Kuhn remembered that the swimming pool on his ship had been converted into a latrine. "We'd climb down the latter and go into the corners where the drains were," he wrote, and commented that "the smell made it a hurry up trip."[94]

GIs endured other noisome miseries. Poor ventilation and the crush of humanity often meant that it was uncomfortably warm in the holds. "We were so hot," recalled Raymond Gantter, "we slept naked and dripped waterfalls of sweat through the thick canvas of our bunks."[95] "The air was warm and close," recalled

---

[85] Sheridan, *They Never Had It So Good*, p. 40.
[86] Keith Winston, *V-Mail: Letters of a World War II Combat Medic*, Chapel Hill/NC 1985, p. 101.
[87] Elevitch, *Dog Tags Yapping*, p. 74.
[88] Wells, *From Anzio to the Alps*, p. 25.
[89] Charles Wise, *My Encounter with Mt. Vesuvius*, privately publ. 2007, p. 5.
[90] Hartman, *Tank Driver*, p. 39.
[91] Letsinger, "And How Was Your Trip Abroad?"
[92] Dean Joy, *Sixty Days in Combat: An Infantryman's Memoir of World War II*, New York 2004, p. 51.
[93] Obermayer, *Soldiering for Freedom*, p. 87.
[94] Kuhn, *I Was Baker 2*, p. 65.
[95] Raymond Gantter, *Roll Me Over: An Infantryman's World War II*, New York 1997, p. 1.

Robert Welker, "smelling of humanity."[96] Most soldiers described it less eloquently. "Our quarters constantly smelled like a locker room in a gymnasium," declared Ted Hartman.[97] Lloyd Wells remembered that many of his fellow passengers were seasick, and "the smell of their vomit did nothing to improve the quality of the air." He noticed other smells emanating from his cohorts. "On the basis of impressionistic, but I thought, very convincing evidence," he wrote, "I estimated that roughly two-thirds of the American army was uncontrollably flatulent."[98] For those quartered near the engines, there were still other olfactory challenges. Roscoe Blunt remembered that "the nauseating stench of diesel fuel" permeated his sleeping quarters.[99]

Blunt could not just smell the engines, but hear them. "Throbbing turbines and the grinding of stretching metal would be my orchestral accompaniment for the next 13 days," he complained.[100] Noise prevented sleep in other ways. "There were voices even during the hours of sleep," wrote Robert Welker.[101] "Beneath me was a murmur of voices, much coughing, and a certain amount of shouting," remembered Leon Edel.[102] Other problems conspired against sleep. On many ships, the lights were kept on at all hours, making it "almost impossible to sleep for more than one or two hours consecutively," according to Herman Obermayer.[103] James Lord complained that "drowsing off in the airless half dark was not easy."[104] In the hold, enlisted personnel suffered still other indignities. They could not smoke in their quarters, for example, and smokers had to wait anxiously each morning for the blackout to end before they could light up on deck. To top it all off, Lloyd Wells also recalled that "a thin skim of oily dirt covered the floor."[105] "The hold was at best no pleasant place," Welker wrote. "There seemed no hours, no days, only existence."[106]

Conditions in the hold were so terrible that many soldiers opted to sleep outside on deck. "At first I could not find a solitary vacant space," Kenneth Gowen remembered, but he eventually found one underneath a gun emplacement "just

---

[96] Welker, *Different Drummer*, p. 132.
[97] Hartman, *Tank Driver*, p. 39.
[98] Wells, *From Anzio to the Alps*, p. 25.
[99] Blunt, *Foot Soldier*, p. 5.
[100] Ibid.
[101] Welker, *Different Drummer*, p. 132.
[102] Edel, *Visitable Past*, p. 29.
[103] Obermayer, *Soldiering for Freedom*, p. 86.
[104] Lord, *My Queer War*, p. 145.
[105] Wells, *From Anzio to the Alps*, p. 25.
[106] Welker, *Different Drummer*, p. 135.

big enough to crawl into, with my legs drawn into a fetal position."[107] Sleeping on deck was impractical in the winter months, and not permitted on all ships. "Sometimes we tried to sneak up to the decks to sleep," recalled Raymond Gantter, "but always the guards would discover us and make us go back down."[108] On some troopships soldiers had no choice but to sleep on deck. These ships were "double loaded," meaning that one shift of soldiers slept in the hold at night and spent the day on the deck, while another slept on deck at night and spent the day below. "I drew the assignment of being topside at night and down in the hold during the day," recalled J.J. Kuhn, who crossed the North Atlantic in October. "I took my two blankets up on deck at night," he wrote. "Even fully clothed, two blankets were not enough to keep me warm."[109]

The enlisted GI, though already accustomed to the Spartan life of the barracks, found quarters on the troopships appalling. Some compared their conditions to those of slaves. "Our bunks were ... so close together that it reminded me of stories I had read of the Slave trade," claimed James Knox, who sailed on the luxury liner *Ile de France*.[110] "I remember reading history books of slave transportation," wrote Richard Letsinger, "and how a slave ship could be detected miles away by its odor. I believe it."[111] Some soldiers expressed feelings of dehumanization. Arnold Boettger remembered that some "cried in their hammocks at the thought [of] being herded out to sea like animals."[112] There were other animal analogies. "We are suspended in the hold like bees in a hive," complained Eugene Alexander.[113] Marvel Rowland used the most common animal comparison when he complained that he and his fellow soldiers were "packed like sardines."[114] Some took conditions in stride. "We were packed in a bottom birth like sardines," William Perkins wrote, "but I was glad to lay down and rest."[115]

---

[107] Gowen, *Granddaddy*, p. 33-35.
[108] Gantter, *Roll Me Over*, p. 1.
[109] Kuhn, *I Was Baker 2*, p. 63.
[110] Knox, "The Bluffers at Home and Abroad", p. 13.
[111] Letsinger, "And How Was Your Trip Abroad?"
[112] Untitled reminiscence, Arnold Boettger Papers, Wisconsin Veterans Museum, Madison, Wisconsin.
[113] Diary of Eugene P. Alexander, 25 July 1944, Eugene P. Alexander Papers, Wisconsin Veterans Museum, Madison, Wisconsin.
[114] Marvel B. Rowland, *Marvel B. Rowland's Story of WW II*, privately published, n.d., p. 8.
[115] Diary of William Perkins, 5 Nov 1944, William Perkins Papers, University of Oklahoma Archives, Norman, Oklahoma.

Officers were crowded too, and their descriptions of their living conditions sometimes mirror those of the enlisted men. "There are eighteen of us ... in my particular cabin," wrote Henry Heyburn, "sleeping in triple decker bunks." [116] Robert Chapman "discovered that the 'state-room' to which I had been assigned had also been assigned to eleven other guys." Bunks were "piled one on top of the other, four deep," he remembered, and claimed that "you needed a slipper spoon to pry yourself in and out of bed." Chapman also noted that "one fat guy had to sleep on the top bunk because he couldn't squeeze between the lower ones." Officers also complained about the toilets and the bathing facilities. "Tonight I have to take a salt water bath,"[117] Cecil Chapman wrote his wife, "which I can't say that I am looking forward to with a great deal of pleasure."[118] Though hardly luxurious, officers enjoyed amenities enlisted soldiers did not. Their quarters were usually in staterooms located in the upper reaches of the ship, providing more light and air. Fear of U-boats made Brendan Phibbs "happy with the geography of the upper deck." He believed that "the nether spaces" of the ship "shriek of entrapment" while from the upper decks "it's a short sprint to the rail."[119] Staterooms usually had their own toilet and bathing facilities, affording a little more privacy than the enlisted passengers had. Officers were allowed to smoke in their quarters, and often had their own lounge and recreational facilities. Leslie Bailey remembered that on the *Aquitania* the officers had "the grand ballroom ... with its rich furnishings and beautiful paintings set aside as the recreation room and bar."[120] Cunard treated officers particularly well. "We had an English steward who made our beds," remarked David Eichhorn of his trip on the *Queen Mary*.[121] "Cunard did not lose sight of the fact that a proportion of the troops, particularly amongst the officer classes, were likely to be fare-paying passengers in the future," claimed Alistair Satchell, a crewman on the *Aquitania* during the war. "Deck officers, pursers, stewards, and crew members were always well turned out, maintaining politeness under trying circumstances," he recalled, and noted that "the officer's library was well stocked with publications, fully illustrated, depicting the grandeur of peacetime travel." [122]

---

[116] Heyburn to parents, 31 Oct 1944, Heyburn Papers.
[117] Chapman, *Tell It To the Chaplain*, p. 66.
[118] Cecil W. Chapman to Claudia Chapman, "Letter No. 3," n.d. [c. Oct 1944], Cecil W. Chapman Papers, University of Georgia Archives, Athens, Georgia.
[119] Phibbs, *Other Side of Time*, p. 45.
[120] Leslie W. Bailey, *Through Hell and High Water: The Memoirs of a Junior Combat Infantry Officer*, New York 1994, p. 11.
[121] Greg Palmer and Mark S. Zaid (Eds.), *The GI's Rabbi: The World War II Letters of David Max Eichhorn*, Lawrence/KS 2004, p. 64.
[122] Stachell, *Running the Gauntlet*, p. 25.

While enlisted men were critical of their accommodations, officers were more charitable. "The officer's quarters are crowded but really much more comfortable than I had hoped for," claimed Henry Heyburn.[123] "In the areas reserved for ... officers," opined Tracy Sugarman, "the packing of humanity was somewhat more manageable."[124] Of course, as the voyage dragged on the passengers' patience wore thin. On April 17, 1943, Lawrence Collins wrote his wife that he and his roommates were "quite comfortable even if a little crowded" on their way to North Africa. By April 30, his tone had changed dramatically. "Did I say earlier that our stateroom was of ample size as well as clean?" he now asked. "Do strike out any such intimations at once." In particular, he complained about the state of his bed linen "after being wallowed upon eighteen to twenty four hours per day without being laundered for seventeen days."[125]

Aboard ship, the two military castes were kept segregated. Officers had free reign of the ship, but enlisted personnel were not allowed in "Officer's Country." Bill Mauldin remembered that on his ship "incredibly complicated routes were laid out between each hold and the soldier's galley" so that "troops who desired could get exercise and fresh air without encroaching on Officer's Country."[126] Segregation by rank continued while on deck. Portions of the deck – on large boats, the upper decks – were for officers only. "An imaginary demarcation line had been drawn," recalled enlisted man James Knox, "officers on one side – 'untouchables' on the other."[127] Robert Welker and some friends once "slipped past the relaxing guards" into the officers' deck area, but were soon confronted by an enraged officer who told him to "get below, and stay the hell out of here in the future."[128] Enlisted personnel bitterly resented the contrast between their own conditions and those of officers. "From what I can see," Keith Winston wrote his wife, "the small percentage of officers on board have as much room as the combined troops." He continued that "it has aroused a resentful feeling, not only in me, but in everyone around me," and claimed that rather instilling respect for his superiors, the situation instead promoted "a complete lack of respect for the officers and the System."[129]

---

[123] Henry Heyburn to parents, 31 Oct 1944, Heyburn Papers.
[124] Sugarman, *My War*, p. 14.
[125] Collins, *The 56th Evac Hospital*, p. 4, 6-7.
[126] Mauldin, *Brass Ring*, p. 157.
[127] Knox, "The Bluffers at Home and Abroad", p. 14.
[128] Welker, *Different Drummer*, p. 129.
[129] Winston, *V-Mail*, p. 101-102.

Food

Rank also determined the quality and quantity of food. Ship galleys were constantly preparing food for the passengers, but because of the immense number of soldiers to feed, enlisted personnel were only served twice a day. At the appointed time, GIs lined up outside the dining hall, mess kits in hand. They "waited in sweating lines strung far up through the ship," wrote Robert Welker, "and [we] held our mess kits for what might be offered when at last we reached the [serving] line."[130] After having their food unceremoniously deposited onto their mess kits, the soldiers searched for a place to eat it. Enlisted men ate standing up, gathered around long tables. "The tables were wide and high," remembered Alan Cope, "with a lip four inches high around the edge" to contain spills.[131] It was crowded too. Daniel Inouye remembered that "men were jammed elbow to elbow in a great echoing cavern" that was the enlisted dining hall on his ship.[132] "While you gobble your food with marathon haste," wrote Leo Bogart, dining hall workers "urge you on to finish quickly, quit stalling, stop eating so much."[133] After finishing their meals, soldiers were then required to do their own dishes. They "filed through the steaming room past stone tubs," recalled Jack Sheridan, "near scalding themselves as they washed out their mess kits." [134] Bogart found he was hurried through the indignity of the washing line too. "At every step of the way, there is some minor authority to crack the whip and urge you along at greater speeds."[135]

GI reviews of the food varied. Dean Joy found his meals on his ship "exceptionally good."[136] Most were critical. "Food was scanty and very poor," claimed Robert Welker. "Two slices of bread, a pale bit of butter, a hard-boiled egg, execrable coffee, and some jam – such was breakfast." He described a typical dinner as "two frankfurters, a forkful of tasteless sauerkraut, a single boiled potato, bread and coffee."[137] Daniel Inouye remembered "an endless river of chipped beef and beans."[138] Food on British-run ships was universally panned.

---

[130] Welker, *Different Drummer*, p. 132.
[131] Guibert, *Alan's War*, p. 84.
[132] Daniel Inouye, *Journey to Washington*, Englewood Cliffs/NJ 1967, p. 102.
[133] Bogart, *How I Earned the Ruptured Duck*, p. 44.
[134] Sheridan, *They Never Had It So Good*, p. 43.
[135] Bogart, *How I Earned the Ruptured Duck*, p. 44.
[136] Joy, *Sixty Days in Combat*, p. 50.
[137] Welker, *Different Drummer*, p. 132.
[138] Inouye, *Journey to Washington*, p. 102.

"The first time I saw corned beef on the menu," wrote Norman Bussel, who sailed on the *Queen Elizabeth*, "I was salivating over the prospect of good old-fashioned deli beef on rye bread, slathered with mustard." He was chagrined to find the meat "so tough, you couldn't chew it."[139] "Ships are noted for good food," wrote Don Edwards, but found the British liner Stirling Castle "the exception." Edwards described peas "like tiny rocks" and potatoes with "a bad odor," and claimed that "in the twelve days spent on the ship, I ate only five meals." He also noted that "each day as the convoy progressed eastward, the mess line became smaller and smaller."[140] "It's really a misnomer to call it food," claimed James Knox, who sailed on the British-run *Ile de France* . "Actually it more resembled the slop that they feed to hogs. I have never tasted anything – before of after – that was so lousy." [141] "The British can't cook worth a darn," Frank Summers concluded.[142] Many ships had a small canteen (known as a Post Exchange or "PX" in American military parlance) where soldiers could purchase snack foods. James Knox claimed that he "managed to subsist" on "cookies and candy" sold at the canteen. "I ate so many damn vanilla wafers that before I left the boat I swore I'd never look at another one."[143] Jack Sheridan remembered "long, sweating lines in front of the PX."[144] Demand was so high on these facilities that they often ran out of items. On some ships, a black market emerged to feed hungry enlisted men. Lloyd Wells was "shocked to learn that members of the crew ... were selling steak sandwiches to army personnel at the outrageous, unheard-of price of one dollar per sandwich." [145] Richard Welker discovered that "civilian mess boys," in cahoots with one noncommissioned officer, "set up a traffic in sandwiches" on his ship. "By the end of the voyage they were asking – and getting – five dollars for each fat sandwich."[146] There was "intense bidding for a spare five cent candy bar or an orange or an apple hoarded from the last mess," wrote Frederick Olson, "any edible item could easily fetch a dollar."[147]

For officers, it was an entirely different gustatory experience. "While the men ate terrible food twice a day standing up," recalled Paul Fussell, "the officers, in an

---

[139] Bussel, *My Private War*, p. 84-85.
[140] Donald A. Edwards, *A Private's Diary*, Big Rapids/MI 1994, p. 23, 35.
[141] Knox, "The Bluffers at Home and Abroad", p. 13.
[142] Frank W. Summers to Harriet Charles Bennett, 23 Dec 1943, Frank W. Summers Papers, Indiana Historical Society, Indianapolis, Indiana.
[143] Knox, "The Bluffers at Home and Abroad", p. 13.
[144] Sheridan, *They Never Had It So Good*, p. 42.
[145] Wells, *From Anzio to the Alps*, p. 26.
[146] Welker, *Different Drummer*, p. 134.
[147] Frederick I. Olson, *Dear Jane: A Soldier's Letters from West Africa and the Middle East*, Milwaukee 1994, p. 48.

elegant restaurant several decks above, sat down to white table linen, nice cutlery, friendly service by stewards, and infinitely better food, hardly different from the cuisine rich transatlantic passengers had enjoyed before the war."[148] "The chow is the best yet," wrote James May several days into his crossing. "Yesterday's breakfast was hot cakes, bacon, and wonderful coffee. Dinner was chopped steak, tomatoes, potatoes, celery soup, and lemon pie."[149] "Each delicious meal lingers in my memory," wrote June Wandrey. She remembered that an acquaintance on board was "a connoisseur of good food," and during one meal he "rolled his eyes and said, 'Something must be up, such good food, is it our last meal before the killing?'"[150] Some officers were unhappy with their victuals, especially those on British ships. William Dreux remembered with disdain the "Brussels sprouts" on the *Aquitania* "which were served to us both at lunch and dinner swimming in a pale and scummy juice."[151] "The food was pronounced by all and sundry as the worst they had eaten in their military careers thus far," wrote Frank Smith while aboard the *Queen Elizabeth*, though he noted that he enjoyed "being served in luxury style by efficient white-coated waiters." [152]

Duties and Leisure Time

Some GIs were assigned to work details while aboard ship. "Each junior officer was assigned to be 'Officer-of-the-Day' at least once during the voyage," wrote Edward Reep, which usually involved supervising the guard detail.[153] For the enlisted personnel, "duties ranged from K.P. to Guard to sweeping down the decks," recalled Richard Letsinger, who worked as an administrative orderly on his crossing.[154] Those given such duties may have been unhappy about it at first, but complaints ceased when they discovered that they received special privileges. Robert Ellis was given guard duty while on the West Point and was glad to be "assigned a stateroom" because of it.[155] Richard Letsinger found that as a result of his administrative duties "waiters brought me food from the Officer's dining

---

[148] Fussell, *Boy's Crusade*, p. 15.
[149] James W. May to Mrs. James W. May, 2 Dec 1944, May Papers.
[150] Wandrey, *Bedpan Commando*, p. 10.
[151] Dreux, *No Bridges Blown*, p. 22.
[152] Frank E. Smith, *Battle Diary: The Story of the 243rd Field Artillery Battalion in Combat*, New York 1946, p. 25.
[153] Reep, *Combat Artist*, p. 18.
[154] Letsinger, "And How Was Your Trip Abroad?"
[155] Robert B. Ellis, *See Naples and Die: A World War II Memoir of a United States Army Ski Trooper in the Mountains of Italy*, Jefferson/NC 1996, p. 98.

room."[156] One of the most common details was KP – working in the kitchen. This could be hard and dirty work. "Our bare arms and backs became streaked with jam and gravy spots," wrote Morton Elevitch. "The front of our pants resembled a pig's snout which had just emerged from the garbage can."[157] KP duty could also involve serving as waiters in the officer's mess. Tough as it was, KP duty provided access to good food. "There was chicken left on the tables after the officers had eaten," Kenneth Gowen wrote, and "after the waiters had eaten all they could hold, there was still chicken left."[158] Transporting food to and from the kitchen, Elevitch wrote that he "learned to inhale food en route."[159] "I asked to go on permanent KP duty," recalled Ted Hartman, "so I could eat decently."[160] But for most GIs, their only duties were to appear for daily musters, lifeboat drills, and calisthenics. The rest of the time was their own. Some complained about boredom. "There is absolutely nothing to do on this ship," Keith Winston told his wife.[161] Many others welcomed the respite from rigid military life. "We had no responsibilities," crowed Robert Kotlowitz. "We may have been caged on our ship, but it still represented a kind of freedom to most of us."[162] Soldiers found various ways to pass the time. They read and wrote letters. Music also helped. "At night we sang," recalled Robert Welker. He noted that most songs dated from the years before the First World War, and speculated that this was because the men sought "such light spirits" that "we did not extract from our own time."[163] GIs spent much of the time immersed in conversation, which revolved around "the usual big three," according to Jack Sheridan: "home, sex, and food." Sheridan noted that in these discussions home had "slipped to the past tense."[164] As it was for peacetime tourists, the voyage afforded soldier-passengers the opportunity to mingle with people of other cultures. Some chose not to. "White and Negro soldiers don't appear to be mixing socially," observed Leo Bogart, but "there have been no racial clashes that I know of."[165] Troopships were often the first place GIs had extended contact with the British and other foreigners, be they members of the ship's crew or Allied soldiers returning from an assignment in

---

[156] Letsinger, "And How Was Your Trip Abroad?"
[157] Elevitch, *Dog Tags Yapping*, p. 70.
[158] Gowen, *Granddaddy*, p. 33.
[159] Elevitch, *Dog Tags Yapping*, p. 72.
[160] Hartman, *Tank Driver*, p. 39.
[161] Winston, *V-Mail*, p. 99.
[162] Kotlowitz, *Before Their Time*, p. 56.
[163] Welker, *Different Drummer*, p. 135-136.
[164] Sheridan, *They Never Had It So Good*, p. 41.
[165] Bogart, *How I Earned the Ruptured Duck*, p. 46.

the United States. "These 'Limeys' (as we called them) had definite accents," wrote Morton Elevitch, "which we attempted to copy, and did poorly, irritating them 'no end.'"[166] British crewmen could be equally curious about Yanks. "The bloomin [sic] limeys gave us lots of laughs," James Brown wrote his family. "They all try to use American slang, so you can imagine the results."[167] Lloyd Lane was interested to see Scottish "Highlanders in skirts" on his ship.[168] Leo Bogart found it interesting that "British soldiers mix with colored ... almost as readily as with us."[169]

Passengers played various kinds of games. Dean Joy and a friend played "game after game of chess with a small pocket set."[170] "I played endless games of checkers," wrote Marshall Hardy.[171] Card games were most popular. Herman Obermayer claimed that he had "played more cards" on his voyage than he had "played during the first eighteen years of my life."[172] Games were not always just for fun. Gambling was perhaps the most common pastime aboard the troopships. Many games were between friends and for low stakes, but "gambling got bigger and better as the hours began to stretch out," according to Jack Sheridan, who claimed that his ship was "gripped in a gambling wave." Gaming took place on deck, in the holds, and even in the stairwells. Officers gambled as much as the enlisted personnel. Poker was perhaps most popular, but there were many other games. "Blackjack, dice, faro, and what looked like a fan-tan game came into their own," observed Sheridan.[173] Some ships seemed like floating casinos. "Self-appointed croupiers presided over the high stakes games," recalled Obermayer. "They announced the odds on crap points, matched bets, changed big bills, and kept kibitzers and amateurs away from the big time poker games," and "nobody objected to their taking their cut" since "they maintained essential order."[174] Fortunes rose and fell quickly. "Pvt. Springer created a mild sensation when he lost all his money and watch one night in a game of dice," remembered Bill Etheridge, but "the sensation was heightened the following night when he

---

[166] Elevitch, *Dog Tags Yapping*, p. 71.
[167] James Brown to family, December 1943, James Brown Papers, California State Library, Sacramento, California.
[168] Lloyd Lane, *All My Love, Forever: Letters Home From a World War II Citizen Soldier, Written in 1943 – 1945*, Bloomington, Indiana: 1st Books, 2001, p. 91.
[169] Bogart, *How I Earned the Ruptured Duck*, p. 46.
[170] Joy, *Sixty Days in Combat*, p. 50.
[171] Hardy to Sis, 21 June 1942, Hardy Papers.
[172] Obermayer, *Soldiering for Freedom*, p. 97.
[173] Sheridan, *They Never Had It So Good*, p. 43-44.
[174] Obermayer, *Soldiering for Freedom*, p. 87-88.

regained his watch and nineteen hundred dollars."[175] Virgil Richardson made more than $3,000 gambling during his first week at sea. "I had so many ones, fives, and tens in my possession," he remembered, "when I laid down in my bed, it felt like my money was pressing me up to the bunk above." Richardson gave the chaplain $1,000 to send home to his pregnant wife, but he lost the remainder in subsequent gambling adventures.[176] "Money had little meaning on a voyage of uncertain duration to an unknown destination," surmised Frederick Olson.[177]

The vast majority of military passengers were male, but some ships transported female personnel. While men and women had separate sleeping quarters, they mingled on deck and at mealtimes. Romances bloomed, and in some cases they went to an advanced stage rather quickly. "Many sexual encounters appeared to be taking place," recalled Robert Ellis, who had guard duty on the West Point. Some women were "wild," in his estimation, but others were not, noting that "we also had our hands full" protecting "those ladies not wanting to participate."[178] June Wandrey claimed that shipboard romances were "no respecter of rank,"[179] but in the competition for female attention officers clearly had an advantage. "Enlisted men aren't allowed to mingle with [nurses] socially because it's detrimental to proper discipline," observed James Knox sardonically, "yet a nurse, who is usually a 2nd or 1st Lieutenant, can go out with officers of any grade and discipline suffers not a bit."[180] Many ships had no women passengers at all. "A rumor made the rounds that one of the smaller transports plowing along behind us had nurses and Wacs,"[181] wrote Dean Joy. "I remember one GI jokingly threatened to jump overboard in the hope that he would be picked up by that smaller ship and make the rest of the trip in the company of females."[182] For most, sexual options onboard were limited. A few turned to homosexuality. In his capacity as an orderly on the *Queen Elizabeth*, Richard Letsinger remembered that one GI came to the office complaining about "a strapping big Italian GI" who coaxed another soldier to "get into his bunk with him late at night."[183] Most

---

[175] Etheridge, *ETO Diary*, p. 4.
[176] Ben Vinson and Virgil Richardson, *Flight: The Story of Virgil Richardson, A Tuskegee Airman in Mexico*, New York 2004, p. 54.
[177] Olson, *Dear Jane*, p. 47.
[178] Ellis, *See Naples and Die*, p. 97-98.
[179] Wandrey, *Bedpan Commando*, p. 10.
[180] Knox, "The Bluffers at Home and Abroad", p. 14.
[181] "Wac" is an abbreviation for Women's Army Corps. Members of the corps are also referred to as Wacs.
[182] Joy, *Sixty Days in Combat*, p. 49.
[183] Letsinger, "And How Was Your Trip Abroad?"

commonly, the sexually-frustrated GI had to settle for what Ty Carpenter referred to as a date with "Lady Five Fingers."[184]

Morale officials tried to provide passengers with more wholesome and structured activities. On many ships, there were movies and shows. On the *U.S.A.T Brazil*, remembered Herman Obermayer, the mess hall was nicknamed the "Chaplain's Night Club" and "was used for some kind of entertainment every evening when the sea was not too rough," including "movies […] sing-alongs, and variety shows with soldier vocal and instrumental groups, pantomimists, and magicians."[185] On the *Queen Elizabeth*, Norman Bussel was treated to boxing exhibitions by Joe Louis, the heavyweight champion who served as a sergeant in the army. "It was obvious he was pulling his punches," Bussel remembered, "but once in a while he wasn't able to slow his momentum in time and the force of the blow registered clearly on his sparring partner's face." Bussel even had a chance to speak with Louis and get his autograph.[186] Not all shows were so wholesome. James May witnessed a "male strip-tease" act organized by the morale officials on his ship. With an orchestra blaring in the background, a soldier who billed himself "Miss Lotta Stuff" sang and stripped away various items of military clothing. "His disrobing was with all the seduction and rhythm of the accepted burlesque manner," he informed his wife, a scene made all the more hilarious by the fact that the soldier "must not have shaved since boarding the ship." The army chaplain confessed that "I guess it's kinda obscene, but G.I. humor always seems to save the day."[187]

Sporting events kept soldiers physically active. "On clear afternoons there were supervised boxing matches on deck," wrote Herman Obermayer. "Each card was organized so that there would be a *USAT Brazil* champion in each weight classification before we reached Europe."[188] For the more studiously minded, troopships often had plenty of reading materials. Robert Kotlowitz believed that "every time the *SS Argentina* crossed the Atlantic from the States, it unloaded another well-read division in the ETO."[189] Many ships published newspapers, usually edited by the GIs themselves, containing news and sports reports from back home, as well as information about events and activities on the ship. "The captain turned out to be remarkably tolerant of our flippant editorial policy," wrote Bill Mauldin, whose cartoons entertained the passengers on the James

---

[184] Carpenter and Yeatts, *Stars Without Garters!*, p. 84.
[185] Obermayer, *Soldiering for Freedom*, p. 87.
[186] Bussel, *My Private War*, p. 83.
[187] James W. May to Mrs. James W. May, 7 Dec 1944, May Papers.
[188] Obermayer, *Soldiering for Freedom*, p. 87.
[189] Kotlowitz, *Before Their Time*, p. 55-56.

O'Hara. "My first target was Officers' Country, my second was the chow line, [and] the third drawing was about the shower facilities."[190] Herman Obermayer believed that the The Trip Over News on the *Brazil* was "somewhat distorted by clumsy GI hands," but was nonetheless grateful that it gave passengers "some vague idea of what is happening in the world around us."[191]

The vast majority of GIs had never been to sea before. Not all were impressed. "There was nothing to see except the broad level of the Atlantic," claimed Jack Sheridan.[192] Others were curious, if not fascinated, by this strange new environment. "To such a landsman as I," wrote Robert Welker, "the very ocean itself was the main experience."[193] Some were awed by its vastness. "The world seemed bigger in the middle of the ocean," claimed Emiel Owens.[194] Many witnessed an abundance of birds and sea animals – dolphins, sharks, flying fish, and even whales. Robert Welker was thrilled to see for himself a Portuguese man-of-war, "a creature I had [only] seen in pictures." Five days out Welker also remembered that "a great sea turtle surfaced to port, the brown hues of his shell seeming very rich against the tones of water."[195] GIs from the American heartland seemed particularly impressed with ocean creatures. "I saw some fish as long as a man," an astonished William Perkins of Oklahoma recorded in his diary. "They call them porpuses [sic]."[196] Nighttime brought still more wonders. Many were intrigued to see bioluminescent organisms glow when agitated by ships passing through the water. "I watched for hours the astonishing bursts of greenish light which phosphorescent plankton flashed in the white of the bow wave," wrote Welker.[197] Henry Heyburn noted what he believed were "bright particles of phosphorous" that "leap and glisten in our wake at night. They are the only light then for we are in complete blackout."[198] "On quiet nights I love standing near the keel, tracing the wake," wrote Robert Peters, "its phosphorescence producing an acute sense of distance traveled."[199]

Some went to great lengths to describe the beauties of the ocean. Letters home sometimes seemed like exercises in creative writing. "I wondered," wrote James

---

[190] Mauldin, *Brass Ring*, p. 160.
[191] Obermayer, *Soldiering for Freedom*, p. 96.
[192] Sheridan, *They Never Had It So Good*, p. 42.
[193] Welker, *Different Drummer*, p. 131.
[194] Owens, *Blood on German Snow*, p. 38.
[195] Welker, *Different Drummer*, p. 131.
[196] Diary of William Perkins, 9 Nov 1944, Perkins Papers.
[197] Welker, *Different Drummer*, p. 131.
[198] Henry Heyburn to parents, 31 Oct 1944, Heyburn Papers.
[199] Peters, *For You, Lili Marlene*, p. 33.

May, "if I could ever describe how beautiful it is when a rainbow flashes through the wind-blown spray on the crest of a tall wave."[200] "The sky is a rich blue," wrote Eddie Sato, "with puffs of fleecy clouds drifting towards the horizon."[201] Marshall Hardy wrote that he "never tired of the changing beauty of the sea. The vast variety of colors of sunrise and sunset in an atmosphere free from dust, the flawless blue of the sky and the fathomless green of the sea, the snowy white of the wave caps at mid day and the mystery of the sub-arctic twilight were fascinating."[202] The majesty and sheer power of the ocean overwhelmed some. "The seas were mammoth," wrote Tracy Sugarman, which made him "quite aware of the very Lilliputian qualities of man and man-made things."[203] Alan Cope was mesmerized by the stormy North Atlantic. "We weren't allowed to go outside" during storms, he recalled, but on one occasion he and a friend "found an unlocked door that opened onto a small observation post" where they could sit and watch the storm's fury. "In the morning the waves were huge," he remembered. "When the ship was at the base of a wave, you could see the sunrise through the water."[204]

For some, ocean travel inspired reflection. "To stir memory I recommend a Spartan ocean voyage," wrote Brendan Phibbs. "There's something about the isolation, the indifference of the watery masses ... that quiets triviality."[205] Many GIs thought about their families. "I found myself thinking a great deal about my grandparents," recalled Daniel Inouye, and "what an irrevocable passage their voyage from Japan must have been."[206] Other loved ones came to mind. "Somehow [on deck] with everything so quiet and the sky full of bright stars you seem close to me," Milton Glatterer wrote his wife. "Possibly you were looking at them at the same time."[207] "I ache for home," wrote Wisconsin farm boy Robert Peters, "kitchen odors, resinous pine blazing in the living room heater, fresh milk striking a pail, even the rancid smells of the hen house."[208] En route to war, they also thought about death. "Every inch of the teak rail that ran entirely around the ship had initials carved into it by the thousands of military men who had preceded

---

[200] James W. May to Mrs. James W. May, 2 Dec 1944, May Papers.
[201] Eddie Sato to Rose Niguma, 8 May 1944, Rose Niguma Papers, Washington State Historical Society, Tacoma, Washington.
[202] Marshall B. Hardy to Sis, 27 June 1942, Hardy Papers.
[203] Sugarman, *My War*, p. 22-23.
[204] Guibert, *Alan's War*, p. 87.
[205] Phibbs, *Other Side of Time*, p. 52.
[206] Inouye, *Journey to Washington*, p. 102.
[207] Milton Glatterer to Mrs. Milton Glatterer, 14 Nov 1944, Milton Glatterer Papers, EUA.
[208] Peters, *For You, Lili Marlene*, p. 33;

me," wrote A. E. Hotchner of his voyage on the *Queen Elizabeth* in 1945. "As I walked down the deck, running my hand across the endlessly passing initials, I thought about how so many of those soldier-passengers who had carved those initials ... would never go back home, their initials on that teak railing their tombstones."[209]

Separated from home and heading off to an uncertain future, many yearned for spiritual sustenance. "Religious services ... are held every day in almost continuous performance," Leo Bogart reported.[210] Army chaplain James May was inspired by the enthusiasm for religion on his ship. "The place was jammed," he wrote of one Protestant service. May found the moment when the congregants belted out the lyrics "Jesus, Savior Pilot Me, over life's tempestuous sea" from one hymn to be "the most powerful part" of the service. "It was so right good watching all those men standing there on the rocking deck," he wrote, "singing it like they had known it all their lives." He also noted that even before they could finish their last hymn, the ship's public address system announced the beginning of Jewish services and "the Jewish boys were coming down the steps before the benediction was finished."[211] Others perceived less interest in religion. "Only the barest handful of men came up on deck for church services," remembered Daniel Inouye, although as the ship drew nearer to the European battle zone he noticed that attendance increased. "They seemed to come blinking into the sunlight as though they had been all their lives below deck."[212]

Landing

After several days or weeks at sea, soldiers began to detect signs that they were approaching land. "On the twelfth day," Roscoe Blunt saw "an antiquated, World War I, canvas-covered, open-cockpit bi-plane emblazoned with the Royal Air Force (RAF) insignia circling protectively overhead."[213] Others noticed an increase in bird life. "Early dawn saw us greeted by gulls," wrote Eddie Sato, "and as the light of a new day lifted its hazy veil, a thin strip of land could be seen in the distance."[214] Like all transatlantic travelers, the soldier-passenger was glad to reach the other side of the ocean, but for the GIs who endured seasickness, U-

---

[209] Aaron E. Hotchner, *The Day I Fired Alan Ladd and Other World War II Adventures*, Columbia/MS 2003, p. 127-128.
[210] Bogart, How *I Earned the Ruptured Duck*, p. 43.
[211] James W. May to Mrs. James W. May, 4 Dec 1944, May Papers.
[212] Inouye, *Journey to Washington*, p. 102-103.
[213] Blunt, *Foot Soldier*, p. 8.
[214] Sato to Niguma, 8 May 1944, Niguma Papers.

boats, cramped quarters, and bad food, land was a particularly welcome sight. Sato claimed that he now understood "how the men of Christopher Columbus must have felt when they discovered America."[215] James Knox claimed that he "felt like Noah in the Ark."[216]

As the Old World grew larger on the horizon, so did the fascination with seeing it. "Men clung to every available spot on the decks and at the portholes to watch the land pass by," Jack Sheridan observed.[217] "We awoke to see a coastline," wrote Robert Kotlowitz. "Green hills, modest cliffs, white beaches came into view; an unexpected prospect. It was France, we were told." Kotlowitz had long wanted to see France, and he would never forget the moment. "It was a first taste of Europe, never to be repeated, and I found it strangely moving."[218] Some felt a personal connection to the Old World. "I dashed out to the bow and struggled through the growing crowd at the rail," James Knox remembered, "to gaze upon the land of my ancestors – Bonnie Scotland."[219] "The immensity of the Rock of Gibraltar was impressive," remembered Mel TenHaken of his entrance into the Mediterranean, "as we glided past it seemed close enough to touch."[220] But for others, the sight of the Old World provoked more ominous thoughts. "Passed through Gibraltar this morning," Robert Ellis wrote in his diary. "Beginning to realize this is no dry run."[221] Indeed, the sight of land often brought mixed feelings. Kotlowitz wrote that as his vessel sailed along the French coast "an electric hush fell over the ship."[222]

The GIs had reached terra firma again, but they arrived in lands which – unlike their own – had been wracked by years of savage conflict. Some could not believe they had landed in a war zone. As the *Queen Elizabeth* pulled into Gourock, Scotland, Bill Etheridge gazed out at "quaint little town, tinted in pastel shades of a gorgeous sunrise" and wondered: "How could a place appear so remote from the destruction of war and yet be so close?"[223] For others, the war was immediately evident. "The strange thing about our arrival in Liverpool was that there were no lights on in the city," remembered Emiel Owens as his ship pulled into port in the early morning hours. "It was completely dark. This was our first

---

215 Sato to Niguma, 8 May 1944, Niguma Papers.
216 Knox, "The Bluffers at Home and Abroad", p. 15.
217 Sheridan, *They Never Had It So Good*, p. 44.
218 Kotlowitz, *Before Their Time*, p. 56.
219 *Knox, "The Bluffers at Home and Abroad",* p. 15.
220 TenHaken, *Bail-Out!*, p. 23.
221 Ellis, *See Naples and Die*, p. 98.
222 Kotlowitz, *Before Their Time*, p. 56.
223 Etheridge, *ETO Diary*, p. 4.

introduction to wartime conditions."[224] Dean Joy landed at the battered port of Le Havre. "We crowded the rails," he wrote, "gaping at the destruction of war."[225] Sometimes their arrival was strangely similar to their departure. Ty Richardson remembered that as he walked down the gangplank in Liverpool, "American Red Cross workers greeted us with coffee and donuts."[226]

The transatlantic voyages of American GIs during the Second World War had many similarities to those of peacetime travelers, though with odd wartime twists. No two people experienced the crossing in quite the same way. Various factors – such as rank, gender, or the kind of ship that carried them – affected each soldier-passenger differently. Some boarded enthusiastically in search of adventure, while others were reluctant travelers. However, all of them encountered a world on the troopship in which peace and war seemed impossibly intertwined. The GIs struggled with seasickness, read guidebooks, enjoyed shows, played games, marveled at the beauty of the high seas, and sometimes even had sex – just like any peacetime vacationer. At the same time, they had also entered a war zone, where they pondered the gruesome work that lay ahead while lurking U-boats hunted them. Ordinary tourists travel for pleasure and expect to return home. The GI was a special kind of business traveler who understood that their journey could be a one-way trip.

The strange juxtaposition of sights, sounds, and smells that the war crossing engendered provoked in the GI a maelstrom of diverse emotions. Anger, fear, homesickness, and resentment mingled incongruously with curiosity, exhilaration, and even pleasure. The crossing also left many soldiers feeling disconnected from the land and people they were traveling to defend. Although they had already been pulled out of civilian society and inducted into the military, the GI serving stateside still felt close to home. Family and friends were just a phone call away, or could be visited while on furlough. The troopship severed those links. As the GIs sailed eastward, they could feel their connections to home stretched more thinly than ever before. Enlisted personnel in particular, subjected to demeaning second-class status, often felt light years away from America's democratic culture. The GI's first war experiences in the Atlantic combat zone, however mild, also separated them from the folks back home. After arriving at their destinations, the GI encountered a world of warfare that was vastly more bizarre than life on a troopship. Bearing witness to civilized nations savagely destroying each other, and being active participants in that madness, alienated the

---

[224] Owens, *Blood on German Snow*, p. 40.
[225] Joy, *Sixty Days in Combat*, p. 54.
[226] Richardson and Yeatts, *Stars Without Garters!*, p. 85.

GI from home even more. In some small way, the troopship prepared American troops for life in a war zone.

"Few wartime experiences," concluded Frederick Olson, "putting aside combat itself – were as unsettling as life on a troopship."[227] Even seasoned travelers sensed that the wartime crossing was somehow different. Henry Heyburn was the son of a prominent Kentucky attorney and had traveled to Europe with his family several times before the war. In 1944 he went over again, this time as an artillery officer. "This trip is not exactly like the other trips we have taken together," he confessed to his parents. "For some reason it is for me utterly divorced from these and I don't know when I have felt so far away from everything I know and hold dear."[228] The peculiar nature of the Atlantic war crossing left the GI confused and grappling to make sense of it all. Bound for the battlefields of the Second World War, the American GI was suspended between two worlds – no longer at peace, but not yet quite at war.

---

[227] Olson, *Dear Jane*, p. 47.
[228] Henry Heyburn to parents, 31 Oct 1944, Heyburn Papers.

7. The Experience of a Lifetime: Lydia DeGuio's Journey across the North Atlantic

Birgit Braasch

Introduction

In 2001 Lydia DeGuio decided to donate the memorabilia of her 1953 trip on the *SS United States* from the United States to France to the Independence Seaport Museum in Philadelphia. She included photographs she had of the trip as well as her narrative, which she had written down after the trip. Her donation of the papers indicates the importance she placed on her travels across the North Atlantic and suggests that she deemed her memories relevant for other people. Indeed, the materials Lydia DeGuio gave to the museum are valuable historical sources that inform us about her experiences while crossing the North Atlantic within the context of that time.

In my analysis I focus on Lydia DeGuio's 1953 journey across the North Atlantic and compare and contrast her experiences with the experiences made by other people who crossed the North Atlantic Ocean on an ocean liner during the same period. My analysis is led by the following questions: 1. How did Lydia DeGuio experience her North-Atlantic crossing? 2. How does her experience relate to other experiences? 3. How do Lydia DeGuios's experiences relate back to life on shore?

In order to explore these tourist experiences, I follow conceptualizations that consider the experience of the individual as one aspect in the construction process of different spaces. By focusing on the experiences of crossing the North Atlantic I ask specifically how the space of the North Atlantic was constructed. With this framework I follow Jason Throop who expands on Dilthey and Turner and emphasizes that the experience of an event is also closely connected to the experience that preceded this particular experience and influences the experiences that happen after this particular experience. Specifically, the meaning that is given to and articulated with regard to living through an event turns it into experience.[1] Such an emphasis on experience, as meaningful lived experience, can be linked back to the material, social and cultural constructions of Atlantic

---

[1] Jason C. Throop, "Articulating Experience", in: *Anthropological Theory* (2003), p. 219-243: 223; Victor Turner, *From Ritual to Theatre: The Human Seriousness of Play*, New York 1982, p. 14.

spaces in that those are one means through which tourists' experiences become meaningful.

While the construction of the space of the North Atlantic Ocean can be theorized in a similar way as other tourism spaces, the sea and ships are, at the same time, considered as specific spaces that are also represented in specific ways since permanent markers do not exist in the water. For example, the construction of oceanic spaces has been analyzed by geographer Philip Steinberg who focuses on representations of the ocean and relates these images back to changing capitalistic needs, although he emphasizes that the images are socially constructed and that the sea's materiality is always important.[2] Regarding the Atlantic Ocean, William Boelhower uses linguistic theory in order to analyze how ships and maps created Atlantic space and how they can, in turn, be used to read this space. He sees the ships as semiotic operators that are vital in defining Atlantic space by drawing connections across it.[3] In a different vein, Claudia Schnurmann shows the importance of the relation between technologies, such as ships, and the image of the ocean by following the change of oceanic images from the Middle Ages to the establishment of European colonies in the Americas.[4]

The analysis of ship spaces in conjunction with the people on board adds the dimension of experience of the specific historical spaces. The constructions of the spaces are specific and depend on the means of transportation and the people on board. For example, a canoe in Polynesia affords different constructions than a sailing ship, which is similarly built for the Pacific.[5] The means of transportation contribute to different experiences of the ocean while moving across the water. For example, geographer James R. Ryan analyses how Lady Brassey's view of the *Sunbeam* between 1874 and 1887 as well as her relation

---

[2] Philip E. Steinberg, *The Social Construction of the Ocean*, Cambridge 2001, p. 209.

[3] William Boelhower, "'I'll Teach You How to Flow': On Figuring Out Atlantic Studies", in: *Atlantic Studies* 1 (2004), p.28-48: 46.

[4] Claudia Schnurmann, "Frühneuzeitliche Formen Maritimer Vereinnahmung: Die Europäische Inbesitznahme des Atlantiks," in: Bernhard Klein and Gesa Mackenthun (Eds.), *Das Meer als Kulturelle Kontaktzone: Räume, Reisende, Repräsentationen*, Konstanz 2003, p. 49-72: 49ff.

[5] For two different constructions of the Pacific in relation to reconstructions of a canoe in Hawai'i and of Captain Cook's *Endeavour* see Bernhard Klein and Gesa Mackenthun (Eds.), *Das Meer Als Kulturelle Kontaktzone: Räume, Reisende, Repräsentationen*, Konstanz 2003, p. 17-47.

to the ocean was influenced by the social and political order in Britain, the ship's point of departure.⁶

His analysis of the ship as a "private and movable place" can be linked to Foucault's characterization of ships. Foucault famously states, "the boat is a floating piece of space, a place without a place, that exists by itself, that is closed in on itself and at the same time is given over to the infinity of the sea".⁷ In this characterization he shows the mutual construction of ship and ocean through the juxtaposition of open space and closed place.

Whereas social and political aspects and different space images influence the tourists' experiences of the spaces, theorists concerned with the experience of spaces have emphasized people's agency in relation to the control of landscapes. Michel de Certeau describes this agency in relation to walking in the city.⁸ In a similar vein, Tim Edensor explains the interconnectedness of representations and experience in the construction of landscapes. While he maintains that representations are relevant for landscapes, a consideration of peoples' experiences allows for the inclusion of their individual contribution to the construction of spaces and places.⁹

As one kind of representation of ship and ocean space, images play an important role. Historian Cord Pagenstecher states that suggestions of experiences in advertisements are mostly conveyed in a visual format.¹⁰ By adding that tourists also produce their own visual culture, Crouch and Lübbren point to the important aspect of individuality regarding experience and space construction.¹¹ Orvar Löfgren adds that the visual remains important for the narration of tourists' experiences. In contrast to experiencing with other senses, visual impressions

---

6   James R. Ryan, "'Our Home on the Ocean': Lady Brassey and the Voyages of the Sunbeam, 1874-1887", in: *Journal of Historical Geography* 32 (2006), p. 579-604· 583.
7   Michel Foucault, "Of Other Spaces", in: *Diacritics* 16 (1986), p. 22-27: 27.
8   Michel de Certeau, *The Practice of Everyday Life*, Steven Rendall trans. Berkeley, Los Angeles, London 1988, p. 98.
9   Tim Edensor, "Sensing Tourist Spaces", in: Claudio Minca and Tim Oakes (Eds.), *Travels in Paradox: Remapping Tourism*, Lanham et al 2006, p.23-45: 29.
10 Cord Pagenstecher, *Der Bundesdeutsche Tourismus: Ansätze zu einer Visual History: Urlaubsprospekte, Reiseführer, Fotoalben 1950-1990*, Hamburg 2003, p. 29.
11 David Crouch and Nina Lübbren, "Introduction", in: David Crouch and Nina Lübbren (Eds.), *Visual Culture and Tourism*, Oxford, New York 2003, p.1-20: 11.

become manifest in images, such as photographs from the holiday, and the language for describing these images is well developed.

These images are a means through which the experience of a sight is framed for future viewers.[12] As Julia Harrison points out, these framings are selective. She cites an example of selective memory by mentioning tourists who were sick on their journeys but gave much more room to the positive experiences that were connected to their travels in their narratives.[13] Harrison's observations can be linked to anthropologist Jason Throop's discussion of experience. This connection means that the selective framing of images of a journey contributes to creating meaningful experiences. However, because of the process of selection the experience of a place also changes over time.

The sources that Lydia DeGuio left, provide information about different aspects of her Atlantic crossing. The pictures she took show us the materiality of the ocean liners. Furthermore, the situations in which she took the photographs indicate what she deemed important about her journey across the North Atlantic. These photographs together with her narrative indicate which of the events she lived through actually became experience because they were meaningful for Lydia DeGuio. Since her narrative seems to have been written quite a while after the trip, the aspects she names condense and frame the events that are still meaningful after such a long period of time.[14]

One indication of how certain events became meaningful for her can be found in the wording of her travel narrative, which seems to be heavily influenced by advertisements to travel with the *United States* across the North Atlantic.[15] Some descriptions are very close to the ones in a brochure that is also part of the donation to the archives. The publications can be considered a representation of Atlantic space that influenced the experience of it.

---

[12] Mike Crang, "Picturing Practices: Research through the Tourist Gaze", in: *Progress in Human Geography* 21 (1997), p. 359-373: 365.

[13] Julia Harrison, *Being a Tourist: Finding Meaning in Pleasure Travel*, Vancouver, Toronto 2003, p. 93.

[14] Aleida Assmann, "Wie wahr sind unsere Erinnerungen?", in: Harald Welzer and Hans J. Markowitsch (Eds.), *Warum Menschen sich erinnern können Fortschritte in der interdisziplinären Gedächtnisforschung*, Stuttgart 2006, p. 95-110: 102; Astrid Erll, "Kollektives Gedächtnis und Erinnerungskulturen", in: Ansgar Nünning and Vera Nünning (Eds.), *Einführung in die Kulturwissenschaften: Theoretische Grundlagen - Ansätze - Perspektiven*, Stuttgart, Weimar 2008, p. 156-185: 157; Harald Welzer, *Das Kommunikative Gedächtnis: Eine Theorie der Erinnerung*, München 2005, p. 43.

[15] Brochure: United States Lines, "*S.S. United States, S.S. America*", n.d. Independence Seaport Museum (ISM), Lydia DeGuio Papers.

My focus lies on the materials that Lydia DeGuio has left. In addition, I conducted oral-history interviews with former passengers. I further based my research on publications by shipping companies and airlines, mainly advertisements and press releases. In addition to company publications, newspaper articles contributed to constructing an image of travel across the North Atlantic.[16] I concentrate on Cunard as the main English shipping company and the United States Lines as its US counterpart. These companies were also market leaders. This is the period in which the ocean liners were used again for pleasure travels after the Second World War and then were overtaken by airplanes as the main means of transportation for crossing the North Atlantic.

In 1947 the Cunard Steam Ship Company (hereafter Cunard) was the first shipping company to offer a regular passenger service across the North Atlantic between Britain and the United States, after its biggest ocean liners, the *Queen Mary* and *Queen Elizabeth*, had served as troop ships during the war.[17] Other companies followed suit, either with newly built or with refitted ships. One of the newly built ocean liners was the *United States*, which made her maiden voyage in 1952 and immediately earned the Blue Riband for the fastest North-Atlantic crossing.[18] However, by the mid 1950s the speed of ocean liners could not compete with the airlines anymore, which had reduced these crossings to a few hours and by 1958 carried the majority of passengers across the ocean.[19]

---

[16] For the role of advertisements in forming images of different spaces of travel see: Cara Aitchison, Nicola E. MacLeod and Stephen J. Shaw, *Leisure and Tourism Landscapes: Social and Cultural Geographies*, London, New York 2000, p. 17f; John Frow, "Tourism and the Semiotics of Nostalgia," *October* 57 (1991), p. 133; Jürgen Hasse, "'Nordseeküste' - Die touristische Konstruktion besserer Welten: Zur Codierung einer Landschaft", in: Norbert Fischer, Susan Müller-Wusterwitz and Brigitta Schmidt-Lauber (Eds.), *Inszenierungen der Küste*, Berlin 2007, p. 239-258: 243; George Hughes, "Tourism and the Semiological Realization of Space", in: Greg Ringer (Ed.), *Destinations: Cultural Landscapes of Tourism*, London, New York 1998, p. 17-32: 19; Pagenstecher, Bundesdeutscher Tourismus, p. 64ff.

[17] Russell Galbraith, *Destiny's Daughter: The Tragedy of RMS Queen Elizabeth*, Edinburgh 1988, p. 101ff.

[18] Arnold Kludas and Karl-Theo Beer, *Die glanzvolle Ära der Luxusschiffe: Eine illustrierte Kulturgeschichte im Spiegel zeitgenössischer Quellen*, Hamburg 2005, p. 194; William H. Miller, *Crossing the Atlantic*, Portland 2007, p. 21.

[19] Terry Coleman, *The Liners: A History of the North Atlantic Crossing*, London 1976, p. 183.; R.E.G. Davies, *History of the World's Airlines*, London 1964, p. 470; Francis E. Hyde, *Cunard and the North Atlantic 1840-1973: A History of*

On the *S.S. United States*

In her travel narrative Lydia DeGuio establishes as the background to her journey across the Atlantic that her mother had died early in 1953 and that she was left at home with her father, three brothers and her uncle, and with many of the household chores. After two of her brothers had left home, her uncle decided to travel to France with her to see their relatives there in the summer of 1953. For their trip they decided on the *S.S. United States*. The choice of this liner was one important aspect of Lydia DeGuio's experience of her North-Atlantic crossing since it was included in the travel narrative. In the narrative, Lydia DeGuio mentions the speed of the liner in comparison with the British liners *Queen Mary* and *Queen Elizabeth* of Cunard and emphasizes that the ship was "America's luxury liner".[20] By mentioning that the *United States* was faster than the *Queen Mary* and *Queen Elizabeth*, DeGuio also points to the competition for the fastest crossing between the ocean liners. This competition was not only a competition between shipping companies but also between nations and was carried out as the "Blue Riband". The Blue Riband was the reward for the fastest average speed, and from 1935 on the shipping company that owned the fastest liner was awarded a trophy.[21] The *Daily Mail* wrote about the different nations that ran ocean liners across the ocean, and mentioned that the *United States* was the first large North American one.[22] In the case of the *United States*, the name of the ship already establishes the importance of the ship's nationality. The liner's sparse décor reflected its dual use as troop transport and ocean liner, both defender and envoy of the nation.[23] John G. Bunker claims that passengers sang the national anthem when the *United States* arrived back in New York from her record-breaking maiden voyage on Independence Day.[24]

The connection between the purpose of a ship as a troop ship and an ocean liner also becomes clear in Lydia DeGuio's travel narrative. The narrative of her trip

---

Shipping and Financial Management, London, Basingstoke 1975, p. 296; Kurt Ulrich, Monarchs of the Sea: *The Great Ocean Liners*, London 1998, p. 133.

[20] Lydia DeGuio, "Narrative of the Trip", 2001, ISM, Lydia DeGuio Papers.

[21] Newspaper Article: C.H. Milsom, "Tremendous Achievement by the Queen Mary", in: *Journal of Commerce*, 3.9.1966, UoLSC&A, PR3/21/2.

[22] Newspaper Article: The Daily Mail, "The Ocean Challenge", 14. June 1952, UoLSC&A, D42/PR3/24/42.

[23] William H. Miller, *The Last Atlantic Liners*, London 1985, p. 54.

[24] John G. Bunker, *Harbor & Haven: An Illustrated History of the Port of New York*, Woodland Hills 1979, p. 138.

uses the language of an advertisement brochure for the *United States*.²⁵ Lydia DeGuio writes:

> "I was a very excited young lady. My goodness, to go on a trip to Europe on a great new liner which everyone was talking about – faster than the *Queen Mary* or *Queen Elizabeth* ships and America's luxury liner, although I was told it was a steel streamlined ship made for easy conversion into a troop ship."²⁶

In her narrative, DeGuio does not simply reproduce the images that were used of the *United States* in advertisement brochures, but her memories speak of an experience of national superiority that related to the ocean liner as well as to a superiority of the United States over Europe. Near the end of her travel narrative both aspects appear. She writes, "[i]t was a great education, and I certainly appreciated my country America for how far advanced it was and much better off we all were".²⁷ DeGuio's experience of being on the *United States* seems to have been similar to what Tim Edensor describes, in that moving through the national landscape forms a connection to one's nation.²⁸ In Lydia DeGuio's case the technology and luxury of the *United States* as an American liner stood in contrast to her experiences in Europe and increased her appreciation of America; it also conformed to the national imagery of the shipping company.²⁹ Therefore, one aspect that made travel on the ocean liner meaningful for Lydia DeGuio appears to have been her experience of progress and the superiority of US technology.

Lydia DeGuio's anticipation of the journey that she also mentions in the abstract features in other memories of North-Atlantic crossings, too. For example, Richard Faber speaks of his first crossing on the *France* in 1967 in similar terms. He emphasizes the importance of the farewells at the ship, and he describes the anticipation he felt as a passenger:

> "Months and months before this was a fantasy. I had the ticket in my bedroom and I was looking at it. [...] it was just something I just couldn't wait for the day, and in those days you dressed just to go to

---

25	Brochure: "United States Lines: *S.S. United States, S.S. America*", ISM, Lydia DeGuio Papers.
26	DeGuio, "Narrative of the Trip".
27	Ibid.
28	Tim Edensor, *National Identity, Popular Culture and Everyday Life*, Oxford, New York 2002, p. 40.
29	Christopher Endy, *Cold War Holidays: American Tourism in France*, Chapel Hill, London 2004, p. 37f.

a bon-voyage party, so [...] I had to get a new suit just for the bon-voyage. I had a lot of people from my office down to see me off."[30]

For Richard Faber, dressing up on the day of departure was something special that was not a part of his everyday life. This practice of dressing up and having farewell parties also indicates that such a trip across the North Atlantic was a very special occasion for both the tourists and those who had to stay at home.

Passengers who had left the shore started to find their place on the ocean liner. Finding one's place literally meant to find the way around the ocean liner and also to socially establish oneself among the passengers. Both aspects were closely related to the class passengers were traveling in. One publication that made these social aspects manifest were the passenger lists. The shipping companies gave out passenger lists that were divided according to the class people were traveling in. Lydia DeGuio traveled in tourist class, on most liners the third and lowest class.[31] Being on the list meant being distinguished from those who could only come to the harbor to say goodbye but could not travel, which could be affirmed by markings on the list. At the same time the practice of consulting the passenger list, which Vincent Lowe names as a typical aspect of embarkation, established oneself as part of the community of passengers.[32] To further record a connection with other passengers on the list, additional information such as the city of residence was added by the passengers themselves.[33]

In order to assist passengers with their orientation on the ocean liners, shipping companies provided deck plans. On some deck plans, the class and cabin style was marked by a certain color. This coloring draws attention to the social distinction that existed between the passengers according to the class they were travelling in. At the same time, being on the same ship connected the passengers. Since they were traveling in different classes, their cabins were very different. While a first-class suite had more than one room, so that guests could be welcomed like in a home, passengers like Lydia DeGuio in tourist class needed to share their cabin with other people. Lydia DeGuio traveled with a "room-mate" who also was not accompanied by a husband or parent in a cabin with a bunk bed.[34]

---

[30] Richard Faber, interview with author, 13 October 2008, min. 10.
[31] Booklet: United States Lines "Lists of Tourist Class Passengers SS United States", 7.8.1953, 23./24.10. 1953, ISM, Lydia DeGuio Papers.
[32] Vincent Lowe, interview with author, 8 October 2008, min. 52ff.
[33] The list was donated by Pamela Cohen and probably used by a relative of hers, since the name „Mrs. Tilly Cohen" appears in the list. Booklet: United States Lines, "List of First Class Passengers SS United States", ISM, Ephemera Collection United States Lines Material.
[34] DeGuio, "Narrative of the Trip".

The class passengers were traveling in not only influenced the design of the cabin but also determined the location of the cabin on the ship, which in turn influenced how passengers could experience the ocean since the amount and kind of movement as well as the view of and proximity to the water differed. While first class was mostly situated on the upper decks, cabin class was literally "in between" the two other classes, and tourist class was either forward or aft and mostly on the lower decks.[35] This removed position of tourist-class cabins was one of their defining features. Apart from the heat in her cabin, this remote position of the cabin on the lower decks has a prominent place in Martha Martin's memory of her 1955 journey on the *Neptunia*. She emphasizes the long time needed to reach her cabin.[36]

Despite the location of their cabins down below, which were surrounded by the space assigned to each class, tourist-class passengers had access to a part of the deck and could go outside.[37] However, the view of the ocean from the interior of the ship was mainly reserved for first-class passengers. The deck plan of the *Queen Elizabeth* shows that the cabins of the first class in particular came with a view of the ocean.[38] Also, the public rooms, such as the first class observation lounge or the Verandah Grill, had windows offering passengers a panorama of the ocean while dining, whereas the tourist restaurant was confined to the interior of the ship.[39] A view of the ocean was considered a privilege, which was mainly reserved for first-class passengers.

On the ocean liners the spaces for each class were strictly separated from each other by barriers, not allowing passengers from the lower classes to move up while enabling passengers from the upper classes to move down. These divisions

---

[35] See e.g. Booklet: Cunard Line, "Queen Elizabeth Plan of First Class Accomodation", NMM. E/Cunard; Booklet: Cunard Line, "Queen Elizabeth: Plan of Cabin Class Accomodations", NMM. E/Cunard; Booklet. Cunard Line "Queen Elizabeth: Plan of Tourist Class Accomodations", NMM. E/Cunard.

[36] Martha Martin, interview with author, 29 September 2008, min. 6.

[37] See e.g. Booklet: Cunard, "Queen Elizabeth: Plan of Tourist Class Accomodations", n.d. NMM, E/Cunard ; Photograph: Cunard "Queen Mary Tourist Sport Deck", UoLSC&A. D42/PR2/1/97/G28; Booklet: United States Lines, "Miniature Deck Plan *S.S. United States*", n.d. ISM, Lydia DeGuio Papers.

[38] Booklet: Cunard, "Queen Elizabeth Plan of First Class Accomodation", NMM, E/Cunard.

[39] Photograph: Cunard, "Queen Mary First Class Observation Lounge", UoLSC&A. D662/2/7; Booklet: Cunard, "Queen Mary: Plan of First Class Accomodation", NMM. E/Cunard; Cunard, *"Queen Elizabeth Plan of Tourist Class Accomodations"*; United States Lines, *"SS US, Deck Plan"*.

were the manifestations in the construction of controlled ship space. Vincent Lowe explains that the barriers which separated the classes were open when the ships were in harbor and the visitors were on board, but once the ships started to move away, these barriers were closed for the duration of the journey.[40] Referring to the *United States,* he explains that the ship had crash gates that looked like barriers to the passengers as divisions between the classes.[41] My interviewees emphasize that these divisions were not meant for everyone to stay in the class they were traveling in; they unanimously indicated that movement from top to bottom was possible. Therefore, the main reason for these barriers seems to have been to ensure that upper-class passengers could stay amongst themselves. The importance ascribed to keeping the classes apart becomes clear through a report by Captain Nicholas from the *Queen Mary* from 1956. He reported,

> "On the outward passage it was reported to me the following morning, that Mr. Randolph Churchill and Sir Phillip Dunne entertained two Tourist Class Female Passengers in the Verandah Grill. As no complaints were received from any First Class Passengers, this incident was accepted with tactful discretion."[42]

This report indicates that the shipping companies tried to ensure that no passenger from the lower classes moved up, in case first-class passengers felt disturbed by tourist-class passengers who entered their spaces. This example shows how well surveillance worked on the ocean liners. The staff of the Verandah Grill knew the limited number of first-class passengers who usually used the restaurant and probably spotted these two women. Similarly, the stewards in first class were reported by my interviewees to have been very good at detecting who was not supposed to be there.[43]

While most accounts of the time indicate that the class system on the ships was taken for granted, complaints by passengers show that they did not agree with all aspects of the division of spaces. These complaints could be related to the prevalent idea of a classless society in the United States and the growing confidence of tourists.[44] For example, a few years later Captain Nicholas also had to deal with complaints by passengers on the *Queen Elizabeth* about the use of

---

[40] Vincent Lowe, min. 39.
[41] Ibid. min. 40.
[42] Letter: R.J.N. Nicholas, Voyage Report Tourist Passengers in First Class, 13.8.1956, UoLSC&A, D 371/2/2.
[43] Ted Scull, interview with author, 20 October 2008, min. 11; Bill Miller, interview with author, 22 October 2008, min. 45; Vincent Lowe, min. 39.
[44] Barbara Ehrenreich, *Fear of Falling: The Inner Life of the Middle Class*, New York 1989, p. 17ff.

the first-class swimming pool by tourist passengers, which was only allowed at certain hours, and about the lack of a bar for tourist passengers.[45] These complaints suggest that about ten years after Lydia DeGuio traveled across the North Atlantic just being able to cross the ocean on an Atlantic liner in tourist class was not something to be proud of in itself, but passengers were self-confident enough to request all the amenities and luxury associated with transatlantic travel. Accordingly, better facilities were available for tourist-class passengers on the newer ships.[46]

Overall, traveling on the ocean liners seems to have involved a social demarcation of people with a lower social standing than the passengers had and a movement towards people of a higher social standing. For people in tourist class, the demarcation took place within the practices of departure at the harbor, as I show above. The other classes of travel literally had another class below them because of the spatial divisions of the liners. Even for people in first class, the possibility to meet people of a higher social standing played an important role, and the possibility to meet celebrities on board was a central aspect in the constructions of ocean-liner travel and today's nostalgia for this way of crossing the North Atlantic. Passengers who traveled in first class had to be affluent in order to travel on the ocean liners. Nonetheless, travel in first class allowed them to socialize with people whom they would not meet anywhere else, so that a first-class ticket for a North Atlantic crossing allowed them access to an elite meeting place, which they may not have been able to access otherwise.

Julia Harrison writes about middle-class tourists that one aspect that made travel meaningful for them was an encounter with celebrities. She describes one woman who had "sneak[ed] up" from second class to first class to dance there. On the dance floor she met and talked to the Duke and Duchess of Windsor.[47] Vincent Lowe tells a similar story of meeting the Windsors, and he describes a feeling of personal elevation in connection with that encounter.[48] Similarly, in his newspaper diary George Eglin describes a sense of awe concerning the amount of money that other people were able to spend on the daily bets on the ship's position. Nonetheless, he was able to share the spaces on the ships and to

---

45 Letter: R.J.N. Nicholas, Voyage Report: Tourist Letter of Complaint, 2.10.1962. UoLSC&A. D371/2/2; Letter: R.J.N. Nicholas, *QE Reply to Letter to Staff Captain Nicholas about Swimming Pool*, 22.4.1963. UoLSC&A. D371/2/2.
46 Newspaper Article: "First Ivernia: Modest Standard of 50 Years Ago", in: The Scotsman, 17.6.1955. UoLSC&A, PR3/20/4f.
47 Harrison, *Being a Tourist,* p. 68.
48 Vincent Lowe, min. 44.

participate in other activities with them.[49] Such meetings allow people "to step, if only temporarily, out of the class milieu in which they live".[50] Although the classes on the liners were divided, the class divisions of the liners 'only' depended on the amount of money passengers could pay for a ticket and not on other defining aspects of class. The first-class passengers received a privileged position on board in comparison to the lower classes on the liners, and within their class they met other passengers of a higher social standing whom they may not have come into contact with at home.

This social elevation also appeared in advertisements of the shipping companies. Traveling on the ocean liners was marketed according to the model described by anthropologist Alma Gottlieb as "Queen (King) for a Day".[51] Although there were significant differences between the different classes, the pictures of first-class travel were often used in advertisements and therefore specifically informed the image of traveling on a ship across the North Atlantic. This emphasis on the first class was mirrored by newspaper articles about ocean liners.[52]

In all the classes of travel there were stewardesses and stewards who cleaned cabins and waiters who took care of passengers during the meals. Ted Scull characterizes the relationship between passengers and crew as being one of master and servant, a characterization that can also be found in the rule book for Cunard crew.[53] While for most passengers these arrangements meant that they were treated as a higher social class than they would usually be, the language for advertising travel in first class on Cunard ships was positively aristocratic. *The Rising Tide* booklet states of the first meeting of the stewards in first class,

---

[49] Newspaper Article: George Eglin, "Atlantic Diary", in: Liverpool Echo and Evening Express, 18.11.1959, UoLSC&A, PR 3/20/17.

[50] Harrison, *Being a Tourist*, p. 68.

[51] Alma Gottlieb, "Americans' Vacations," Annals of Tourism Research 9 (1982), p.165-187: 165.

[52] See e.g. Newspaper Article: Gavin Lyall, "New Battle of the Atlantic", in: *The Observer*, 21.7.1965. UoLSC&A, PR3/21/17; Newspaper Article: Willy Müller, „Rendez-vous mit einer Queen", in: *Letzeburger Journal*, 4.3.1960, UoLSC&A, D42/PR4/27; Eglin, "Atlantic Diary"; Newspaper Supplement: The TIMES Supplement, "The Cunard Steam-Ship Company", 12.7.1965. UoLSC&A. PR 3/21/19.

[53] Book: Cunard Steam Ship Company Ltd., "Regulations to be Observed in the Company's Service" April 1950. NMM, 347.792 Cunard, p. 31,71.

"[f]rom this moment on, the passengers whom each individual steward or stewardess is looking after, becomes his or her lady or gentleman".[54]
For Lydia DeGuio's experience of crossing the North Atlantic on the *United States* this aspect of social elevation also seems to have been important. In her travel narrative she speaks of all the "pampering" on board. Furthermore, she relates her journey to the recent death of her mother and the resulting situation at home. Through this relation she creates a contrast between the good service on board and her responsibilities at home. She further assesses her social situation positively by adding a comparison to the situation in Europe, which she encountered during her travels. She writes about the crossing back to the United States: "The other passengers and I compared our adventures and experiences while enjoying the splendour of a beautiful cruise on the Atlantic. [...]"[55] Therefore, the exchange with passengers who were as privileged as she was as well as her nationality both added to her experience of social elevation.

Spending Time

Although in 1953 traveling across the North Atlantic on an ocean liner was still the most common way of crossing the ocean and the ocean liners therefore served as means of transportation, Lydia DeGuio calls her crossing a "cruise" in her travel narrative, which suggests that she remembers the time on the ocean liner as a leisure time and being on the ship pleasurable for its own sake rather than only to reach a destination for getting somewhere. The photographs that Lydia DeGuio had taken of herself indicate that she considered the ocean liner a holiday destination not only in retrospect but also while she was traveling since her poses are those typically associated with holidays, e.g. at the beach. One photograph shows Lydia DeGuio with a magazine and notebook on a deck chair on the sundeck of the *United States*. Around her are other passengers who are sleeping or enjoying the sun.

---

[54] Advertisement Booklet: Cunard Steam Ship Company Ltd., "The Rising Tide", 1965, UoLSC&A, PR 3/22/28.
[55] DeGuio, "Narrative of the Trip".

Figure 22: Lydia on the sundeck of the SS *US*.

Lydia DeGuio poses for the camera in summer clothing, wearing sunglasses and a smile on her face. The descriptions in her travel narrative suggest that the possibility to relax during her Atlantic crossing made this crossing memorable in contrast to the work she had to do at home. At the same time the depiction of Atlantic crossings by advertisements and other passengers suggest a similar interpretation of the journey. They indicate that the images of Atlantic crossings as holidays were widely spread and indeed became one of the most frequently used topics in the years following Lydia DeGuio's journey on the *United States*.[56]

---

[56] See e.g. Advertisement Booklet: Cunard Steam Ship Company Ltd, "Travel in its

In comparison to long oceanic voyages, on which passengers and crew alike had a lot of time available that they needed to fill, North-Atlantic crossings were short. However, since these crossings still took between four and six days in the time between 1947 and the 1960s, there were days at sea that passengers filled with various activities. As Dagmar Bellmann shows in her contribution, various shipboard activities had been well established by the 1950s, but it was only in the late 1950s that the construction of ocean spaces as tourism spaces moved into the foreground. Terry Coleman maintains that the ocean liners, which used to compete for the prize of fastest crossing, offered "leisure, and, in first class, opulence".[57]

The relaxation and leisure activities offered on board the ocean liners were not only important for constructing the spaces of the ocean liners but they also represented the North Atlantic Ocean in a certain way. In advertisements the ocean was attributed qualities that are often closely connected to holiday destinations.[58] The ocean was depicted as always offering good weather and relaxation, and passengers who are shown on the North Atlantic seem to be in a good mood. In addition to depictions of happy-looking passengers on the ocean, Cunard, for example, advertised the sea's positive effects on the passengers' health. One advertisement emphasizes the "invigorating effect of the good sea air", which, together with the luxury of the ship, helps to "overcome even the most obstinate strains and stresses in a matter of hours".[59] This development towards a more touristic North Atlantic can be read in conjunction with the introduction of the airplane. Shipping companies depicted the fast airlines as stressful and countered the image of hectic life with advertisements that

---

Finest Sense", NMM. E/Cunard/Brochures 1; Advertisement Booklet: Cunard Steam Ship Company Ltd, "Atlantic Fairway", 1956-62. NMM. E/Cunard/Brochures.

57 Coleman, *Liners*, p. 187.
58 John K. Walton, "British Tourism Between Industrialization and Globalization", in: Hartmut Berghoff, Barbara Korte, Ralf Schneider and Christopher Harvie (Eds.), *The Making of Modern Tourism: The Cultural History of the British Experience, 1600-2000*, Basingstoke, 2002, p. 109-131: 117; Wright, Sue. "Sun, Sea, Sand and Self-Expression: Mass Tourism as an Individual Experience", in: Hartmut Berghoff, Barbara Korte, Ralf Schneider and Christopher Harvie (Eds.), *The Making of Modern Tourism: The Cultural History of the British Experience, 1600-2000*, Basingstoke, 2002, p. 181-202: 187; John Beckerson and John K. Walton, "Selling Air: Marketing the Intangible at British Resorts", in: John K. Walton, *Histories of Tourism: Representation, Identity and Conflict*, Clevedon, Buffalo, Toronto 2005, p. 55-68:55.
59 Cunard, "Travel in its Finest Sense".

emphasized the possibility for relaxation on board the ocean liners. Importantly, the North Atlantic Ocean became a key aspect of this relaxation and a part of a touristic space.[60]

Another aspect of the construction of the Atlantic as a touristic space consisted of the activities that were offered on board. Cunard emphasized the different possible ways of spending one's time on the ocean.[61] In the advertisements, the evening entertainment stood out, showing people in their formal clothing, which were also indicators of the class they were traveling in. The shipping lines made an effort to provide the appropriate settings for the evening entertainment. An advertisement of the United States Lines states "[i]n First Class, chances are when friends on the *United States* say "Meet you later," they'll designate the majestic Ballroom Lounge. For this is the main social room of the ship".[62] In the lounge, entertainment as well as dancing was provided. In *Gracious Living at its Best* the narrator advertises:

> "Aboard the *Queen Elizabeth* after dinner they, literally, roll back the carpet to uncover what the experts tell me is a superb dance-floor. The dance-band appears and the couples take the floor. It's all very jolly, whether you are one of those god-like creatures that skim across the floor with icy aplomb, or whether you perform an amiable jog-trot and think of the brandy you left on the table".[63]

While Lydia DeGuio kept the memorabilia of the trip and remembered it in a positive way as a possibility to relax in agreement with what the United States Lines and other shipping companies advertised, other passengers could not handle the journey across the North Atlantic in such a way. For example, Ron Dawson remembers his trip with the *Queen Elizabeth* in 1968 as being very boring. While he claims that he is glad that he took part in what is now a "bygone age", he really noticed the length of time that it took to cross the ocean. Whereas his teenage daughter found things to do, so that he "lost" her every day, Ron and his wife were bored, because playing table tennis was the only activity that suited them, and this did not provide enough entertainment for them.[64] Martha Martin crossed the North Atlantic in different ships between 1955 and 1958. From the

---

[60] Ibid.
[61] See e.g. Advertisement booklet: Cunard Steam Ship Company Ltd., "Gracious Living at Its Best", UoLSC&A. D42/PR3/19/57.
[62] Advertisement booklet: United States Lines, "New *S.S. United States*", probably 1952, Mystic Seaport Museum, Manuscripts Collection, G. W. Blunt White Library, Coll. 283, Box 14/3.
[63] Cunard, "Gracious Living at Its Best".
[64] Ron Dawson, conversation with author, 13 November 2008, min. 3.

first two crossings between North America and Europe she has kept diary entries and pictures; however, from the last crossing she did not record anything after the ship left the St. Lawrence River on the way from Quebec to Southampton, saving her film for taking pictures in Europe.[65] In doing so she emphasized that traveling on an ocean liner was mainly a means of getting to Europe. Richard Faber explains that passengers had to fend for themselves, because "there was practically nothing to do".[66]

However, the passengers who had trouble filling their time on their ships journey seem to have been a minority. In addition to music performances, dancing and films, other typical ways of spending one's time on a ship had been long established: deck games formed an important aspect of being at sea. Another traditional pastime consisted of betting on the progress the ship made every day. Cunard advertised this competition as one of the entertainments on board. *The Rising Tide* advertisement describes the activity in detail, ensuring that passengers knew what to expect:

> "[t]he next time we catch sight of her husband, he has put aside his high finance in favour of a more lowly kind, at which you and I, too, can play. He is standing in the Main Hall, just before noon, and staring at the totalisator board, on which there is inscribed a list of numbers running from 700 to 745. How many miles has the Queen travelled in the last day and night 'I'd like 723, please' says the Glasgow industrialist, and lays down seven shilling on the Assistant Purser's table. 'I guess we've done better than that,' says the man from Wall Street, laying down a dollar, 'I'll take 739'".[67]

The description of this activity on board provided information about the progress across the North Atlantic by emphasizing the distance they had traveled across the ocean. The information about the position that was given out every day was turned into a game in which passengers could exercise their knowledge about the ocean and their daily speed. The entertainment on board thus suggested that the Atlantic Ocean was a space for relaxation because of its unique oceanic qualities. Furthermore, the practice of betting on the daily progress let passengers experience their progress and speed across the Atlantic. The advertisement also takes up the aspect of social prestige because it names the high-ranking occupations of the passengers.

As mentioned above, the speed of the *United States* seems to have been important to the anticipation Lydia DeGuio felt before the journey. In addition, the speed of

---

[65] Martha Martin, min. 22.
[66] Richard Faber, min. 28.
[67] Cunard, "The Rising Tide".

the liner as an affirmation of the United States' technological superiority seems to have been more important for her experience of the crossing than a possible discomfort caused by the fast journey. Other passengers did not necessarily agree that the speed of the ship contributed to making the crossing on the *United States* a better experience. Speaking about the period of the mid 1960s, my interviewee Richard Faber claims that "nobody that was a real enthusiast would go on there. She was vibrating; she went very fast and because of that the vibration was a lot, and very few people did that".[68] By emphasizing the discomfort that was caused by the speed of the *United States*, Richard Faber shows that for him the ocean liners were not mainly a means of transportation but were supposed to be comfortable. My interviewee John Maxton-Graham speaks about the change in the experience of ocean-liner travel in a similar vein, when he describes how the movement of the ship could be felt. The average speed of the *QE2* was changed in order to save fuel from 28.5 to 24 knots.

> "And when you lost that urgency it lost some of the drama. It's a very subtle thing and most passengers don't even think about it, but I noticed it, because I remember it from the old days. And the same as the two Queens. They used to rumble along. […] And looking out of the stern you would see a four-propeller wake, which is something you don't see any more".[69]

This wake seems to have been a central aspect for the experience of movement across the ocean, and it points to the importance of remembering through pictorial representations.[70] The collections of Lydia DeGuio and John Clark's shipboard photographs show an image of the wake from the *United States* and the *France* respectively.[71] Among the pictures of herself taken at different locations on the ship Lydia DeGuio left one of the wake of the ship.

---

[68] Richard Faber, min. 17.
[69] John Maxtone-Graham, interview with author, 25 October 2008, min. 38f.
[70] Pagenstecher, Bundesdeutscher Tourismus, p. 29; Orvar Löfgren, *On Holiday: A History of Vacationing*. Berkeley 1999, p. 9, 85.
[71] Photograph: Lydia DeGuio, Wake of the Ship, October 1953, ISM, Lydia DeGuio Papers; Photograph: John J. Clark, "Photograph in Scrapbook of John J. Clark", August/September 1963, ISM, John Clark Papers.

Figure 23: Lydia DeGuio, Mid Atlantic.

This wake can be seen as the pictorial representation of the *United States* as the fastest ocean liner at the time. As such it is also an aid to her memory of the speed of the ship. The wake of the *United States* indicates the power of the liner's engines and shows the movement of the ship across the ocean.

Eating on Board

Among the occupations of passengers on board the ocean liners, the meals on board seem to have been an outstanding event in constructing the space of the North Atlantic and in making the journey meaningful for passengers. In the sources that Lydia DeGuio left, the meals on board are explicitly and extensively named in her travel narrative, and among the photographs pictures of having food on board stand out. These photographs seem to represent one of her most important experiences while crossing the North Atlantic Ocean on the *SS United States*. Two photos show DeGuio as she is having her breakfast in bed. In one picture she sits in her bunk bed with her breakfast tray in front of her. The upper bunk is so low that she can hardly sit upright. Despite the rather uncomfortable position for eating, the picture shows Lydia DeGuio as she sits smiling behind her breakfast tray.

Figure 24: Lydia in Bed (with breakfast tray).

Her narrative of the trip suggests that she fully embraced the idea of the luxury connected to having breakfast in bed that was promoted by the advertisements. These advertisements depicted breakfast in bed as one aspect of the luxurious treatment that awaited passengers on board. In contrast to the household chores Lydia DeGuio had to do at home, she did not even have to get up in order to have breakfast on the liner.[72] This photograph can also be assumed to be an example of how the personal experience of Lydia DeGuio was influenced by the publications of shipping companies. Mainly, advertisement pictures for first-class travel show stewardesses bringing in the breakfast tray and people eating in bed.[73] The possibility of having breakfast in bed was not only advertised as a very luxurious way of eating, in that breakfast was an occasion that was marked by the practice of serving in the cabin, but also provided a certain structure for the day. On the ocean liners, breakfast was followed by hot bouillon at around 11:00 a.m. on deck, sitting in a deck chair. This tradition of having a warm soup on deck was specifically connected to crossing the sometimes-chilly North Atlantic. Ted Scull

---

[72] DeGuio, "Narrative of the Trip".
[73] See e.g. Cunard, "Travel in its Finest Sense".

fondly recalls sitting on deck wrapped in a warm blanket against the wind.[74] His memory indicates the multi-sensuous experience of food as an important aspect of the experience of ocean-liner spaces.[75] This memory includes the bouillon served in connection with the wind on the ocean. In contrast to Ted Scull's positive memories, Gavin Lyall mentions the tradition of serving bouillon rather critically as a fancy of transatlantic passengers in a newspaper article in 1965, when the passenger trade with ocean liners was in decline.[76] Both references point to the importance of this tradition for the experience of ocean-liner space as well as the experience of passengers. By having bouillon on deck, the time between breakfast and lunch was divided to include another meal, and the space of the deck was turned into an area for food.

On the ocean liners people then met in the restaurant for lunch, which was usually a three-course meal. Except in first class on the *Queen Elizabeth* and *Queen Mary*, this meal was precisely timed on Cunard ships, since there were two sittings, so that the first had just over an hour to eat.[77] In 1965 Cunard advertised for the time after lunch that people could have

> "the kind of pleasurable treat that is permanently denied to the shore people [...]. On a Queen, the siesta reclaims its rightful place in the pattern of 20th century Anglo-Saxon life. After a Cunard luncheon you feel you really owe yourself a relaxed hour or two, stretched out in a deck chair [...]. And, when you next open your eyes, it is to see a steward bending over you, with afternoon tea."[78]

This advertisement can be read in contrast to hectic life elsewhere, and it emphasizes the luxury of being served one's food on the liners by considerate stewards. Since people are said to be denied the possibility of relaxing after lunch, the possibility to do so on the ocean liners is also construed as luxurious. The emphasis on the time available to passengers to take a nap on the ocean liner, in contrast to life on shore, was added in 1965, although the tradition of having afternoon tea on deck on the British ocean liners was already emphasized in

---

74   Ted Scull, min. 17.
75   Sally Everett draws attention to food tourism as an essentially multi-sensuous experience, although she differentiates between inauthentic and authentic experiences, neglecting that "staged" experiences are also multi-sensuous. See Sally Everett, "Beyond the Visual Gaze?: The Pursuit of an Embodied Experience through Food Tourism" in: Tourist Studies 8 (2008), p. 337-359: 342f.
76   Lyall, "New Battle of the Atlantic", p. 13.
77   Cunard, "Regulations to be Observed in the Company's Service", p. 71.
78   Cunard, "The Rising Tide".

1958.[79] The time for passengers to retire to their cabin or stay in the deck chair to sleep was located in between two meals. After waking up and having tea in one of the deck chairs, which the United States Lines calls a "pleasant interlude",[80] it was already time to start preparing for dinner, for which passengers dressed in their best clothing. Before dinner was served, passengers could meet in the lounge for cocktails and canapés.[81]

This sequence of meals shows that the meals on board structured the journey to the effect that the various meals provided a set structure for each day and emphasized different locations on deck. For passengers on board, in addition to the menu cards, this structure became manifest in the daily programs that were given out.[82] While these programs structured the day for passengers, newspaper articles, such as Gavin Lyall's piece[83] or the commissioned diary in the *Liverpool Echo* provided information about the meals on board the ocean liners for people who could not travel across the ocean themselves. In this diary the author spends one article solely on food on board and claims that the whole day was spent in anticipation of the next meal.[84] Besides structuring the time of the day, the meals also structured the space of the ocean liner in that they periodically changed the function of certain spaces such as the cabin or the deck and directed the passengers' movements. While the meals on ocean liners primarily structured each day, they were also related to the whole journey in that the various days had a certain theme or dress code. On the first and last night passengers did not have to dress for dinner, because their evening clothes were still or already packed.[85] One night was usually reserved for a special gala dinner.[86] Whether passengers engaged in any activities after dinner, such as dancing, partly depended on the direction they were traveling in. While clocks were put forward each day on eastbound voyages (in the case of the *United States* by 75 minutes[87]), passengers

---

[79] Advertisement Booklet: Cunard Steam Ship Company Ltd., "The Stately Ships of Britain", probably 1958, UoLSC&A, D42/PR4/25.
[80] US Lines, "New *S.S. United States*".
[81] Cunard, "Atlantic Fairway".
[82] Programme Card: Cunard Steam Ship Company Ltd, "Programme for Today", Queen Elizabeth, 1965-1966, UoLSC&A, PR3/21/15 (a-h, j-n, p,q).
[83] Lyall, "New Battle of the Atlantic".
[84] Eglin, "Atlantic Diary", 23.11.1959.
[85] Richard Joseph, "The Captain's Table: Life among the Floating Elite, from the Second Night out to the Last Night in", in: *Esquire*, May 1963, UoLSC&A, D42/PR4/25-26: 88; Cunard, "The Rising Tide".
[86] Menu Card: United States Lines, "Menu Gala Dinner *S.S. United States*", 10.8.1953, ISM, Lydia DeGuio Papers.
[87] Ibid.

received an extra hour on westbound voyages.[88] Therefore passengers effectively experienced a 23- or 25-hour day, dependent on the direction of travel and as a result of adjustment of onboard clocks.

The meals on board the ocean liners not only structured each day but at the same time each meal was an occasion itself. The importance of the food that was served for each of the meals is shown by the menu cards that were given out. The practice of printing menus for the voyage had been established on the ocean liners, on which new menu cards were given out each day and could be taken home.[89] Lydia DeGuio also donated the menu card of the gala dinner from her outbound journey, and explicitly names some of the foods available on board as an example of the "gourmet meals"[90] that were served. This menu card from 10 August 1953 serves as an example of what was served in tourist class on the ocean liners. The meal started with different hors d'oeuvres, and was followed by soup and the main course, for which passengers could choose between fish and meat - which could also be ordered from the grill. The side orders consisted of different vegetables and potatoes as well as a salad. The meal could then be completed by compote, cake or ice cream. Dessert was followed by cheese and crackers, nuts and fruits and coffee.[91]

Even before passengers faced the choices on the menu they were presented with food. In 1965 Cunard advertised:

"And here come the canapés […]: a tray designed by a poet for a king, and brought round to you by a steward who could be half Lord Chamberlain and half a court-jester, bears smoked salmon and caviar and hot liver and bacon in a setting of orange stuck with beetroot roses. Traveler, beware; there is dinner yet to come."[92]

Both, the warning about "dinner yet to come" and the overflowing buffets, concern the amounts and kinds of foods that were served, but they could also be considered as signs of the abilities of the kitchen staff and the quality of food, since the foodstuffs are elaborately arranged and include a variety of different foods. Cunard also promoted the idea of quality food on board by advertising, "[s]uperb food and wine are part of a magnificent service jealously guarded and scrupulously maintained. Cunard cuisine offers only the best, both in quality and presentation. It has many admirers but acknowledges none the better".[93] In this

---

[88] Richard Faber, min. 24.
[89] Marguerite Patten, *Post-War Kitchen*, 2 ed., London 2004 [1998].
[90] DeGuio, "Narrative of the Trip".
[91] Unite States Lines, "Menu Gala Dinner."
[92] Cunard, "The Rising Tide".
[93] Cunard, "The Stately Ships of Britain".

case, the image of luxurious travel was closely connected to the idea of fine dining.

These gourmet meals were supposed to take place in the appropriate setting. For this setting, the architecture of the ocean liners as well as the attire of the passengers was important. Cunard advertised, "[t]here are few things in eating so elaborately generous as dinner in a great Cunarder. The occasion is honored by formal clothes".[94]

Lydia DeGuio had a photograph taken of her at the table from both her trips across the North Atlantic, suggesting that it was common to take a picture at the dinner table. This practice of photographing passengers dressed up at the dinner table presents a reinforcement of the idea of luxurious dining as it was marked by formal clothes. In addition to the photograph, she saved a napkin from the *United States*, on which her first ever alcoholic beverage was served, indicating how special the alcohol served on board was.[95] This napkin is also a memento of her first experience of drinking alcohol.

The photographs of Lydia DeGuio at the dinner table also show that she and her uncle dined together with other passengers. The aspect of establishing connections between the passengers who dined together was considered a central aspect of having meals on the ocean liners. This aspect corresponds with Ferdinand Fellmann's discussion of personal and cultural identity, as they are expressed through various ways of having one's meals. He has identified an important function of these meals in forming relationships between the people at the table.[96]

Since the dinner table was so important for forming connections with other passengers, they took care to reserve a seat just after they had embarked. Concerning seats at the table, the general information for passengers just states: "Seats at table – Passengers requesting particular seats or tables are invited to submit alternatives to their first choice. Whilst every effort will be made to comply with passengers' wishes, specific seating or sitting cannot be guaranteed".[97] However, my interview partners placed the reservation of a seat of

---

[94] Cunard, "Atlantic Fairway".

[95] Dave Bryceson, The Titanic Disaster: As Reported in the British National Press April-July 1912, Somerset 1998.

[96] Fellmann, Ferdinand. "Kulturelle und personale Identität", in: Hans Jürgen Teuteberg, Gerhard Neumann, and Alois Wierlacher (Eds.), *Essen und kulturelle Identität: Europäische Perspektiven*, Berlin 1997, p. 27-36: 35.

[97] Information Leaflet: Cunard Steam Ship Company Ltd. „Cunard Line Embarkation Notice, Liverpool Services", September 1955, UoLSC&A, D.861/1/c

choice within the important ritual of departure. For example, Vincent Lowe related that the first thing passengers did was to go into the cabin and look at the passenger list to see whether they knew anyone. Second, they went to the dining room to arrange their table.[98]

On the ocean liners, the number of choices and the quality of the food marked differences between the different classes, and within each class, the choice of table and companions set a further distinction. The ultimate luxury and sought-after company on board ocean liners could be found at the captain's table, which was situated in first class on Cunard and United States Lines ships. As *Esquire* wrote in 1963, the

> "*[c]rème de la crème* of this leisured aristocracy are the six to eight passengers whose social or professional stature entitles them to a commend invitation to sit at the Captain's table in the dining room. This is a summons that can't be wangled, and one of the Captain's non-nautical headaches is the status-climbing passenger who tries to do so."[99]

As Commodore Thelwell's memo book indicates, the passengers at his table also gave the captain social distinction, because he kept photographs of some of the passengers who sat at his table. Indeed, some of the passengers also seem to have given him some headaches because in September and October 1956 he marked a few of the names with the comment "never again".[100] The officers also dined in first class and were heads of distinctive tables, but the Cabin Assistant Purser had to dine in cabin class, and the assistant purser responsible for tourist class had to take "occasional meals" there each voyage, so that special tables existed in cabin and tourist class as well.[101]

Still, even if passengers were not invited to the captain's table, the people at the dinner table were important to the experience of the journey. This importance of making reservations early mirrors the centrality of the dinner table for making connections with other passengers, with whom the table was shared for three meals a day. Whereas advertisements and publications about ocean liner travel

---

[98] Vincent Lowe, min. 55.
[99] Joseph, "The Captain's Table", p. 86.
[100] Book: Commodore Robert G. Thelwell, "Memo Book", 1946-1956, UoLSC&A, D335/3/4.
[101] Cunard, Regulations to be Observed in the Company's Service. 65; Joseph, "The Captain's Table", p. 86.

only focus on companionship in a general way, personal documents suggest the specific importance of the dinner table.[102] Vincent Lowe explains:

> "And I, as I have said before, the dining room experience is very important. I think, that's where you meet people. And on the ships when I was in the transatlantic business; that's, you tag along with these people; you meet your tablemates, and that's your little group for the trip. That's from my experience."[103]

For Vincent Lowe, who was often traveling on his own, making connections with other people seems to have been especially important; he even kept in contact with one woman he met as a student.[104] Similarly, Martha Martin formed a group with the companions at her table.[105] The value that Vincent Lowe and Martha Martin place on these encounters might stem from what Julia Harrison calls the "sociability impulse," which she found an important aspect for giving meaning to travels.[106] While the travel enthusiasts, whom Julia Harrison interviewed, could form connections with local people, passengers on the ocean liners mostly met groups of people from a similar background.[107] For example, the class divisions of the dining rooms largely ensured that similar people would meet at one table.

In order to make travel with fellow passengers agreeable, the shipping lines tried to ensure that people around the table fit to each other. Ted Scull recalls that the maitre d' "had a knack of what to do", and would put people of the same age at one table.[108] He remembers one trip on which he played scrabble with his table mates, who were all university-educated and came from different English-speaking countries - New Zealand, Canada and England - so that they had to agree on the spelling and idioms of the words that could be used in the game. In this case the people had a very similar educational background, yet their differences allowed for an entertaining voyage. The time people spent together on board, especially during the meals, can be seen as forming communities and networks of travelers across the North Atlantic.[109]

---

[102] One Cunard advertisement, for example, states: "The authentic social conviviality that certainly does exist on a giant liner – you can take it or you can leave it alone". Cunard, "The Rising Tide".
[103] Vincent Lowe, min. 70.
[104] Ibid. min, 65.
[105] Martha Martin, min. 20.
[106] Harrison, *Being a Tourist*, p. 46.
[107] Ibid: 47, 74f.
[108] Ted Scull, min. 13.
[109] Ibid. min. 14.

Sometimes these communities only lasted for the voyage and were based on the shared time and information around the table, and in some cases the networks have been kept active long after the original connection on the voyage.[110]
For Vincent Lowe, Martha Martin and Ted Scull meeting new people over food was an important characteristic of the journey by ocean liner. Similarly, in Donald Sultner-Welles' reports about his North Atlantic crossings his fellow passengers at the table take centre stage, and they convey some of the excitement that he connected to meeting different people on board. In 1962 he noted in his postcard diary,

> "[a]nother reason I like to take these trips by boat is because of some of the contacts .. I am at a table for four .. one is a lady from Chicago (formerly from Czec.) & the man Mr. Arlington Valles from Hollywood says he won an Occar [sic] for the art work in the movie "Spartacus" .. his traveling companion is a Miss Julia Gamble, a middle aged redhead and a color specialist ... amazing how one can meet folk such as this."[111]

On his second ocean crossing to Europe in 1962, where he went to give some concerts, Donald Sultner-Welles could draw the connections with the people he sat with at the table beyond the meeting on the North Atlantic. He reported,

> "AND, here is another funny one: There were only two other peoppe [sic] at my table last evening, one an Indonesian woman married to a Hollander who is at the moment a mine engin. In N[orth] D[akota] (she has a horror of going there..does one blame her?) and the other a German doctor ... We began talking about what I do and suddenly he pointed his finger as me and said: "I've met you!" ... and sure enough he was, or is a friend of Dieter Hepp's who visited us at "Glen Hill" .. I met his chap in Plainfield last November. Strange !!!!!"[112]

---

[110] Joseph, "The Captain's Table", p. 88; Ted Scull, min. 13; Vincent Lowe, min. 65.
[111] Postcard: Donald Sultner-Welles, 25.4.-3.5.1962, National Museum of American History, Smithsonian Institution, Archives Collection (NMoAH, SI, AC), Donald H. Sultner-Welles Collection # 145, Series 1, Box 6.
[112] Postcard: Donald H. Sultner-Welles, 1.8.1962, NMoAH, SI, AC. Donald H. Sultner-Welles Collection # 145, Series 1, Box 6. See also Postcard Diary: Donald Sultner-Welles, 23.7.1965. NMoAH, SI, AC. Donald H. Sultner-Welles Collection # 145, Series 1, Box 7 and Postcard Diary: Donald Sultner-Welles, 19.-28.4.1966. NMoAH, SI, AC. Donald H. Sultner-Welles Collection # 145, Series 1, Box 7.

Figure 25: *S.S. United States*. Lydia, Theresa, Genen (at the dinner table).

It is striking that the people at the dinner table also feature in other personal accounts. This reference to the tablemates in the dining room suggests that stories about and reference to the other people at the table seem to have become an important aspect of remembering the journey. This aspect has been emphasized by the time spent with the people at the table, and mentioning these people seems to have become a part of the scripts for narrating the experience of crossing the North Atlantic. The second photograph Lydia DeGuio kept of herself in the dining room indicates the importance of her tablemates for the journey.
On the photograph she noted the first name of one of the women who sat at the table besides Lydia DeGuio and her uncle.[113] Since these photographs stem from a gala dinner, and since the people at the other table are wearing paper hats, it stands to reason that these pictures were taken by a photographer on board. Such a practice points to the importance that the United States Lines ascribed to depicting people at the dinner table. These pictures can be seen as emphasizing

---

[113] Photograph: Lydia DeGuio, "Lydia DeGuio at the Dinner Table (2)", 26.10.1953, ISM, Lydia DeGuio Papers.

the importance of having dinner together, since they show the people and not the food they would have had later on.

The food that was served later on was not only important as an aspect of the experience of luxury but it also contributed to an experience of the nationality of the liners and of the destination. In her travel narrative Lydia DeGuio emphasizes that she crossed the North Atlantic on "America's luxury liner".[114] The liner's nationality, its technological advancement as well as its destination was mirrored in the food. Similarly, the food that was served on board the ocean liners also contributed to marking the spaces of the liners as national, although most passengers were US American and the food was tailored to their tastes.[115] As Arnold Zingerle states, food as a marker of identities is not bound to a certain place and can be varied and still function as a marker.[116] Taking the ocean liners to Europe provided a first opportunity for US American passengers to engage with a European nation. Accordingly, the menu card Lydia DeGuio kept features French food terms.[117] The ways of preparing meals on board were used by shipping companies and airlines to promote their technological achievements; passengers perceived the meals as authentic to the nationality of the ocean liners. Interestingly, the spaces of the harbor, which were marked as national spaces through different controls, also became international in the close relation between the harbor and the ocean liners, since the liners docked in the harbor mostly belonged to a European nation. This internationality was especially evident in New York, where all the European ships docked.

Ocean-liner enthusiasts remember New York Harbor in summer, above all, for the sight of the ocean liners, which docked there and could be visited by everyone who could afford the small entrance fee.[118] On board they could, above all, drink beverages that were associated with a certain nation. Ted Scull recounts that he went on the liners without being a passenger while they were docked in New York. He told me,

---

[114] DeGuio, "Narrative of the Trip".

[115] In critical commentaries of Americanization, one comment is that Americans increasingly did not have to adjust to foreign tastes any more. See e.g. Gerhard Herm, *Amerika Erobert Europa*, Düsseldorf, Wien 1964, p. 7.

[116] Arnold Zingerle, "Identitätsbildung bei Tische: Theoretische Vorüberlegungen aus kultursoziologischer Sicht," in: Hans Jürgen Teuteberg, Gerhard Neumann, and Alois Wierlacher (Eds.): *Essen und kulturelle Identität: Europäische Perspektiven*, Berlin 1997, p.69-86.

[117] Unite States Lines, "Menu Gala Dinner."

[118] Bill Miller, min. 25.

"I would get a date and I would say we're going to have a very good time tonight. 'Where are we going?' 'Down to the docks'. And she would be like: 'What are we going down to the docks for?' You go down and you go to the German ships, and they had a beer licence in port and they had a band and you danced, and the French had a champagne licence in port. Five dollars for a bottle of Moët & Chandon, which wasn't cheap, but it was affordable. [...] And then the French line had a glass dance floor with coloured lights underneath, and that was really fun. You danced two or three hours and then half an hour before the ship sailed, you would get off. So it was easy; it was easy to get on".[119]

The stereotypical national drinks that were served on board marked the ocean liners as having a European nationality for US American visitors. During the time the liners were docked at the harbor, New Yorkers could engage with the respective nations as tourists, although they did not travel far. The ocean liners brought the foreign world of the ocean and of European nations into the harbor, and visitors could get an idea of what it would be like to cross the North Atlantic on an ocean liner. On Atlantic crossings the liners were also advertised as preparing passengers for the drinks they would find once they had reached Europe. Cunard advertised

that "all of the Queens' bars serve a draught beer from the cask. A touch heavier than most American beers, but not as abruptly British to the first-time American taste as English 'bitter' or Scotch ale, it provides a gentle introduction for American visitors to the pints they'll find people drinking in Pubs ashore".[120]

These constructions of the ocean liners as national spaces were aimed at US Americans who were the majority of passengers and experienced the food served on board as tourists. At the same time, the British perceived the Cunard liners as British ships, and the origin of most passengers in the United States and their eating and drinking habits were met with mixed feelings.[121] The *Times* supplement on Cunard wrote in 1965, the "dining rooms and bars on ships which are British to the backbone in every other way are dominated by American culinary and drinking habits".[122] For example, the different tastes associated with being British and being US American were related to Americans enjoying their

---

[119] Ted Scull, min. 27.
[120] Cunard, "The Rising Tide".
[121] For nationality as an aspect of shaping tastes see Stephen Mennell, *All Manners of Food: Eating and Taste in England and France from the Middle Ages to the Present*, Oxford, New York 1985, p. 17.
[122] TIMES Supplement, "Cunard".

drinks on ice; whereas the British had theirs without ice.[123] The perceptions of these different habits show the role of food as an expression of national pride and of food as a distinction between "us" and "them".[124] The British national pride in their ocean liners is contrasted with the spending power of US Americans, most of whom could afford to cross on the liners, reflecting their better spending power, which also influenced the political and economic relationships between the two nations in the post-war period.[125]

However, from the point of view of US Americans the adjustment of food to American tastes did not always work, as Donald Sultner-Welles reports from his 1966 crossing from New York to Amsterdam. His comments bring out how the perceived cultural differences between Americans and people from the Netherlands were associated with varying eating habits. He wrote,

"the food on this ship, in fact on all the HA [Holland-America Line] ships is not up to the SS INDEPENDENCE .. although the service is far superior on these ships ... not having a regular breakfast as we do in their own country the chefs couldn't care less apparently about how the prepare breakfast for Americans... when frying bacon, for instance, they simply take up a handful and thro it into a pan... and you can imagine the results."[126]

Donald Sultner-Welles apparently expected to be served American food, which he found on the *Independence*, which was American, and he expressed dismay at foreign ways of preparing breakfast. In contrast, Americans seem to have embraced foreign food which was not adjusted to their tastes as part of the tourist experience of crossing the North Atlantic on a European liner. For example, the tradition of serving tea with scones or biscuits in the afternoon on the ocean liners was an important aspect of identifying Cunard ships as British. Richard Faber portrayed the British ships as having a particularly good service, and they were seen as British because tea was served in the afternoons.[127] According to George Eglin, Americans enjoyed the tea even more than the Britons did.[128] This

---

[123] Eglin, "Atlantic Diary", 14.11.1959, 18.11.1959.
[124] David Bell and Gill Valentine, *Consuming Geographies: We Are What We Eat*. London, 1997, p. 168; Jennie Germann Molz, "Eating Difference: The Cosmopolitan Mobilities of Culinary Tourism", in: Space and Culture 10 (2007), p.77-93: 80.
[125] Kathleen Burk, *Old World, New World: The Story of Britain and America*, London 2007: 566ff.
[126] Sultner-Welles, "Postcard Diary", 1966.
[127] Richard Faber, min. 25.
[128] Eglin, "Atlantic Diary", 18.11.1959.

enjoyment of British food by Americans presents an appreciation of British culinary traditions and can be linked to a struggle of the British to "identify themselves as [people] of taste".[129] Janet Floyd identifies such a struggle as a culinary mirror of the post-war question whether Britain should lean towards Europe or the United States as an ally. She states that "there is no doubt that France dominates the gastronomic arena", but the food of the United States was also attractive.[130] In between these poles the appreciation of British culinary traditions seemed vulnerable.

While Cunard ships were mentioned in relation to the services on board, the French Line was repeatedly mentioned in my interviews as serving the best food, as restaurants in France had the reputation of being superior to other restaurants.[131] Richard Faber supports this claim by mentioning that the restaurant on the *France* was rated the finest restaurant in the world in the 1960s.[132] Ted Scull remembers that its further advantages consisted of a bottle of wine from its own vineyards for lunch and dinner.[133]

However, according to Bill Miller, the food on the European liners was considered too complicated by some US Americans because they, for example, did not understand the French gourmet terms. These passengers were "far more comfortable with American food" and therefore chose the *United States*.[134] The food served on the *United States* was perceived as American because of what was served and how it was served. According to Bill Miller, the "substantial portions so typified European impressions of America: abundance".[135] In addition to the American food served, the United States Lines also advertised for the international cuisine available on board, and the line emphasized the importance of the food's quality in the competition with other companies. In an advertisement

---

[129] Janet Floyd, "The Restaurant Guide as Romance: From Raymond Postgate to Florence White", in: David Bell and Joanne Hollows (Eds.), *Historicizing Lifestyle: Mediating Taste, Consumption and Identity from the 1900s to 1970s*, Aldershot 2006, p. 41-53: 46.

[130] Ibid.

[131] Gerald W. Whitted, New Horizons World Guide: Pan American's Travel Facts About 108 Countries. 11th ed. New York 1963, p. 61.

[132] Richard Faber, min. 15.

[133] Ted Scull, min. 67.

[134] William H. Miller, *SS United States: The Story of America's Greatest Ocean Liner*, Sparkford 1991, p. 111. These findings correspond to the communication problem that Cohen and Avieli found with food tourism. See Erik Cohen and Nir Avieli, "Food in Tourism: Attraction and Impediment," Annals of Tourism Research 31 (2004), p.755-778: 765.

[135] Miller, *SS United States*, p. 111.

it states: "You'll enjoy the finest American and international dishes prepared by master chefs whose specialty is pleasing you – expertly. The menus from which you choose have earned United States Lines its high reputation for cuisine unsurpassed afloat or ashore".[136]

Vincent Lowe mainly recalls that the food on the American ocean liners was very American, and he mentions the excellent steaks as an example.[137] In literature about the association of food and nations, beef is closely linked to Britain,[138] but of course the British also brought their eating habits to the United States,[139] and in Vincent Lowe's perception, steaks signified American food. According to Vincent Lowe, the steaks on the *United States* were prepared with microwave ovens, but although he speaks of the excellent steaks, he was less happy with their preparation. He states, "the *United States* was very progressive, so when it came out in 1952, among other things, it had microwave ovens, which was very very new in 1952 […] but the steaks would have sort of a grey look, they'd be cooked, but they didn't have that nice grilled look."[140]

Nonetheless, preparation with microwave ovens was an important aspect of constructing the spaces of the *United States* as national spaces, and the use of this technology fits into the narrative of technological progress used by the shipping companies. The use of microwave ovens can be considered as quintessentially US American, since the development of the microwave oven can be linked to the Cold War and the US-American goal to be viewed as superior to the Soviet Union through its consumer goods. According to Richard A. Schwartz, technologies that enabled the building of microwave ovens were heavily funded by Cold-War related agencies.[141] These ovens can also be associated with American ways of preparing food. Stephen Mennell claims that the American cuisine of the second half of the 20th century was characterized by the speed of preparing and eating food.[142]

---

[136] US Lines, "New S.S. United States".
[137] Vincent Lowe, min. 48.
[138] Bell and Valentine, *Comsuming Geographies*, p. 167; Menno Spiering, "Food, Phagophobia and English National Identity," in Food, Drink and Identity in Europe, ed. Thomas M. Wilson (Amsterdam, New York, 2006): 31ff.
[139] Stephen Mennell, "The Culinary Culture of Europe Overseas", in: Hans Jürgen Teuteberg, Gerhard Neumann, and Alois Wierlacher (Eds.), *Essen und kulturelle Identität: Europäische Perspektiven*, Berlin 1997, p. 459-464: 460.
[140] Vincent Lowe, min. 49.
[141] Richard A. Schwartz, *Cold War Culture: Media and the Arts, 1945-1990, Cold War America*. New York 1998, p. 65.
[142] Mennell, "Culinary Culture of Europe Overseas", p. 462.

To sum up, each meal on the ocean liners can be interpreted as an occasion in itself. At the same time, the different meals taken together formed a structure for the spaces and time of the journey. This structure marked ocean-liner travel as luxurious, since passengers had so much free time available that such a structure seemed welcome. As Vered Amit argues, time is one of the resources that privileges people to undertake voluntary journeys.[143] The sources that Lydia DeGuio left indicate that she experienced the food as luxurious in contrast to the situation at home and that her experience was influenced by publications about ocean-liner travel. Lydia DeGuio was served luxurious food, which she explicitly names in her narrative in contrast to preparing everything herself. She also kept memorabilia of her dining experiences which included dressing up and socializing with other people at the dinner table. Her experience of eating on board the *SS United States* seems to have emphasized the aspect of the ocean liners as a holiday destination.

Conclusion

Lydia DeGuio crossed the North Atlantic Ocean on the *United States* from New York to LeHavre and back in the summer of 1953, one year after the ocean liner was put into service. She traveled across the North Atlantic at a time when ocean liners were the most common way of crossing the Atlantic, a few years before airplanes started transporting the majority of the passengers. As an American she came from a country that was overall economically better off than the European countries on the other side of the ocean.

One of the sources that can serve as an example for an analysis of the different aspects of Lydia DeGuio's experience of crossing the North Atlantic is the photograph of her having breakfast in bed. For the researcher, this photograph provides information about the materiality of the ocean liner, specifically of a part of her cabin. Since Lydia DeGuio had a picture taken of herself while she was having breakfast in bed, this event seems to have been important enough to warrant taking this picture. That Lydia DeGuio kept a photograph of this specific event indicates the influence of advertisements on her experience and suggests that they were one means that made her experience meaningful. Advertisements of the United States Lines suggest that having breakfast in bed was one of the amenities that came with a journey on the liners and something that you did on board. Furthermore, getting served in the cabin was one indication of the

---

[143] Vered Amit, "Structures and Dispositions of Travel and Movement," in: Vered Amit (Ed.), *Going First Class? New Approaches to Privileged Travel and Movement,* New York, Oxford 2007, p. 2.

"pampering" Lydia DeGuio received on board. Therefore, the photograph can also be understood as a memory aid that reminded Lydia DeGuio, for example, of the luxury of being served her meals.

This luxury of being served her meals is one aspect of the answer to the first research question of how Lydia DeGuio experienced her North Atlantic crossings. The sources suggest that she experienced them as events that made her feel privileged and elevated her social status because she was among the people who could travel on a liner that "everyone was talking about". Although she traveled in tourist class, her pictures, markings on the deck plan as well as her narrative show that she embraced the narratives of luxury travel, which were, for example, presented in advertisements. In addition to being served her meals, she comments on the luxury of the food and kept the napkin on which she was served her first ever alcoholic drink, so that her experience of being on the liner also seems to have been marked by special things that were not necessarily allowed at home. Furthermore, the photographs Lydia DeGuio had taken on board show behavior typically associated with tourist destinations, such as enjoying the sun in a deck chair. Therefore, she seems to have experienced the time on the *SS United States* as holiday time.

As an answer to the second research question of how Lydia DeGuio's experience relates to the experience of other passengers it can be said that most other passengers agreed with her experience of the time on the liners as a holiday destination and described similar aspects of the anticipation they felt and the luxury and structure that was provided by the food that was served on board, which can also be found in publications about traveling on the ocean liners. However, at least one example from the 1960s indicates that the experience of privilege was not just about being on the liner any more but had changed to an expectation of certain amenities, such as the swimming pool, even when traveling in the lowest class. This expectation might have been an expression of a growing self-confidence of a growing number of tourists.[144]

Lydia DeGuio's different experiences correspond to what other research has found to be meaningful for tourists. Her experience of social elevation seems to be similar to what Alma Gottlieb calls being " Queen (King) for a Day",[145] and this elevation corresponds to Julia Harrison's finding of tourists who temporarily move up from the milieu they usually live in.[146] Furthermore, the spaces of the

---

[144] Endy, *Cold War Holidays*, p. 132.
[145] Gottlieb, "Americans' Vacations", p. 165.
[146] Harrison, *Being a Tourist,* p. 68.

Atlantic liner seem to have allowed for behavior that was different from home.[147] Although in the early 1950s crossing the North Atlantic on an Atlantic liner was basically the only way to travel across the ocean, the spaces of the liner have been constructed as tourist spaces. As such they seem to have remained meaningful to Lydia DeGuio because she connects her journey on the *United States* to her later love for cruising, which in contrast to crossing the ocean is fully aimed at providing holiday destinations rather than transportation.

Furthermore, Lydia DeGuio's experience of being privileged extended beyond her individual situation and included the United States as her home country, and the space of the North Atlantic was one that showed the national superiority of the United States. Lydia DeGuio was proud of being US-American, and this pride was represented by the *SS United States* as an example of advanced US-American technology. In relation to the North Atlantic the Blue Riband represented the ship's superior technology. At a time when the United States was confirming its status as world power after World War II,[148] its new ocean liner won the long-established trophy for the fastest North Atlantic crossing. As an example of the speed of the ocean liner a photograph of its wake is included in Lydia DeGuio's memorabilia. Therefore, the North Atlantic is here constructed as a space that shows the technological advancement of the United States, which could be experienced through the latest technology and speed of the *United States*.

Again, the experience of the technological advancement of the *United States* can be linked to advertisements by the shipping line and media coverage, which hailed the technological advancements of the liner. These publications can be seen as another example of contributions to making certain aspects of the voyage meaningful. Lydia DeGuio's experience of the ocean liner as a specifically US-American space is also found in other sources in that other passengers agree that the ocean liners were distinctly national spaces. This common aspect of the experience is therefore another part of the answer to the second research question of how Lydia DeGuio's experience related to the experience of other passengers. However, for the other passengers the technological advancement of the ocean liner carried less of a positive connotation because some of them experienced the rumble that went along with the speed of the liner as uncomfortable.

Since Lydia DeGuio makes the link herself in her travel narrative, her positive experience of the *United States* seems to have been influenced by her personal situation at home, which stood in contrast to life on board because she had to do

---

[147] Rob Shields, *Places on the Margin: Alternative Geographies of Modernity*. London, New York 1991, p. 261.

[148] Jürgen Heideking and Christof Mauch, *Geschichte der USA*, 6th ed. Tübingen, Basel 2008, p. 285ff.

most of the chores. Furthermore, as an answer to the third research question of how her experience relates back to life on shore, the differences in the post-war development in the United States and Europe seem to have made Lydia DeGuio's crossing meaningful in that she could appreciate her privileged position as an US American, which was reinforced by the positive reception she encountered in Europe.

To conclude, besides showing that Lydia DeGuio deemed her Atlantic crossing important enough to donate her memorabilia, this donation and her travel narrative suggest a certain nostalgia for North Atlantic crossings on the ocean liners. An analysis of her experience as an aspect of the construction of North Atlantic space indicates that nostalgia for the ocean liners originated from the clearly ordered privilege that was an important aspect of Atlantic crossings in the 1950s and also in the 1960s. For Lydia DeGuio this privilege consisted of a social elevation related to her position on the liner and her position as an US American. The space of the North Atlantic allowed a measurement of privilege since it served as the basis for showing the advancement of technology through the speed of the ocean liner and as the space in between America and Europe connected these continents and through this connection allowed for a comparison of the differences in development after World War II.

8. A Floating Carnival: P. G. Wodehouse and the Atlantic Crossing

Eric Sandberg

Introduction

P. G. Wodehouse is remembered today as one of English literature's finest comic writers, but as little more. A typical assessment would see him as an author of unsurpassed levity whose books resist all forms of seriousness. Indeed, reading his work critically has been described as "taking a spade to a soufflé," a form of unrewarding, unsophisticated, unnecessary and ultimately destructive behavior.[1] Recent republications of Wodehouse's work have further entrenched this position by including a laudatory back cover blurb from Stephen Fry, who claims that "you don't analyse such sunlit perfection, you just bask in its warmth and splendour."[2] This approach to Wodehouse simultaneously heaps him with praise and leaves little to say: to characterize Wodehouse as "gaiety in print," for instance, is to rather effectively end any further discussion of his work as a literary or cultural phenomenon.[3]

Yet elements of Wodehouse's work can be productively viewed as a form of what might be described as Atlantic carnivalesque, an approach that yields a clearer view of his literary accomplishment and its broader significance. This is a term, however, that requires a certain amount of explication. Wodehouse has been acknowledged by a number of critics as a "trail-blazer" of transatlantic narrative, a "peripatetic writer" who crossed and re-crossed the Atlantic incessantly on the great liners that were such a prominent cultural and physical feature of the pre- and inter-war years.[4] One of the great themes of his work is the contrasting cultures of America and England, and as David Damrosch points out, he achieved his greatest success as a comic interpreter of British culture for the American market, and American culture for the British market.[5] But Wodehouse can also be viewed as a writer of the Atlantic crossing itself, for a significant strand of his

---

[1] Allan Ramsay, "The Green Baize Door: Social Identity in Wodehouse Part One" in: *Contemporary Review* 285.1667 (2004) p. 352-357: 352.
[2] P. G. Wodehouse, *The Luck of the Bodkins*, London 2008.
[3] Mary Jane Kneen, "Recommended: P. G. Wodehouse" in: *The English Journal* 73, (1984), p. 77-78: 78.
[4] Benny Green, *P. G. Wodehouse: A Literary Biography,* London 1981, p. 64, 95.
[5] David Damrosch, *What is World Literature?*, Princeton and Oxford 2003, p. 210.

work is directly related to the experience of the four- to seven-day Atlantic crossing, drawing inspiration from the "true culture" of the steamship liners, which, while reflective of the social world of their home countries, was in many ways independent of particular English or American cultural formations.[6] "Transatlantic crossings became," Robert McCrum writes, "an integral part of Wodehouse's life," and they also became an integral part of his fiction, most particularly in *The Girl on the Boat* (1922) and *The Luck of Bodkins* (1936).[7] Both of these novels employ the Atlantic crossing as a temporal and spatial setting for a carnivalization of society involving freedom from the confines of traditional authority, romantic possibility, and the disturbance of hierarchical systems. In these novels, the ocean crossing itself is as important as arrival in New York or Southampton, for on-board the SS Atlantic the normal rules of society can be evaded, reformulated, or at least temporarily suspended, in an imaginative space of personal freedom similar in many ways to what Mikhail Bakhtin describes as "the atmosphere of joyful relativity characteristic of a carnival sense of the world."[8]

The Carnivalesque Sensibility

The carnivalesque sensibility is part of the "boundless world of humorous forms and manifestations" of "folk carnival humor."[9] These range from fairs to feasts, from comic skits to curses, and have fed into, Bakhtin argues, a "carnivalized literature" which reflects a life "drawn out of its usual rut."[10] While Bakhtin's discussions of carnivalized literature are directed towards the elucidation of the particular literary practices of Rabelais and Dostoevsky, his analysis of the roots of carnivalized literature provides a literary-historical context for a reading of Wodehouse's Atlantic novels, and offers insight into the themes and situations developed in them.

Bakhtin traces the origins of carnivalized literature to the serio-comic genres of classical antiquity – Socratic dialogues, bucolic poetry, and Menippean satire – all of which are "saturated with a specific carnival sense of the world."[11] The novel, Bakhtin argues, arose from epic, rhetorical, and carnivalistic roots, the

---

[6] Lorraine Coons and Alexander Varias, *Tourist Third Cabin: Steamship Travel in the Interwar Years.* New York 2003, p. 3.
[7] Robert McCrum, *Wodehouse: A Life*, New York 2006, p. 95.
[8] Bakhtin, *Dostoevsky's Poetics*, p. 107.
[9] Bakhtin, *Rabelais*, p. 4.
[10] Bakhtin, *Dostoevsky's Poetics*, p. 107.
[11] Ibid., p. 107.

latter stream emerging from the Socratic dialogue and Menippean satire, flowing through the carnivalized parodic literature of the middle ages and the great carnivalesque works of the Renaissance epitomized by Rabelais and Cervantes. From the Socratic dialogue carnivalized literature took the notion of the "dialogic nature of human thinking about truth" as opposed to "official monologism, which pretends to possess a ready-made truth."[12] From Menippean satire, it derived a "bold and unrestrained use of the fantastic and adventure" in which the "the content of life was poured into a stable form that possessed an inner logic."[13] It is interesting to note that critics have identified commonalities between Wodehouse's work and the Latin comedy of antiquity, particularly his shared reliance on stock characters.[14] In addition, the internal logic and symmetry of his "beautifully restrained" work has also been widely recognized.[15] Certainly, both the resistance to monologic truth claims and the introduction of whimsical or fantastic elements into a stable literary form are characteristics of Wodehouse's writing: pompous certainty never emerges intact from his novels, and for all their comic energy his stories are as rigorously patterned as any classical drama.

Of perhaps even greater relevance, however, to a reading of Wodehouse's Atlantic novels are the identifying traits of the carnivalesque. According to Bakhtin, one of these is the suspension of the "laws, prohibitions, and restrictions" that structure and order ordinary life, particularly with reference to the hierarchical structures which govern social existence.[16] This allows for the emergence of a "new mode of interrelationship between individuals" based on the "free and familiar contact among people."[17] Another factor is the way carnival connects and even unites "the sacred with the profane, the lofty with the low, the great with the insignificant, the wise with the stupid."[18] The result of this is a laughter which indicates a free and open relationship to a non-determined world about which the "ultimate word" has not been spoken and never will be spoken, a world that is oriented toward an eternal and self-perpetuating freedom.[19] Finally, these carnivalistic impulses are played out, in reality or in fiction, in public spaces, ideally the public square, but also in

---

[12] Ibid., p. 110.
[13] Ibid., p. 114, 119.
[14] George McCracken, "Wodehouse and Latin Comedy", in: *The Classical Journal*, 29 (1934), p. 612-614: 612.
[15] Edward L. Galligan, "P. G. Wodehouse Master of Farce", in: *The Sewanee Review 93* (1985), p. 609-617: 610.
[16] Bakhtin, *Dostoevsky's Poetics*, p. 122.
[17] Ibid., p. 123.
[18] Ibid., p. 123.
[19] Ibid., p. 166.

any meeting point of heterogeneous groups of people such as "streets, taverns, roads, bathhouses," and most significantly for this discussion, "decks of ships."[20]

The Atlantic Crossing: Opportunity and Anxiety

The Atlantic crossing is in many ways a particularly suitable setting for a work of carnivalized literature, for by the early twentieth century this voyage had come to signify a peculiar mixture of opportunity and anxiety. The opportunity was initially associated with the opening, settlement and exploitation of the new world. The steamship companies which ferried Wodehouse, and his characters, back and forth across the Atlantic for purposes of business, cultural exploration and sheer pleasure had their roots in the mass transshipment of European immigrants, 72 million of whom left for North America between 1820 and 1920.[21] While conditions aboard the transatlantic steamers in steerage class were by no means idyllic, they were a monumental improvement on those that had prevailed aboard sailing ships. The steam-powered crossing was brief, and the dream of a new life in the new world awaited. However, if most Atlantic travellers viewed the voyage itself as only an unpleasant but necessary step, others could look forward to the crossing itself as an opportunity for unbridled consumption and unbelievable luxury. Ironically, these first-class passengers were to some degree subsidized by the immigrant masses, who provided the steamship companies with a steady stream of revenue from their fully booked westward passages.[22] Underwritten by the poor, the liners offered incredibly luxurious surroundings in a wild range of styles to privileged first-class passengers, whose enjoyment of this extraordinary level of luxury was widely remarked upon.[23]

Part of the anxiety associated with the Atlantic crossing arose directly from this contrast between wealth and poverty, or more specifically from the simultaneous presence on one ship, and thus in one limited space, of ultra-rich first-class and extremely poor – and ethnically diverse – steerage passengers. While liners were carefully demarcated by both an inflexible social hierarchy and class boundaries which were intended to be permeable in only one direction, anxiety about the

---

[20] Ibid., p. 128.
[21] Coons, Varias, *Tourist Third Cabin*, p. 7.
[22] William H. Miller, Jr., *Picture History of British Ocean Liners, 1900 to Present*, Mineloa 2001, p. 11.
[23] Crosbie Smith, Ian Higginson, and Phillip Wolstenholme. "'Avoiding Equally Extravagance and Parsimony': The Moral Economy of the Ocean Steamship", in: *Technology and Culture 44,* (2003), p. 443-469: 454.

effectiveness of these prophylactic measures was common.[24] To minimize this problem, some British lines went so far as to refuse to carry central European immigrants, and were thus considered a better choice for the hygienically-minded Anglo-Saxon than continental passenger lines less discriminating in their choice of client.[25] Passengers were informed of company regulations against inter-class fraternization, and physical barriers were proposed as a means of combating the problem, but there was no fully effective way of preventing the infiltration of the poor into prohibited areas.[26]

Another significant set of anxieties focused on the possibilities for sexual licentiousness in the confined, unrestrained, and relatively unsupervised setting of the transatlantic liner. These anxieties arose from a number of causes. Firstly, the shipping lines themselves actively sought out independent women travellers, particularly following World War I, and they did so with considerable success: it was not uncommon for a liner to carry twice as many women as men in all classes.[27] While this was no doubt good business, it raised a number of 'moral' issues: wealthy middle-aged widows might prey upon younger men, or young single women prey upon the "unattached male passenger."[28] At its strongest, this anxiety became a fear of prostitutes using the ship as a commercial venue. Third-class female passengers were, for example, subject to a 10 p.m. inspection on Cunard boats to ensure that they were in their cabins rather than on deck soliciting.[29] All of this meant that the ocean liner was perceived as both a site of romantic opportunity and of sexual danger. The adventures of the gold-digging Lorelei Lee on the Majestic in Anita Loos' 1925 Gentlemen Prefer Blondes (immortalized by Marilyn Monroe in Howard Hawks' 1953 adaptation) are a fine example of the social and sexual tension surrounding interwar steamship culture. The existence of these anxieties should alert readers of Wodehouse's Atlantic novels to levels of cultural signification more pronounced than their humorousness might suggest.

---

[24] Coons, Varias, *Tourist Third Cabin,* p. 7, XXII.
[25] R. A. Fletcher, *Traveling Palaces: Luxury in Passenger Steamships*, London 1913, p. 275.
[26] Coons, Varias, *Tourist Third Cabin,* p. 41-43.
[27] Ibid., p. 31-32.
[28] Ibid., p. 32-33.
[29] Ibid., p. 44.

The Girl on the Boat
Transatlantic and Atlantic Readings

Wodehouse's *The Girl on the Boat*, which first appeared in serial form in 1921 in *Women's Home Companion*, is certainly funny. Wodehouse himself felt that "as farce" it was "pretty well all to the mustard," which is to say that it was "darned funny."[30] It can also be read as both a transatlantic and Atlantic novel. By this I mean firstly that it is an example of Wodehouse's typical strategy of offering comic cross-cultural stereotypes to audiences on both sides of the Atlantic. Here we find, for example, an Englishman preparing for a trip to America by practicing with a revolver in order to face the dangers of "the Underworld," and Americans complaining bitterly about England's lack of "ice, central heating, corn-on-the-cob" and "bathrooms," an exchange of querulously humorous preconceptions that would still function today.[31] The novel also opens with a typical feature of Wodehouse's transatlantic mode: Mrs Horace Hignett, English author of theosophical works, is on a lecturing tour to get her share of the "easy-money to be picked up on the lecture platforms of America" by the intellectuals of England, an example of what has been described as "Wodehouse's mid-Atlantic convention," a trade agreement run on "strict profit-and-loss lines" in which each partner "has something which the other half covets desperately."[32] Mrs Hignett's house, Windles – or more accurately her son Eustace's house – is just such an object of transatlantic desire: Mr Bennett, a wealthy American, has been pestering her to rent out the house during her time in America, a notion which Mrs Hignett rejects out of hand. In her eagerness to protect Windles, Mrs Hignett has even stolen her son's trousers to prevent him from attending his own wedding and thus providing a presumptive new mistress.

The Girl on the Boat is thus clearly concerned with transatlantic themes. In addition, it also activates the carnivalesque energies of the Atlantic crossing. It might in fact be described as a transatlantic novel enclosing an Atlantic carnivalesque novella. In the transatlantic portion of the novel, by preventing her son's marriage through the symbolic emasculation of trouser-theft, Mrs Higgnet demonstrates the "theory of the aunts," which argues that for Wodehouse

---

[30] P. G. Wodehouse, *A Life in Letters,* Sophie Ratcliffe (Ed.), Hutchinson 2011, p. 127, 129.
[31] P. G. Wodehouse, *The Girl on the Boat,* New York 2007, p. 111, 125.
[32] Ibid., p. 12.; Green, *Wodehouse,* p. 76.

authority is generally vested in the figure of the elderly female.³³ This incident is thus an example of the type of official dominance that the carnivalesque exists to subvert, and it allows Wodehouse to establish the oppressive rule against which the shipboard carnival will react. Mrs Hignett sends her disgraced son back to England aboard the Atlantic, along with his cousin Sam Marlowe, and it is from this point that the novel begins to develop its carnivalesque tendencies. Although Hignett and Marlowe's adventures on board occupy a limited portion of the narrative, they offer a strong contrast to the social worlds of both America and England: life aboard the Atlantic is qualitatively different to life on land.

This difference is marked in a number of ways in *The Girl on the Boat*. The transition from land to sea is first mediated by the transitional space of "the cavernous Customs sheds" through which Sam Marlowe must force his way "by employing all the muscle and energy which Nature had bestowed upon him," a formulation which arguably emphasizes the difficulty of escaping the conventions and restrictions of ordinary life.³⁴ However, once the setting of the novel has shifted, the ship seems at first to offer little more than a floating replica of the hierarchical and authoritarian social word of normal life. For example, the crew is carefully delineated into "sailors" as opposed to "junior officers" as opposed to "white-jacketed stewards," all of whom operate under the captain's authority.³⁵ However, the captain is notable by his absence: "Probably, the captain," the narrator speculates, "though not visible, was also employed on some useful work."³⁶ As historians of liner culture have pointed out, these ships attempted to offer a "reflection of the old feudal order" through the maintenance of a strict social hierarchy amongst both passengers and crew.³⁷ Yet as the conspicuous absence of the captain from Wodehouse's novel implies, it was difficult to preserve a land-based social order during a crossing when "ship life was pure escapism for both passengers and crew."³⁸ It may be true that class is "inscribed in modes of transport" through the physical demarcation of space, but this is an inscription that demands unceasing and potentially unavailing effort to police.³⁹ It is difficult to maintain distinctions between hierarchical levels within limited spaces, and this is all the more true when the apex of the hierarchy is missing.

---

33 Francis Donaldson, *P. G. Wodehouse, A Biography,* New York 1982, p. 97.
34 Wodehouse, *Girl on the Boat*, p. 25.
35 Ibid.
36 Ibid., p. 25.
37 Coons, Varias, *Tourist Third Cabin,* p. xix, xxii.
38 Ibid., p. 50.
39 David Simpson, "Tourism and Titanomania" in: *Critical Inquiry 25* (1999), p. 680-695: 681.

The transition from land to sea in *The Girl on the Boat* is characterized as not just a simple movement away from hierarchical authority, however, but as a form of mysterious transformation: cabins, for example, are "curious things" that have different dimensions when viewed from land and from sea, swelling and shrinking as perspectives shift.[40] On shore, in the passenger-office, they seem spacious; then they shrink when first encountered, only to expand again with familiarity. And this sense of transformation is very much what the Atlantic offers its passengers: an opportunity for the change, play, development and rebellion that are absent from dry-land, ordinary, non-carnival life. While I will be tracing these transformations in more detail in the pages that follow, it is worth pointing out here that once the crossing is over, the rules and regulations of mundane life reassert themselves. Immediately after arriving at Southampton, Sam goes, for no good reason, to Bingley-on-the-Sea, an English town which is a hyperbolically dreadful synecdoche for the land as a whole. Even the "very waves that break on its shingle seem to creep up the beach reluctantly, as if it revolted them to have to come to such a place," a disgust that may be more readily comprehensible when we realize that the great lesson the land offers the newly arrived travellers is that "life is real, life is earnest."[41] This is a sentiment that the carnivalized shipboard sensibility can do nothing but reject.

The Carnivalization of Authority

The frame Wodehouse provides for the Atlantic crossing thus prepares us to encounter a space of transformative possibility and freedom from authority on board the Atlantic; "a life," in Bakhtin's phrase, "turned inside out."[42] This transformation takes place in a number of ways: through the rejection of parental authority, through the challenging of gender-based hierarchies and roles, and, perhaps most significantly, through a consistent, repeated inversion or conflation of elevated and debased values.

The rejection of parental authority, or in Wodehouse's work of the tyranny of the aunts, is carried out through the novel's romantic plotting. As we have seen, the ocean liner was construed as a site of simultaneous sexual opportunity and danger. Northrop Frye has argued that resistance to parental disproval of youthful "erotic intrigue" is a key element in the structure of the comic, and this is certainly the case here.[43] It is worth noting that *The Girl on the Boat* is one of the few places

---

[40] Wodehouse, *Girl on the Boat*, p. 28.
[41] Ibid., p. 107, 115.
[42] Bakhtin, *Dostoevsky's Poetics,* p. 122.
[43] Northrop Frye, *Anatomy of Criticism*, London 1990, p. 44.

in Wodehouse's oeuvre in which genuine parents, rather than aunts and uncles, are found: as William Vesterman has pointed out, the presence of an actual parent involves issues of filial duty limiting to comic vivacity.[44] Yet in this case, the presence of the parents is critical in establishing a state of authoritarian domination against which the carnivalesque can react.

Eustace Hignett, as we have seen, is under the control of his mother, particularly in terms of his love life. On board, however, he meets and falls in love with Jane Hubbard, in clear defiance of his mother's mercenary aversion to his forming romantic attachments. Similarly, Hignett's former fiancé Wilhelmina Bennett (stood up at the altar due to Hignett's lack of trousers) has long been regarded by one Mortimer Bream as his destined mate. But Bream is far too closely aligned with the world of parental authority for romantic success: he is in the words of Wilhelmina's father "a thoroughly estimable young man," and any man in Wodehouse's world who wins the approval of a parent is justly doomed.[45] Bream is repeatedly described as looking "much more like a parrot than most parrots do," and like a parrot he is unable to speak for himself. Instead, he merely repeats that which the world tells him to say.[46] Only on shipboard can Wilhelmina find her true companion, Sam Marlowe. The two relationships that are established on board the Atlantic are both the motors of the novel's plot – once the ship has docked, the rest of *The Girl on the Boat* concerns first the reassertion, and then the gradual overcoming of, parental disapproval – and indicators of the suspension of authority within the carnivalesque atmosphere of the Atlantic crossing.

Some critics have condemned Wodehouse's handling of romance: "Some of his early stories," Roger Kimball writes, "attempt to include a love interest" but the result is "always embarrassing."[47] In fact, Wodehouse's novels almost always include a romantic plot, indeed several, but they are generally treated with an extreme lightness of touch and a lack of seriousness that makes them appear unimportant. However, in *The Girl on the Boat*, the inclusion of romantic elements is far from being trivial or an embarrassing failure. It is essential for the development of the novel's carnivalesque themes.

---

[44] William Vesterman, "Plum Time in Nevereverland: The Divine Comedy of P. G. Wodehouse" in: *Raritan – A Quarterly Review 25* (2005), p. 92-113: 99.
[45] Wodehouse, *Girl on the Boat*, p. 184.
[46] Ibid., p. 19.
[47] Robert Kimball, "The genius of Wodehouse", in: *The New Criterion 19* (2000), Web, http://www.newcriterion.com/articles.cfm/wodehouse-kimball-2327, accessed 20 Feb 2012.

The Carnivalization of Gender Roles

Established gender roles also face carnivalesque inversion. The first indication that *The Girl on the Boat* will unsettle traditional social demarcations between men and women arises from its use of names. Eustace Hignett has been engaged to Wilhelmina Bennett, and while their relationship was comically brief, a firm intention to marry indicates a certain personal familiarity. Yet Eustace knows his ex-fiancée as "Wilhelmina Bennett," which is the same name that the egregious Bream Mortimer refers to her by.[48] As far as the reader is concerned, on land this formally feminine name, for surely one of the things a name like Wilhelmina draws attention to is its feminized nature, is Miss Bennett's proper appellation. But when Sam Marlowe meets his future bride on board the Atlantic, she introduces herself as "'Wilhelmina Bennett. My friends,' she said softly as she turned away, 'call me Billie!'"[49] Although gender-neutral, Billie is more commonly used as a man's name than a woman's. Sam muses over this name in a way that both stresses its difference from Wilhelmina, and draws the reader's attention to it:

> "He was sorry for poor old Eustace, but he really could not permit the suggestion that Wilhelmina Bennett – her friends called her Billie – had not behaved in a perfectly splendid way throughout. It was women like Wilhelmina Bennett – Billie to her intimates – who made the world worth living in.
> Her friends called her Billie. He did not blame them. It was a delightful name and suited her to perfection. He practised it a few times. 'Billie. . . Billie. . . Billie. . .' It certainly ran pleasantly off the tongue. 'Billie Bennett.' Very musical. 'Billie Marlowe.' Still better. 'We noticed among those present the charming and popular Mrs. 'Billie' Marlowe . . ."[50]

The repetition of 'Billie' nine times in this short passage highlights the unusual masculinity of Billie Bennett's shipboard name. Eustace, whose romance with Billie was conducted outside of the carnivalesque atmosphere of the Atlantic, does not even recognize 'Billie' as his ex-fiancée's name, indignantly correcting Sam: "'Wilhelmina Bennett. Where on earth did you get the idea that her name was Billie?'"[51] The girl on the boat in *The Girl on the Boat* is Billie, by name a

---

[48] Wodehouse, *Girl on the Boat*, p. 30.
[49] Ibid., p. 48.
[50] Ibid., p. 50
[51] Ibid., p. 51.

different person from the girl on land, Wilhelmina. In many ways, however, Wilhelmina-on-shore and Billie-at-sea share stereotypically feminine qualities. She despises "weak men," and is romantically inclined towards the "strong and brave and wonderful."[52] Yet Billie certainly behaves with greater freedom on ship than Wilhelmina does on shore, and is described in stereotypically masculine ways, "striding along the deck with the breeze playing in her vivid hair like the female equivalent of a Viking."[53] However, these moments are relatively rare, and we must look further to find a stronger example of carnivalesque gender inversion and questioning of monolithic gender categories.

Billie's new shipboard friend Jane Hubbard – and one may doubt if such a friendship could have arisen on shore – is a "splendid specimen of bronzed, strapping womanhood" who is also a big-game hunter.[54] Even without the resounding 'manliness' of this profession, the description of her as a splendid specimen of strapping womanhood would be enough to alert readers to her transgressive status, for splendid and strapping specimens are linguistically construed as male. Jane's romantic desire is also transgressive, an inverted version of Billie's longing for a manly man. When she finds herself deep in the jungle on the track of some inoffensive beast destined by a cruel fate to decorate her wall, Jane dreams "of some gentle clinging man who would put his hand in mine and tell me all his poor little troubles and let me pet and comfort him and bring the smiles back to his face."[55] This is a clear inversion of the socially-accepted male-female relationship. Given the open affront to conventional gender roles Jane represents in the novel, it may not be an act of excessive exegetical energy to point out that her surname, Hubbard, is linguistically proximate to husband, the figure whose role she will eventually perform in her relationship with the emasculated and ineffectual writer of vers libre, Eustace Hignett. While the blurring of gender roles in evidence during the Atlantic crossing both precedes the crossing – remember Hignett's dominating mother – and persists once the characters have arrived in England, these disruptive energies are at their fullest during the brief but significant period on board the Atlantic.

The Carnivalization of Value

The rejection of parental authority and the questioning of received gender roles in *The Girl on the Boat* are accompanied by a conflation of high and low values.

---

[52] Ibid., p. 76.
[53] Ibid., p. 56.
[54] Ibid., p. 75.
[55] Ibid., p. 76-77.

By this I mean that socially accepted evaluative binary pairs, what Claude Lévi-Strauss would describe as unequal diametric social structures, such as age versus youth or pure versus impure, are confused and challenged in the carnivalesque atmosphere of *The Girl on the Boat*'s Atlantic crossing.[56] Take, for instance, the tropes of chivalric heroism and courtly love, and the ways that they are consistently undercut in the novel. Sam and Billie's first meeting on board the ship (they have previously met in the Customs sheds when Billie's dog bites Sam) occurs as a result of an act of mock heroism. As the Atlantic pulls away from the quayside in New York, Billie's father's clerk attempts to toss a package of cash (for travelling expenses) to her. Inevitably, the package falls short, bursts open, and deposits its contents into the water. This is, incidentally, in itself another sign of the weakening of parental authority, for the strongest, if not the only, parent-child bond in the world of Wodehouse tends to be financial. Sensing a once-in-a-lifetime opportunity, a denizen of the harbor-front leaps in to fish out the money. When viewed from the departing ship, this looks like an emergency, and as a crowd gathers at the railings to await the outcome, Sam realises that this is "a wonderful chance of making the most tremendous impression" on this beautiful girl.[57] All he would have to do is dive overboard and swim to the rescue, "and there were men," he thinks, "who would be chumps enough to do it."[58] Sam is no hero, and it is only the literal propulsion of an unexpected blow in the back that sends him tumbling over the side of the ship to meet his romantic destiny. From Billie's perspective, of course, Sam has behaved with extraordinary courage, fulfilling her fantasies of a heroic man "like the stories of knights who used to jump into lions' dens after gloves," a reference to Friedrich Schiller's ballad "Der Handschuh" or "The Glove".[59] In Schiller's poem, Sir Delorges is genuinely heroic, but disdainfully rejects Cunigund's romantic rewards; in Wodehouse's version Sam is only mock-heroic and is only too happy to accept his unearned prize.

Billie's misinterpretation of Sam's leap is but the first instance of a sustained inversion of chivalric values. Eustace, for example, complains that Billie wanted him to separate two fighting dogs on one occasion during their courtship. His refusal is compared, again, to a standard of chivalric behavior: "Sir Galahad would have done it like a shot," a comparison that conflates chivalric heroism

---

[56] Claude Lévi-Strauss, *Structural Anthropology*, Claire Jacobson and Brooker Grundfest Schoepf (Trans.), Garden City 1967, p. 135-136.
[57] Wodehouse, *Girl on the Boat*, p. 35.
[58] Ibid., p. 35.
[59] Ibid., p. 45.

with the ludicrous attempts of a man to intervene in a dog fight.[60] Billie is not unique; she is, as Allan Ramsay has pointed out, a member of the "species of Wodehouse heroine who [...] sees courtship primarily as a series of knightly tests to be accomplished by her betrothed."[61] While these mock-chivalric occurrences continue throughout the novel – Sam ends the novel, in fact, with a knight's helmet firmly stuck on his head – the point has, I think, been made. This is an instance of what Bakhtin describes as the "the carnivalistic nature of parody," of a laughter directed "toward something higher."[62]

Before moving on to the second substantial target of *The Girl on the Boat*'s parody, romantic love, it is worth noting that carnivalized laughter is, according to Bakhtin, "deeply ambivalent."[63] On the one hand it ridicules its object, exposing it to the withering force of unrestrained laughter. On the other hand, however, carnivalized laughter is a rejuvenating force that allows, or forces, the objects of its mockery to "renew themselves."[64] Carnivalized parody does not reject its object, but transforms and revivifies it through a purifying laughter, a force which strips away accretions of convention and falsity while preserving or refreshing the genuine nature of its target: its laughter "revives and renews."[65] Thus a Wodehouse text can parody the conventions of romantic love while simultaneously acting out a fantasy of its fulfillment. This perspective offers a potential rebuttal to critics who believe that Wodehouse is capable of dealing with love in only "superficial terms": while he certainly does not, as some remark, explore the realm of the carnal, his carnivalized parody of romance is in a way a powerful affirmation of its value.[66]

Broadly speaking, *The Girl on the Boat* as a whole could be read as a romantic parody, but there are specific elements of the Atlantic crossing that mock the afflatus of romance with particular energy. In the first romantic scene between Sam and Billie, for instance, Sam, attempting to find a conversational opening for a proposal of marriage, comments rather mundanely upon the weather, a tactic the "goofily talkative" narrator describes as ubiquitous:[67]

---

[60] Ibid., p. 55.
[61] Ramsay, "Green Baize Door", p. 40.
[62] Bakhtin, *Dostoevsky's Poetics,* p. 127.
[63] Ibid., p. 126.
[64] Ibid., p. 127.
[65] Bakhtin, *Rabelais,* p. 11.
[66] Ramsay, "Green Baize Door", p. 40.
[67] David Heddendorf, "When Plummie Met Sally", in: *Sewanee Review 118* (2010), p. 411-416: 413.

> "How strange it is that the great emotional scenes of history, one of which is coming along almost immediately, always begin in this prosaic way. Shakespeare tries to conceal the fact, but there can be little doubt that Romeo and Juliet edged into their balcony scene with a few remarks on the pleasantness of the morning."[68]

This passage enacts an abrupt collision of high romance with the most mundane elements of life, contrasting romantic intention with conversational necessity, Sam and Billie's love with Romeo and Juliet's, in a juxtaposition of two very different intensities of emotion and text type. The dialogue that follows continues the pattern. Every time Sam offers a romantic platitude, Billie's reply inadvertently undermines the romantic seriousness he is attempting to achieve. When he speaks of pouring out "the stored-up devotion of a lifetime" at the feet of the one he loves, in other words Billie, her reply collapses romantic seriousness into a parody of its pretensions: "How jolly for her. Like having a circus all to oneself."[69] This is not the expected reply, in spite of the fact that Billie herself is feeling more than a little romantic towards Sam; the novel's carnivalistic energies overtake its characters and drive them onwards. Similarly, Eustace, although as deeply in love as it is possible for a sensitive verse libre poet to be, and that is very deeply indeed, is unable to limit his rhetoric to a consistently elevated, romantic register:

> "'Nothing,' said Eustace Hignett gravely, 'could make me do that [forget Jane Hubbard]. Our souls have blended. Our beings have called to one another from their deepest depths, saying [...] There are your pyjamas, over in the corner [...] saying "You are mine!" How could I forget her after that?'"[70]

At his moment of greatest romantic inspiration, Eustace falls flatly back into ordinary life: few things, after all, could be less romantic than pyjamas.

It is perhaps worth reiterating that while the shipboard sections of *The Girl on the Boat* certainly do expose romance to the disruptive energies of a carnivalesque sensibility, this does not mean that romance is thereby diminished or dismissed. On the contrary, the romantic energies ignited by the crossing, by the lack of social control, by the very inversions of value and status that affect romance itself continue to shape the dry-land portions of the novel. On land, the shipboard romances are faced with a reassertion of normal social values and assessments, and eventually overcome these obstacles to find fulfillment in a typical romantic

---

[68] Wodehouse, *Girl on the Boat*, p. 65.
[69] Ibid., p. 68.
[70] Ibid., p. 104.

ending. To expose a value to carnivalistic laughter is not to destroy it, but to mock it and elevate it simultaneously.

The Carnivalization of Discourse

This may be most clear from Wodehouse's use of differing levels of discourse. This is a feature of his work that has been widely remarked upon. Allan Ramsay, for example, notes the presence of a tremendous range of "literary quotation, and deliberate misquotation and juxtaposition" from the classics, the Bible, Shakespeare, and the canonical works of English poetry.[71] Another critic has pointed out that quotation is the "dominant characteristic" of Wodehouse's Jeeves and Wooster series, an observation that could be extended beyond one particular set of Wodehouse's works.[72] It is instead a feature of all of his stories and novels. At the very least it is one of the more prominent features of his style, one which makes, incidentally, translation of his work particularly difficult.[73] The sort of linguistic playfulness I am discussing here, then, is not limited to the shipboard scenes in Wodehouse's Atlantic novels. Instead, it must be viewed as one of the networks of reversals, inversions, and conflations that together make up the carnival atmosphere of the Atlantic. We have already seen two examples of this linguistic assimilation in *The Girl on the Boat* in the chivalrous and romantic dislocation of Schiller's "The Glove" and Shakespeare's Romeo and Juliet. And what we have seen in both cases is that the literary work alluded to is used, as we might expect from the fact that it occurs during the Atlantic crossing, in a transformative context. The relevance of this feature of Wodehouse's work to a discussion of its carnivalesque elements is clear: one of the objects of carnivalization is discourse, or, more specifically, the tendency to attribute hierarchical value to different types of language.

Further instances abound in *The Girl on the Boat*, and it will be worth examining at least one instance in detail in order to see precisely how it works to efface the notional line separating high and low cultural registers. A climactic romantic misunderstanding takes place during the ship's concert: Sam performs – or rather attempts with catastrophic lack of success – what is announced in the program as "A Little Imitation."[74] The narrative frames this scene by collapsing disparate levels of discourse into the same textual space:

---

[71] Ramsay, "Green Baize Door", p. 355.
[72] Mary Lydon, "First Love: Reading with P. G. Wodehouse", in: *Profession* (1994), p. 21-25: 23.
[73] Ramsay, "Green Baize Door", p. 353.
[74] Wodehouse, *Girl on the Boat*, p. 90.

"All over the saloon you could see fair women and brave men wilting in their seats. Imitation […]! The word, as Keats would have said, was like a knell! Many of these people were old travellers, and their minds went back wincingly, as one recalls forgotten wounds, to occasions when performers at ship's concerts had imitated whole strings of Dickens' characters, or, with the assistance of a few hats and a little false hair, had endeavoured to portray Napoleon, Bismarck, Shakespeare, and other of the famous dead."[75]

This seemingly simple passage reveals an extraordinary density of quotation and allusion embedded in the farcical context of the ship's concert. To begin with, this audience is not merely a group of passengers waiting dutifully for the "grim work" of amateur performers.[76] It is simultaneously a group of revelers in Brussels awaiting the battle of Waterloo, the "fair women and brave men" of Byron's Childe Harold's Pilgrimage.[77] The explicit reference to Keats links the audience's expectation of an entertainment in appalling taste to "gallant Sidney's, Russell's, Vane's sad knell," all three of whom were executed for treason after the Restoration.[78] This is followed by a string of references to literary and political figures, conflating the "famous dead" of a lofty and elevated past with the trivial moment of the present, a present that will momentarily involve Sam Marlowe appearing in blackface in an imitation of Frank Tinney, famous vaudeville comedian: "a worse thing had befallen" the audience "than even they had looked for," the narrator informs us with another allusion, in this case to Job 3:25 and to Milton's Samson Agonistes.[79] The worse thing here is of course not the egregious racial politics of this rather common form of shipboard entertainment, but its appallingly low quality.[80] Suffering through this terrible performance is tantamount to the sufferings of Job or the blinding of Samson.

This passage offers the reader a different experience than, for instance, a direct quotation from Shakespeare or another classic author put into the mouth of a character. Here, the very fabric of the discourse is woven out of a weft of literary

---

[75] Ibid.
[76] Ibid., p. 89.
[77] Lord Byron, "Childe Harold's Pilgrimage" in: *The Major Works including Don Juan and Childe Harold's Pilgrimage,* Oxford 2008, p. 19-206: 110.
[78] John Keats, "Lines Written on 29 May The Anniversary of the Restoration of Charles the 2nd" in: *The Complete Poems,* London 1988, p. 44.
[79] Wodehouse, *Girl on the Boat*, p. 92.
[80] Cecilia Morgan, *'A Happy Holiday': English Canadians and Transatlantic Tourism, 1870 – 1930,* Toronto 2008, p. 43-44.

high-culture allusion and a warp of farcical humor. Mary Lydon has argued that Wodehouse's use of quotation relies upon the reader's ability, first, to recognize the sources from which he takes his material, and then to note that the familiar material is "out of context" and thus "paradoxically defamiliarized."[81] Of course, as Wodehouse's references tend to be to the "Edwardian schoolboy canon," fewer and fewer readers are actually able to place, or even notice, many of his allusions.[82] Furthermore, some critics emphasize the breadth and range of Wodehouse's allusive practices, arguing that they extend well beyond the public school corpus.[83] Both of these factors make the required recognition a task of some difficulty. This is certainly true, but the familiarity need not be with specific literary works. As Michael Riffaterre has argued, readers need not be aware of the specific intertexts to any given work, but simply of the fact of their existence.[84] When Wodehouse's narrator wants his readers to know exactly what is going on, he is more than happy to help them, for example by providing translations of Latin tags for "the benefit of those who have not, like myself, enjoyed an expensive classical education."[85] However, in most cases, it suffices for the reader to be broadly attuned to levels of discourse, so as to be able to recognize the fact that widely dispersed cultural strata are being brought into collision in *The Girl on the Boat* as part of a "web of idiom and quotation," a clash which contributes to the novel's carnivalesque sensibility.[86]

The Luck of the Bodkins

The Carnivalization of Social Roles

Wodehouse's *The Luck of the Bodkins* is in some ways very similar to *The Girl on the Boat*, most obviously in that it is also set aboard the SS Atlantic, but it develops and extends the carnivalesque themes of its predecessor. This is the only one of Wodehouse's novels that is set almost exclusively at sea. It narrates the shipboard tribulations of Monty Bodkin, Reggie Tennyson and his brother Ambrose, who during the crossing become romantically involved with Gertrude Butterwick, Lottie 'Lotus' Blossom, and Mabel Spence, while movie-magnate

---

[81] Lydon, "First Love", p. 23.
[82] Joseph Bottum, "God & Bertie Wooster" in: *First Things* October (2005), p. 23-27: 27.
[83] Heddendorf, "When Plummie Met Sally", p. 414.
[84] Michael Riffaterre, "Syllepsis", in: *Critical Inquiry* 6 (1980), p. 625-638: 626.
[85] Wodehouse, *Girl on the Boat*, p. 225.
[86] Lydon, "First Love", p. 25.

Ivor Llewellyn attempts to smuggle his wife's pearl necklace through customs. Rather than integrating an Atlantic carnival into a novel otherwise concerned with the comic juxtapositions of American and English culture, *The Luck of the Bodkins* addresses itself directly and almost exclusively to the carnivalization of experience that is possible during the Atlantic crossing. A great deal of this carnival spirit circles around one character in the novel, Albert Peasemarch, bedroom steward to Monty Bodkin, who contributes to the unsettling of both social hierarchies and language itself. Peasemarch has been described as "one of the richest characters in the whole of the Wodehouse creation, absolutely rounded and quite without flaw."[87] He also embodies quite clearly certain principles of the carnivalesque.

As we have seen, the shipboard carnivalesque of *The Girl on the Boat* challenges parental authority, and thus more broadly construed social hierarchies. A similar form of carnivalization occurs in *The Luck of the Bodkins*, but here the challenge to authority occurs in terms of class rather than in terms of generation. One instance of this occurs during a surreptitious meeting between Monty and Lottie which takes place, significantly, on the second-class promenade deck. Reggie Tennyson is clear on the benefits of this arrangement: "First-class passengers don't go strolling all over the second-class," a fact that will preserve the secrecy of the meeting.[88] But in the carnivalized atmosphere of the Atlantic, this is exactly what first-class passengers do, and Monty is caught by his fiancée Gertrude, with the unwitting, or witless, assistance of Peasemarch.

Despite his participation in this particular contravention of the ship's physical hierarchy, Peasemarch is an eager participant in a clearly demarcated class system. As a first-class steward he is hierarchically superior to second- and third-class stewards due to his proximity to and contact with the rich and famous, roles fulfilled in this novel by the wealthy dilettante Monty Bodkin and the movie star Lottie Blossom.[89] He would in all likelihood also consider himself superior to, and in turn be despised by, the rest of the crew, who tended to view stewards as effeminate and unmanly.[90] Stewards' relations with the passengers were in turn shaped by company regulations designed to reinforce class barriers: they were, for instance, "advised to refrain from idle conversation with passengers."[91] In addition, their wages were comparatively meager, as they were expected to supplement their incomes through tips, a practice that encouraged them to "grovel

---

[87] Ramsay, "Green Baize Door", p. 43.
[88] Wodehouse, *Luck of the Bodkins*, p. 246.
[89] Coons, Varias, *Tourist Third Cabin,* p. 79.
[90] Ibid., p. 76-77.
[91] Ibid., p. 71.

to and ingratiate themselves" with their passengers.[92] A first-class steward was thus very much a product of the class-system, reliant on it for both status and income.

Yet Peasemarch seems immune to these pressures. When he first meets Monty Bodkin, he regards him with "a certain disapproval" which leaves Monty feeling distinctly uncomfortable.[93] This is Monty's first crossing, "so he had no means of estimating from past experience what was the average mean or norm of geniality in stewards, but surely, he felt, he was entitled to expect more chumminess."[94] That is to say that given the existing class relations that should structure their attitudes and behavior towards each other, Peasemarch's rude and unpleasant conduct is inexplicable: this is not the appropriate or normal behavior of a man constrained by rule and financial self-interest to make up to his social superiors. Peasemarch goes further, reprimanding Monty (unjustly) for having defaced his bathroom walls with a message written in lipstick. Peasemarch is well aware that in doing so he is contravening the normal social order: "I fear you may think it a liberty, me talking like this," he confesses, but this only the beginning of a carnivalization of social roles that quickly levels any traditional distinctions between Peasemarch and his erstwhile masters.[95] He insists that he could have been Monty's father, based somewhat improbably on their relative ages, and persists in providing ethical guidelines: "you ought not to do that sort of thing."[96] Even Monty, stunned as he is by Peasemarch's incredible transgressions of the social code, eventually attempts to reassert hierarchical norms:

"'Thank you,' repeated Monty, '(a) steward, for telling me the story of your bally life –'
'Only to pleased, sir.'
'– and (b), steward, for giving me the benefit of your dashed valuable advice.'"[97]

Monty's sarcasm is wasted, as Peasemarch continues throughout the Atlantic crossing to cross all of the barriers that normally act to separate society into discrete, hierarchical strata. He is a pure agent of the Bakhtinian carnival, an embodiment of "the working out, in a concretely sensuous, half-real and half-

---

[92] Ibid., p. 77.
[93] Wodehouse, *Luck of the Bodkins*, p. 86.
[94] Ibid., p. 86-87.
[95] Ibid., p. 89.
[96] Ibid., p. 90.
[97] Ibid., p. 98.

play-acted form, a new mode of interrelationship between individuals" which Bakhtin describes as its function.[98]

What makes this especially clear is the way in which Peasemarch consistently frames his relationship with his passengers in terms of feudal hierarchy. According to Peasemarch, for the duration of the voyage his relations to Monty are "those of master and man," or, in his own archaic terminology, "vassal and [...] feudal overlord."[99] This is not an uncommon trope in Wodehouse's fiction: one of the better known Jeeves and Wooster novels, for example, is entitled Jeeves and the Feudal Spirit. One critic has argued that this concept is central to Wodehouse's fiction, identifying it with "a natural and semipaternal social hierarchy, one cemented by reciprocal personal loyalties with duties extending above, below, and sideways."[100] According to this reading, the Wodehousian feudal spirit – which must be carefully distinguished from any sort of historical feudal spirit, to which it is unlikely to bear any resemblance – is a positive phenomenon. Jeeves, for example, "knows his place and never resents it" because his 'place' is a social rather than personal phenomenon.[101] To say that Jeeves is Bertie's "personal gentleman's gentleman" no more defines him as an individual than to say that he is a brother or son: it is a social role entailing rights and responsibilities that he inhabits in relation to other people, not an essential part of who he is.[102] Yet even if we accept this relatively benign vision of the functioning of social hierarchy, Peasemarch's behavior consistently upsets or inverts the relationship to which he commits himself. Rather than serving his 'master' and easing his path, Peasemarch complicates his life through a horrible series of indiscretions and inaccuracies. This can be productively contrasted with the behavior of Jeeves, who, for instance, would simply never be capable of such literary enormities as misattributing Felicia Dorothea Hermans' egregious and frequently parodied ballad of nautical heroism Casabianca, better known by its first line "The Boy Stood on the Burning Deck", to Tennyson.[103] If Peasemarch embodies a feudal relation, he does so in a carnivalized fashion. Throughout the Jeeves and Wooster series, Jeeves is always extremely reluctant to embark on a

---

[98] Bakhtin, *Dostoevsky's Poetics,* p. 123.
[99] Ibid., p. 89.
[100] Vesterman, "Plum Time in Nevereverland", p. 97.
[101] Ibid., p. 94.
[102] P. G. Wodehouse, "Jeeves and the Kid Clementina", in: *The World of Jeeves,* London 2008, p. 572-594: 586.
[103] Jean-Jacques Leclercle, "Parody as Cultural Memory", in: *REAL: Yearbook of Research in English and American Studies 21* (2005), p. 31-44: 40.

steamship; given the carnivalization of status that seems inevitable onboard, this is perhaps understandable.

The Carnivalization of Language

Some critics have recognized that Wodehouse's work is fundamentally about language; Lydon, for instance, identifies Wodehouse as a writer pre-eminently interested in the networks of literary and linguistic codes.[104] In this vein, it can be argued that *The Luck of the Bodkins* is about, more than anything else, language, and more specifically the carnivalization of language, and, by extension, that the primary object of Wodehouse's Atlantic carnivalesque is language itself. This is, in part, the sort of linguistic dislocation which occurs in *The Girl on the Boat* when varying levels of discourse are unexpectedly brought into conjunction. In *The Luck of the Bodkins*, however, much of this carnivalized discourse is placed in the mouth of a character rather than being part of the heterodiegetic narration. This is a typical feature of Wodehouse's high period. Take, for instance, the extraordinarily literate Jeeves who is able to provide an apposite quotation from the classics for any occasion, in contrast with Bertie Wooster's sub-literate, slangy and garbled dialogue. In *The Luck of the Bodkins*, this collision between high and low levels of discourse is embodied, again, in Albert Peasemarch.

This does not occur only through the use and misuse of quotation and allusion, although the misattribution of "The Boy Stood on the Burning Deck" to both Tennyson (by Peasemarch) and Shakespeare (by Monty Bodkin) certainly indicates that this sort of high- and low- cultural collision is certainly going on. In addition, however, *The Luck of the Bodkins* is shaped by a collision between widely different speech registers. Peasemarch tends to speak in a carefully maintained formal register, but he regularly lapses into colloquial idiom. Take the following passage, which has already been discussed as an example of the inversion of social hierarchies, as an example:

> "Until the ship docks in New York harbour our relations are those of master and man. In my dealings with any of the blokes in my sheds – any of the gentlemen who occupy the staterooms under my charge, I always say to myself that for the duration of the voyage I am a vassal and he is – temporarily – my feudal overlord."[105]

Peasemarch's 'elevated' language is not the blending of quotation from and allusion to the classics of Western literature that we saw in *The Girl on the Boat*; instead, it is the pretentiously refined language of the textbook, the academy and

---

[104] Lydon, "First Love", p. 24.
[105] Wodehouse, *Luck of the Bodkins*, p. 89.

the corporate workplace: it is the type of language that would be recommended in handbooks such as "Useful Hints for Stewards" that were issued by steamship companies.[106] But intermittently breaking through the desiccated surface of this official language is a second register of slang and idiomatic speech. Under normal circumstances, these registers would be kept widely separate, belonging to different characters or at least to different situations. Jeeves, for instance, would never use colloquial language, and no more would Wodehouse's range of marginal characters – small time crooks, bookies, gamblers – use official language. Even on shipboard, one register belongs below decks, one above. On the Atlantic, however, this separation fails, and the two linguistic registers are superimposed.

The expected social value of these registers is also questioned: Peasemarch tends to refer, when relaxed, to the various members of the ship's crew by their nicknames. The head waiter is "Scupperguts," the second steward in "the Dooser," and so on.[107] Before long, Monty Bodkins is also referring to these staff members by their nicknames, in an unsuccessful attempt to ingratiate himself with Peasemarch. The linguistic current is flowing in the wrong direction in this instance, as the carnivalized speech of Peasemarch spreads throughout the ship. On other occasions, characters who should be able to use formal language are simply unable to do so. An angered Reggie Tennyson defends his right to speak freely by arguing that "one is scarcely called upon to feel that one requires a formal invitation to induce one to give it as one's opinion that one […] now I've forgotten what I was going to say."[108] In a carnivalized environment, language refuses to remain in its ordinary channels.

The Carnivalization of Communication

The Luck of the Bodkins opens with a scene of letter writing, as Monty struggles first to obtain the needful tools in his schoolboy French, and then to overcome his "unreadiness […] as a correspondent." [109] The novel thus begins by highlighting two ways in which language can resist its communicative function; Monty can no more communicate effectively in French than he can match the written word, even in his native language, to perceived reality. And once on board the Atlantic, the plot hinges around a series of romantic and professional misunderstandings, many of which have a communicative root. Ivor Llewellyn, for instance, is

---

[106] Coons, Varias, *Tourist Third Cabin,* p. 71.
[107] Wodehouse, *Luck of the Bodkins*, p. 99.
[108] Ibid., p. 185.
[109] Ibid., p. 8.

convinced that Monty Bodkin is a Customs agent attempting to arrest him for smuggling his wife's pearl necklace into America. This misunderstanding, which fuels a good portion of the plot's comic arrangements and rearrangements, arises in part because of Monty's inability to spell: his repeated approaches to Llewellyn for assistance in spelling are interpreted as the low cunning of the professional detective rather than the utterances of a man mastered by language. These minor linguistic errors, for we are looking here at the smallest unit of written language, the letter, in turn fuel a series of plot developments ranging from attempts at bribery to broken employment contracts. If this seemingly simple dislocation of language drives the professional side of the plot – which means little more than the attempts of the characters to lay their hands on enough money to realize their romantic ambitions – other failures of communication complicate its romantic side.

Monty and Gertrude move through the novel in an intricate romantic dance, happily engaged at one moment and bitterly estranged the next, and these changes stem from a series of mis-writings and mis-readings. Their first break-up is caused by a single written word, as revealed in this almost impenetrable dialogue:

"'Then who's Sue?'
'Who's Sue?'
'Who's Sue?'
'Who's Sue?'
'Yes. Who's Sue? Who's Sue? Who's Sue?'"[110]

As it transpires, Sue is the name of an ex-girlfriend tattooed onto Monty's chest, a procedure that "hurt like the dickens and cost much more than you would expect."[111] Language, far from being an inert medium of communication, is never free of consequences, and is very capable of causing pain. The next major dislocation in the novel's romantic plotting occurs because of yet another example of writing-out-of-place: Lottie Blossom, under the mistaken apprehension that the stateroom next to hers is occupied by her fiancé Ambrose Tennyson, inscribes Monty's bathroom with the loving message written in lipstick that so infuriates Albert Peasemarch. Wodehouse's description of this event highlights its overwhelmingly transgressive nature: "The wall seemed not so much a wall with writing on it as a mass of writing with a wall somewhere in the background."[112] This is carnivalized communication that quite literally overruns socially accepted margins, writing which refuses to stay in place. It is also writing that is the scene of a radical collision of two different literary

---

[110] Ibid., p. 68.
[111] Ibid., p. 69.
[112] Ibid., p. 92.

contexts, the profane world of Lottie's message scrawled in red lipstick, redolent of Hollywood and the potential for unrestrained sexual adventure, and the words inscribed on the wall during Belshazzar's Feast: "It was even as Albert Peasemarch had said. The writing was on the wall."[113] The divine message "MENE, MENE, TEKEL, and PARSIN" of the Book of Daniel has become the jolly "Hi, baby!" of a Hollywood starlet.[114]

Carnivalized communication thus drives the major plot developments of the novel. But it also constitutes its texture. All of the characters are prone to aphasia, to moments when language slips between their fingers. This forgetting has been identified as a primary feature of Wodehouse's fiction, particularly with reference to Bertie Wooster, who is unable to properly remember any of the tags and allusions that pepper his speech (although he is paradoxically able to remember them perfectly well when it comes times to narrate his forgetting).[115] Here, however, all of the characters struggle to maintain coherence. Gertrude calls Monty a "hickaprit," which is a "new one to Monty," who is of course himself unable to distinguish between a neologism and an error.[116] Peasemarch is certain that lipstick is "undelible," and that an argument can be described as an "imbrolligo."[117] Lydon describes this as the inability of characters to handle "the common coin of English," and it is a frequent problem aboard the Atlantic.[118] On other occasions, language finds itself locked into repetitive patterns, overcome by a sort of denotative paralysis as words somehow begin to take precedence over that which they signify. We have seen this in the discussion between Monty and Gertrude about Sue (who?), and other examples appear throughout the text:

"'I shan't be long. I'm just curing Mr. Tennyson's headache.'
'Mr. Tennyson junior's headache.'
'Mr. Tennyson junior's headache.'
'Not to be confused,' proceeded the patient, 'with Mr. Tennyson senior's headache, if he has one – which, I'm afraid, he hasn't.'"[119]

---

[113] Ibid., p. 91f.
[114] "The Hebrew Scriptures Commonly Called the Old Testament", in: Bruce M. Metzger and Roland E. Murphy (Eds.), *The New Oxford Annotated Bible,* New York 1989, p. 1-1237: 1136.
[115] Vesterman, "Plum Time in Nevereverland", p. 92.
[116] Wodehouse, *Luck of the Bodkins*, p. 67.
[117] Ibid., p. 98, 191.
[118] Lydon, "First Love", p. 24.
[119] Wodehouse, *Luck of the Bodkins*, p. 77.

In a 'conversation' such as this one, while the sense of the words is indeed decipherable, it is almost effaced by a rebellion of sound: in Sausserian terms this would be a carnivalesque triumph of the signifier over the signified.

This sort of confusion extends, as we have seen, from the smallest unit of written language, the individual letter, to larger linguistic structures such as words and sentences. It also extends to broader components of literary systems. The confusion over the author of "The Boy Stood on the Burning Deck" is one relatively minor example of this. Another instance of this larger-scale literary carnivalization is Llewellyn's confusion over Ambrose Tennyson, whom he has hired to write scripts under the misapprehension that he is the Tennyson, "one of the big noises."[120] While Llewellyn's mistake is risible, and is treated as such by the other characters, it is typical of the novel's communicative carnivalization.

Language thus ceases to function in its normal, everyday forms on the Atlantic, instead acting in ways that draw attention towards its intractable playfulness, what might be described as a Barthian Jouissance, "the moment when by its very excess verbal pleasure chokes and reels into bliss."[121] One instance of this has already been discussed from a slightly different perspective; Monty Bodkin's inability to spell words such as "sciatica" and "inexplicable" is a plot device leading to one of the novel's critical misunderstandings, but it is also a sign of the slipperiness of language.[122] The French waiter Monty first asks for help with his problem to spell sciatica "Wit' a ess, wit' a say, wit' a ee, wit' a arr, wit' a ee, wit a' ku, wit'a uh, wit'a ay," a scene that draws attention both to the way different languages assign different verbal tokens to the same concept and to the very physical noise, the rush of breath, out of which words are made.

Language then, in its carnivalized form, is quite simply difficult to use, as even the simplest of instrumental exchanges becomes an opportunity for almost endless difficulties. When Ivor Llewellyn wants to order a cup of coffee from Peasemarch, the word is exchanged ten times before the beverage, "COFFEE," is actually produced.[123] On another occasion, Monty has promised the jealous Gertrude that he will not speak to Lottie Blossom, but, in order to retrieve the plush Mickey Mouse doll belonging to Gertrude that Lottie has dishonestly obtained and is using to blackmail Monty into taking a job with Llewellyn in order to get Ambrose's job with the same back, he has decided to write to her (Wodehouse's plots are nothing if not intricate). He uses Peasemarch as his

---

[120] Ibid., p. 178.
[121] Roland Barthes, *The Pleasure of the Text,* Richard Miller (Trans.), New York 1975, p. 8.
[122] Wodehouse, *Luck of the Bodkins*, p. 17, 59.
[123] Ibid., p. 141.

messenger, and a brisk correspondence ensues. The contents of these notes are fine examples of the way carnivalized language conflates registers of formality; they begin with the archaically formal third-person of "Mr. Bodkin presents his compliments to Miss Blossom" and end with "a single ribald word."[124] What is more interesting in this context, however, is the extreme difficulty with which this communicative act is carried out. Lottie is on the boat deck, and Monty is in his stateroom, and the unlucky Peasemarch as intermediary is required, "sweating about and climbing stairs" to carry the notes between them.[125] The conclusion of the exchange finds the steward "panting like the hart when wearied in the chase," yet another parodic biblical and literary allusion in this text so rich in them, but one emphasizing the extreme difficulty of forcing carnivalized language to do our bidding.[126]

Reading Wodehouse Seriously

The great irony here is that Wodehouse accomplishes with apparent ease the very task his characters grapple with so unsuccessfully. He is able to make the unruly language, which masters so many of his characters in so many of his novels, perform as he wishes. This is his greatest strength as a writer, and it is in this sense that Hillaire Belloc described him in 1934 as "the best writer of English now alive."[127] But the ends to which Wodehouse put his talents have long been seen by most readers and critics as beneath – or in a more positive view, above – serious consideration. To take the spade of criticism to the soufflé of Wodehouse's fiction is to show oneself to be not just a fool, but a vulgar one at that, patently unable to understand that some things are best left alone. My intention here has been, however, to demonstrate that Wodehouse's work is perfectly amenable, and indeed responsive, to a critical reading highlighting its carnivalesque elements.

This approach not only offers a clearer view of Wodehouse's fiction, but may also contribute to a reassessment of this critically neglected author. While Wodehouse is extremely popular with the common reader, and, as Laura Mooneyham has pointed out, has received high praise from some writers and

---

[124] Ibid., p. 227, 233.
[125] Ibid., p. 228.
[126] Ibid., p. 233.
[127] Kimball, "Genius of Wodehouse".

critics, he has been completely excluded from the canon.[128] Any survey of 1922 as the annus mirabilis of modernist literature, for instance, would discuss works such as Joyce's Ulysses, Eliot's The Wasteland, Rilke's Duino Elegies, and Woolf's Jacob's Room; none would include Wodehouse's *The Girl on the Boat*, published in the same year. Similarly, Joseph Bottum has recently identified his prose as transcendently meaningless: "never a weak moment, never a lost sentence, never a word out of place – and never a one of those words mattering in the least, never a one of them aimed at any purpose but their own light comedy, never a one of them anything but wasted."[129] While Bottum later modifies his conclusion, it is representative of Wodehouse's place, or lack of place, in literary history.

Even a confessed devotee such as Robert West can say no more than that his work is "literarily important even though nearly all lighthearted," as if lightheartedness were in itself a disqualification for importance.[130] Mooncyham attempts to refute this type of criticism by looking to Northrop Frye's discussion of comic structures, including its resistance to unjustly restrictive social controls.[131] She situates Wodehouse's comedies against the prevailingly tragic tone of the high-modernist literature initially distributed to a small but culturally elite market and later canonized in university English departments. In this context, Wodehouse was doubly discredited as a comic and popular writer.[132] While modernism certainly contains elements of the comic – writers such as Wyndham Lewis practice a form of satire that is certainly funny, if often incredibly bitter – on balance this view seems to be valid. If we add to this Wodehouse's acceptance of genre standards, embrace of the mass market, disinterest in originality, and reliance on plotting – and frequently recycled plotting at that – as a structuring principle for his novels, we have a portrait of the artist as an anti-modernist, a looking-glass version of a Joyce or Faulkner.[133] Wodehouse was of course aware of his position in relation to the developing artistic impulses of the modernist period, and typically enough responded with a comic parody of futurist prose in a 1914 column on "The Literature of the Future: Or Every Man His Own

---

[128] Laura Mooneyham, "Comedy Among the Modernists: P. G. Wodehouse and the Anachronism of Comic Form" in: *Twentieth Century Literature 40* (1994), p. 114-138: 114-115.
[129] Bottum, "God & Bertie Wooster", p. 24.
[130] Robert H. West, "The High Art of Quality Frivolity" in: *South Atlantic Bulletin 37* (1972), p. 12-19: 13.
[131] Mooneyham, "Comedy Among the Modernists", p. 115.
[132] Ibid., p. 116-117.
[133] Ibid., p. 119-120.

Futurist."[134] Wodehouse's solution, as always, was laughter, but a laughter that seems in the context of the carnivalesque to be meaningful rather than meaningless.

There are a number of ways in which an attempt to read Wodehouse seriously can be made. He can be seen, as Damrosch has argued, as a transatlantic writer, instrumental in establishing an interpretative matrix through which American and British audiences were able to 'read' each other, and themselves as viewed by the other, in humorously distorted images. According to this interpretation, his "cultural double vision" was closely linked to his commercial and popular success.[135] By the end of World War I, Wodehouse had become a best-selling author on both sides of the Atlantic, and although he ultimately took American citizenship and lived there until his death in 1975, to emphasize either the indubitably British roots of many of his works, or the American inspiration of many others, would be to miss the fact that he was very much a writer of the relationship between these closely related yet very different countries. Yet Wodehouse was also, as I have argued here, a writer of the Atlantic crossing itself, a chronicler of the social world of steamship culture and its effects on those who took part in it. Here he found a world in which the social constraints of both America and England were loosened. This is not to say that the rules of society were in some mysterious way in abeyance for the duration of the Atlantic crossing. On the contrary, we have seen that the shipping lines themselves went to extraordinary lengths to police and enforce the prevailing social mores, and Wodehouse's novels remain alert to the constant assertion of social norms. However, the ocean liner seems, as a site of both anxiety and opportunity, to have provided an ideal setting for a literature that corresponds in many respects with the Bakhtinian notion of the carnivalesque.

In both *The Girl on the Boat* and *The Luck of the Bodkins* accepted social values and norms are subject to enormous pressure. They do not vanish, but they are repeatedly and insistently challenged. Parental authority is subverted, traditional gender roles are blurred, and class-based social hierarchies are overturned, if only for the duration of the voyage. Peasemarch's carnivalesque role in *The Luck of the Bodkins*, for instance, ends when he decides to smuggle Llewellyn's pearl necklace through customs for Monty because "he has always proved himself to be a pleasant, agreeable young gentleman, the sort of young gentleman a man

---

[134] Daniel Tracy, "Investing in 'Modernism': Smart Magazines, Parody, and Middlebrow Professional Judgment" in: *The Journal of Modern Periodical Studies 1* (2010), p. 38-63: 52.

[135] Damrosch, *World Literature,* p. 213.

likes to do a good turn for."¹³⁶ Peasemarch here collaborates in the re-assertion of social norms of hierarchical deference. Similarly, in *The Girl on the Boat* once the *Atlantic* docks normative social values are quickly re-asserted: Marlowe's love for Billie is, for instance, lightly dismissed by his father as a mere "shipboard flirtation."¹³⁷ Yet the very re-establishment of traditional social values acts to highlight the temporary period of relative freedom from constraint that occurs during the Atlantic crossing.

A further set of carnivalesque challenges centres on notions of high and low cultural value. Chivalry and romantic love are parodied, although in a fashion that acts as much to rejuvenate and revivify as to subvert. However, language itself is perhaps the primary focus of, and outlet for, the carnivalesque impulses of *The Girl on the Boat* and *The Luck of the Bodkins*. In both novels, a dislocation of genres, registers, and discourses occurs as language, from its most basic components to its most elaborate systems of signification, falls prey to the spirit of carnival. From the dense networks of quotation and allusion that make Wodehouse's novels studies in intertextual virtuosity, to the ways in which language persistently slips out of his characters' control, these novels consistently display an extraordinary linguistic attentiveness. Ultimately, Wodehouse's Atlantic novels offer the attentive reader a sustained meditation on the intersections between self, society, and language that is arguably as effective and as important as the work of any of his more canonical modernist peers. While Wodehouse is often seen as the creator of a "never-never land" upon which the "Sturm und Drang" of the real world barely impinges, this is a view that needs to be modified by a clearer recognition of his work's carnivalesque tendencies.¹³⁸

---

[136] Wodehouse, *Luck of the Bodkins*, p. 357.
[137] Wodehouse, *Girl on the Boat*, p. 117.
[138] Herbert Warren Wind, *The World of P. G. Wodehouse*, London 1981, p. 24-25.

9. Menageries at Sea: Animals and Trans-Atlantic Travel in 1940

Stephanie Beck Cohen

Introduction

> "Through the generosity of Harvey Firestone, an expedition has been arranged for the purpose of penetrating the jungles of Liberia to collect wild animals. This expedition, which I have the honor to head, sailed from New York…on the *S.S. West Kebar*, and by the time this article is printed, will be in Liberia, to stay from three to five months. The Firestones have long been interested in the national zoo, the late Harvey S. Firestone having presented a pygmy hippopotamus to it about 13 years ago."

So begins William Mann's article in the April 1940 issue of the *Scientific Monthly*. Mann goes on, "On a trip of this kind one can never tell what one is going to get; the results are absolutely unprophesiable."

On February 17, 1940, the *S.S. West Kebar* left New York on a 22-day trans-Atlantic journey to Monrovia, Liberia, carrying Dr. William Mann and his wife, Lucile Quarry Mann, along with two keepers from the National Zoological Park. Funded by Firestone Rubber and Tire Company and under the auspices of the Smithsonian Institution in Washington, D.C., the Manns journeyed to Liberia to collect animals for two institutions: the National Zoo and the Firestone company's pavilion at the 1940 New York World's Fair. The expedition to Liberia culminated in one of the largest acquisition projects for the zoo.[1] Included in the trans-Atlantic travelers and one of the most highly publicized acquisitions was a breeding mate for the popular presidential pet and zoo resident, Billy, who had drawn visitors to the zoo since 1927. Millions of American tourists viewed the resulting exhibitions of rare animals at both the World's Fair and in permanent

---

[1] William and Lucile Mann returned to Washington with over 300 live animals for the National Zoological Park, thousands of fish species, entomological samples and plant specimens. The fish, insect and flora specimen were accessioned by the US National Museum. However, cataloging (especially the thousands of fish species) was overwhelming for the USNM staff and several thousand samples were sent to Harvard to be cataloged. The animal lists and personal correspondence between Loveridge and William Mann also confirm this.

installations at the zoo in Washington DC. Many more followed the Manns' expedition through newspaper and magazine articles or through film and lectures given by Dr. and Mrs. Mann after their return.

This chapter considers how the human and animal travelers of the Smithsonian-Firestone Expedition crossed the Atlantic in terms of expedition planning, execution, and exhibition upon reaching their final destinations. Drawing from field journals, personal correspondence, newspaper and magazine accounts of the major figures (both human and animal), I examine the complex mechanisms that supported the scholarly American travelers and their menagerie in the early 20th century. Dr. and Mrs. Mann's experiences were tied directly to corporate, academic and public interests. Together with the animals and with the authority of the Smithsonian Institution behind them, the Manns shaped Americans' understanding of Liberia and the Liberian-American relationship through these exhibitions. On the eve of the Second World War, the Smithsonian-Firestone Expedition brought two Atlantic coastal countries together through travel during this collecting and exhibition project. For American visitors to the 1940 New York World's Fair and to the National Zoo, the expedition allowed for vicarious trans-Atlantic travel at a time when crossing the Atlantic was becoming a dangerous prospect as a result of the Second World War. The exhibitions, especially at the New York World's Fair, projected an image of future success through technological innovation, tied to scientific, economic, and political cooperation between the countries. Crossing the Atlantic as conflict began to rage in Europe, the expedition served as a propaganda and publicity machine for corporate and national interests, drawing visitors to American cities to experience Liberian animals and culture.

The exhibition practices, networks established on both sides of the Atlantic and the personal relationships and narratives of their exhibitions can perhaps speak more broadly to the complex institution of human and animal travel in the transitional period between the Great Depression and the Second World War. Although Dr. and Mrs. Mann are examples of the scientist traveler, on their expedition they met other common Atlantic travelers like the Firestone entrepreneurs and American and German missionaries. Focusing on their menagerie provides the opportunity to focus on the movement of and understudied group of trans-Atlantic travelers. The desire and planning for the animals' capture, their dramatic entrances into American society, and relationships with native peoples on both sides of the Atlantic add new perspectives to the discussion of trans-Atlantic crossings at the beginning of the twentieth century. Additionally, the resulting exhibitions and lectures illustrate the importance of travel for Americans, both physically to world's fairs and zoological parks, as well as imaginary trips across the Atlantic, during a time when it was increasingly difficult or dangerous. The theoretical underpinnings of this study are drawn from literature on tourism, museums and world's fairs and the history of zoos to navigate the complexity of planning and executing such a trans-Atlantic venture and staging travel narratives afterwards.

Staging a Crossing: Zoological Expeditions and Planning Trans-Atlantic Travel on the Eve of War

"Day after day, the Zoo-sounds lure me over, and I make the rounds of my friends, some of whom have been fellow-travelers with me…" – Lucile Q. Mann, 1934.

William Mann took over as director of the National Zoological Park in 1926 and immediately began aggressively collecting, adding rare animal species unmatched by other American zoos.[2] For William Mann, going into the field to collect insect specimens had been a regular part of his life as an entomologist. His appointment to the directorship of the National Zoological Park did not curb his travel; rather, he engaged in several collecting trips to enlarge the zoo's population. By the early 20th century, scholarly expeditions were a regular part of American science and anthropological study. They were also tied to public travel and exhibition, and expeditionary artifacts were a regular part of the late-19th century and early 20th century world's fair and museum collections and exhibitions.[3]
This travel was by no means compulsory, as animals for zoological collections were acquired mainly through gifting or purchase from animal brokers. Instead,

---

[2] Nelson Graburn describes tourism as an institution "humans use to embellish and add meaning to their lives." Although he refers here to leisure travel, he goes on to describe the ways in which tourism meshes with other types of travel, namely as related to "purposeful institutions" like medieval religious travel (i.e. pilgrimage). Today's tourism literature considers a number of different types of travel and multiple motivations for travelers. The type of traveling that the Manns engage in as scientists on expedition falls into "compulsory/serious travel" on Graburn's work/traveling matrix. Nelson H. H. Graburn, "Tourism: The Sacred Journey" in: Valene Smith (Ed.), *Hosts and Guests: The Anthropology of Tourism*, Philadelphia 1977, p. 21-36: 22-23.

[3] For example, Franz Boas' Northwest Coast collections at the 1893 Chicago World's Fair. For the connections between anthropological collecting, national institutions and world's fair exhibitions, see Robert Rydell, *All the World's a Fair*, Chicago 1984.

Mann saw travel as a way to both bolster the collections and create intellectual networks between scholars around the world and connect with potential sponsors for a public institution in need of extra funding. Mann focused his expeditionary ventures on exotic locations. For example, he obtained sponsorship from the Chrysler Corporation to travel to eastern Africa in 1926, and made several other trips (accompanied by his wife) to Central and South America and the South Pacific. The Manns used travel as both collecting mission and networking opportunity at home and abroad. Additionally, Dr. Mann helped establish small national zoos in some of the locations of their expeditions, namely East Africa and India.[4]

The Manns established far-flung networks in order to continue their collecting projects beyond each expedition. As the zoo had a very small acquisitions budget, they relied on gifts and exchanges to build the animal collection.[5] Lucile Quarry Mann's autobiography recounts visits to zoological parks and private collections in Europe, the Caribbean and South America. Her book, *From Jungle to Zoo*, makes clear the dual nature of the Manns' travel: they were both naturalists in the field and tourists far from home.[6] Her account of visiting a wealthy woman's menagerie in Havana, Cuba, and German zoological parks particularly illustrates this point. As a naturalist, she was interested in the different types of animals and their upkeep, but she was equally fascinated by the arts collections, architecture and biographies of people who kept the animals. Her dual interest in zoological and cultural aspects of their trips blurs the distinctions between travel for work and leisure, demonstrating that any attempt to draw distinct lines between types of travel would be inadvisable, since types of travel blended over the course of a trip.

---

[4] Mann also indicated a desire to establish a national zoo in Monrovia at the outset of their journey. William M. Mann, "National Zoological Park Expedition to Liberia", in: *Scientific Monthly* L (Apr 1940), p. 377-379. Smithsonian Institution Archives, Record Unit 7293, William M. Mann and Lucile Quarry Mann Papers.

[5] Lucile Q. Mann, *From Jungle to Zoo: Adventures of a Naturalist's Wife*, New York 1934, p. 37-62.

[6] In "Tourism: the sacred journey," Graburn refers to the complexity of the term "tourism." Although generally tied to leisure, for Graburn "some sanctioned recreation is often another kind of 'hard work.'" The Manns travels often tiptoed on the boundary between work and recreation, and they often reflected on the business and pleasure of their travels in their articles for such publications as *Scientific Monthly* and *National Geographic*. For drafts of these articles, SIA RU 7293, William M. Mann and Lucile Quarry Mann Papers.

In addition to the collecting done by the Manns, the zoo acquired animals through individual donation and from exotic animal vendors, even though acquiring rare animals from vendors was considered unwise because they were prohibitively expensive and generally in unfortunate shape.[7] One important individual donor to the National Zoo was Harvey S. Firestone. After establishing the first rubber plantations in Liberia in the early 1920s, Firestone gifted a pygmy hippopotamus named Billy to President Coolidge in 1927. The President, in turn, gifted Billy to the National Zoo.[8] Billy's popularity was such that Mann declared part of the reason for the 1940 expedition was to bring home a mate for Billy; a task accomplished on the expedition.[9] Billy was so popular that he was even sent to New York as part of the Firestone exhibition. He also holds a prominent place in American zoo history, as the progenitor of nearly every pygmy hippopotamus in US zoos today.[10] Zoogoers viewed Billy as more than an object; they invested in his personal life and family.

The engagement of individual animal biographies and individual animals in zoos and animal parks has been the subject of recent scholarly interest. Although there are a number of approaches to understanding the human-other species encounter, including preservation and conservation policies, one of the most interesting was proposed by Traci Warkentin and Leesa Fawcett. Warkentin and Fawcett propose

---

[7] Elizabeth Hanson, *Animal Attractions: Nature on Display in American Zoos*. Princeton 2002, p. 71-80.

[8] "Baby Hippo for Coolidge is Coming from Liberia" *Special to the New York Times*, May 27, 1927.

[9] Billy's family life was catalogued by major publications like the *New York Times* and *Washington Post*. His first mate, acquired by the zoo in 1929, had difficulty performing her maternal duty (see "Ignored by mother, Infant hippo dies," *The Washington Post*, 30 Aug 1931, p. M3 and "Pygmy Hippo Kills its 3rd Offspring; Jungle Mother Rolls on Latest Infant and Crushes Out Life," *The Washington Post*, 5 May 1933, p. 18). After three unsuccessful attempts at breeding, the zoo decided to acquire another mate for Billy on the Smithsonian-Firestone exhibition. On 27 Feb 1940, a mere 10 days after the expedition departed, she delivered and began to care for the infant. "4th Baby Hippo Arrives at Zoo; Seems Healthy," *The Washington Post*, 27 Feb1940, p. X1.

[10] "Since 1929, 58 of these rare animals have been born at the Zoo. Over the years, the Zoo has sent pygmy hippopotamuses to zoos in Portland, Fort Worth, Chicago, Philadelphia, Pittsburgh, San Antonio, Canada, Venezuela, Argentina, Brazil, Chile, England, South Africa, Sri Lanka, Singapore, and Thailand." From the Pygmy Hippo fact sheet, National Zoological Park, https://nationalzoo.si.edu/animals/asian-elephant, accessed 13 Aug 2017, and in Dr. Mann's correspondence from 1939: William M. Mann and Lucile Quarry Mann Papers, SIA RU 7293.

transforming our understanding of the human-animal encounter. To counter "the patriarchy and colonialism of animal captivity," they suggest restructuring the human-animal encounter to "propose transformative encounters within which the touch of encounter requires responsibility, reciprocity, and recognition of these meetings as intra-active relations." That is, to acknowledge that the animals in captivity not only look back, but also deserve to have their agency respected in the animal encounter. While the Manns' expedition is certainly subject to its time, I would argue that they privileged the animal-human encounter, respecting zoo residents as sentient beings. They often lived and traveled with animals from the National Zoo. Even as they set out on collecting expeditions to capture wild creatures, Lucile Mann reflexively engages the transformative encounter with these same animals in her book *From Jungle to Zoo*, musing on individual relationships zoo animals developed, or refused to, with keepers and visitors. [11]

For the Manns, an expedition to Liberia was a matter of practicality. Travel to many other exotic locations was made difficult by their colonial associations with the battling European powers. Lucile Mann wrote: "[We] chose the little Republic of Liberia as being less likely to be upset by the war."[12] Liberia, as an independent nation, provided a neutral location – port to port – or travel. Additionally, as an interest of an American corporation and because of the history between the two countries, the Manns could be assured of government permissions to collect and local guidance from Firestone plantation managers. Likewise, Liberia was home to a number of animals not found elsewhere on the continent, which Mann attributed in her article to the dense forests that provided barriers that isolate the animals and students of zoology alike.[13] Lucile Mann wrote: "One gets the impression that Liberia is teeming in animal life, smaller in size but perhaps as abundant as that on the great plains of East Africa, but seldom seen because of the dense forests which cover practically all the 42,000 square miles of the Republic."[14] A Liberian expedition could not expect to bring home large game animals like in East Africa; rather, publicity for the expedition highlighted the

---

[11] Traci Warkentin and Leesa Fawcett, "Whale and Human Agency in World-Making: Decolonizing Wale-Human Encounters" in: Ralph R. Acampora (Ed.), *Metamorphoses of the Zoo: Animal Encounter after Noah,* Lanham, Boulder, New York, Toronto, Plymouth 2010, p. 103-122.

[12] Lucile Quarry Mann, "The Smithsonian-Firestone Expedition to Liberia," draft for *National Geographic*, 1941, p. 1, William M. Mann and Lucile Quarry Mann Papers, SIA RU 7293.

[13] Ibid., p. 1-2.

[14] Article draft: Mann, "Expedition to Liberia," William M. Mann and Lucile Quarry Mann Papers, SIA RU 7293.

rarity of the miniature animals (like the pygmy hippopotamus and small deer species), extraordinarily poisonous reptiles, and diverse, brightly colored bird species that the public could expect.

In order to set the stage for the 1940 Smithsonian-Firestone Expedition, it is necessary to outline Firestone's establishment of business in Liberia. During the 1920s, the American automobile industry ramped up marketing and production, increasing the need for rubber in the US. American businessmen like Harvey Firestone saw the need to grow (literally) America's own rubber crop, either in the US or foreign spaces operated by American industry. Rubber plantations were attempted in South America, Mexico and Liberia – with the Liberian plantations emerging as the top choice for economic, spatial and political reasons.[15] Scientific research in Liberia in the 1920s concentrated on rubber and tropical medicine studies, and travel to and from Liberia was primarily related to business and missionary work. Through the Harvard African Expedition, which spent 4 months in Liberia and 4 months in the Congo documenting life and collecting human blood/tissue samples as well as collecting animal and plant material, Firestone and American scientists established the idea that American intervention was necessary to continue the development of infrastructure and progress in Liberia. Firestone began to work closely with both the Liberian government and indigenous populations all over the country, sometimes negotiating directly with local authorities.[16] Firestone's corporate history – the establishment of economic imperialism in Liberia - sets the context for the Manns' expedition.

The Manns' expedition to Liberia was quickly conceived and executed. In a 1939 letter to animal-collector friend Silas Johnson, Mann wrote that he met with Firestone plantation manager George Seybold and was considering a collecting trip to Liberia. Mann discovered that Firestone had employed Johnson in

---

[15] Alfred Lief, *The Firestone Story: A History of the Firestone Tire and Rubber Company*, New York, 1951, p. 3-137. The first ten chapters of Lief's book detail the creation of the Firestone Tire and Rubber Company in the United States, as well as the trial and error approach to growing rubber which finally leads Firestone to plant a series of rubber trees outside of Monrovia, Liberia in 1925. Achieving a successful crop, he extends the operation onto several plantations in the following five years and trains a local population of employees as well as importing officials to run the plantations from the United States section of the company. At this point in time, the Liberian Secretary of State and the Firestone T &R Co enter into advanced negotiations for land use, arrangements that (in general, with few renegotiations) last through World War II.

[16] Richard P. Strong (Ed.), *The African Republic of Liberia and the Belgian Congo: Based on the observations made and material collected during the Harvard African Expedition 1926 – 1927*, New York 1930.

Monrovia in November of that year. Mann wrote about his excitement about possibly acquiring a number of rare animals through his friend's contacts. However, he doubted that he and Mrs. Mann could afford such a trip. Negotiations with Firestone ensued, and at the end of 1939, Harvey Firestone, Jr. agreed to sponsor a collecting expedition that would coincide with the second season of the 1939-1940 World's Fair in New York. Firestone facilitated getting the Manns permits to travel around the country from the Liberian government while Mann secured the necessary permits to import exotic animals, and planned the trip. Mann acquired a number of new technical devices to record the trip, including a Rolleiflex still camera he acquired in Germany, a Kodak Cinespecial to record moving, color film, and a typewriter for Mrs. Mann to record field notes, as she served as the official expedition secretary.[17]

Planning the trip included rousing public interest in the venture. The Manns worked to get public support for their expedition to supplement the funding and administrative support from Firestone. W. H. Shippen, a journalist who wrote for the *Washington Evening Star* and accompanied the Manns on past collecting trips to South America, wrote at least four articles about the expedition in the weeks leading up to the Manns' departure. Shippen's articles, although mainly celebratory, touch upon the broader worldwide context for the trip, including concerns about traveling across the Atlantic at the time. In the first week of February 1940, he wrote that the party planned "to...swing into the South Atlantic to give the war zone a wide berth and touch first, in all probability, at Liberia."[18] This is one of the few references to the war in articles about the expedition, although Lucile Mann describes listening to the radio for war news in her field journal, both during the Atlantic journey and while at Harbel, the base of operations for Firestone. Although the Manns found it difficult to disembark and refuel in European colonies, they did stop in Dakar both on the way to and from Liberia to refresh their food stock.

Shippen also wrote about the World's Fair exhibit from the beginning, mentioning that Dr. Mann "hopes" that at least part of the collection would be temporarily displayed in the Firestone Pavilion. Shippen wrote two other articles of particular interest, both published in the Evening Star before the Manns departed for Liberia.

---

[17] The technology the Manns took to Liberia also included a number of different lenses and a light meter. Details can be found in the repair receipts in William M. Mann and Lucile Quarry Mann Papers, SIA RU 7293.

[18] W. H. Shippen, Jr., "Dr. Mann to Lead New Animal Hunting Expedition to Africa." *Washington Evening Star*, n.d. (article indicates that the Manns sail in a week, so likely first week of February, 1940), from the Manns' scrapbook: William M. Mann and Lucile Quarry Mann Papers, SIA RU 7293.

One article summarizes Manns' past experience collecting in East Africa and discusses a dual need for the expedition; one, for science, as the animals found in the Liberian interior are incredibly rare (for example, the pygmy hippo, potto, and ratel) and two, because the National Zoo had to compete with other prominent zoos on the East coast and in the Midwest for tourist attention and audiences. The second article of interest was titled "Dr. Mann and Wife To Carry Rival Flags Into African Wilds." Shippen highlighted two important points in this article. The first is an issue of audience. The Manns had to appeal to the general American public, but also to the academic communities; the "rival" flags that they carried were for the Explorer's Club of New York (Dr. Mann) and the Society of Women Geographers (Lucile Mann). The article set up a competition as to which society's flag (and, thus, representative) will "penetrate deeper" into the hinterland. These flags appear in the Manns' film and photo albums from the expedition, pinned to the houses that Dr. and Mrs. Mann stayed in during their trips to the interior.

The second important point evolves from the first: Lucile Mann's presence as a female traveler to exotic locations. She was both contributor to the expedition as a researcher and representative of a group of women scholars. A published writer, Lucile Mann also kept all of the records for the expedition, photographed and filmed in addition to her animal caretaking duties. It is her field journal that remains in the Smithsonian collection, and she gave lectures (both with her husband and alone) and published in National Geographic after their return. Additionally, it was Lucile Mann who gifted ethnographic and art objects to the Smithsonian's National Museum of Natural History and the National Museum of African Art between 1940 and 1964.[19]

During the *West Kebar*'s trans-Atlantic journey, public interest in the expedition was maintained through official Smithsonian publicity releases. On April 13, 1940, the Washington Post published the first reports on the expedition's journey.

---

[19] It is not until 1962, after the death of her husband, that Lucile Mann gifts the NMNH Anthropology collection five Liberian objects (a knife in sheath, a stool, an antelope horn, a bow, and a sculpture of a crocodile). In 1979, Lucile Mann further bequeathed objects from her collection to the National Museum of African Art, including several from Liberia. The NMAFA collection includes textiles and jewelry, as well as a second stool. As far as objects collected in the field, we also know (from Lucile's fieldnotes) that the Manns were gifted with many lengths of country cloth and that they also purchased country cloth as gifts (per William Mann's correspondence). William Mann's correspondence indicates that as souvenirs, they also bought a number of animal skins, quickly appropriated upon their return by the US National Museum. National Museum of Natural History Acquisition records and William M. Mann and Lucile Quarry Mann Papers, SIA RU 7293.

According to the Post, Dr. Mann likened the outbound voyage to day after day of Independence Day-type celebrations: "All the top decks, hatch covers, and sides of the ship have brilliantly painted American flags on them and these are illuminated at night." Mann contrasts this gaiety with, "…ships that have passed us in the moonlight, sailing without lights and not answering our radio greetings—I suppose for fear of giving away their positions." In these statements, Mann not only makes light of the dangers of trans-Atlantic travel, but also juxtaposes his American ship with all others, determinedly enjoying the trip across the ocean. The article goes on to indicate Mann's feelings about the travel still to come once he would reach the Liberian shore: "He said he has established contacts in Liberia with missionaries 'who talk casually of places that to [Mann] have always spelled romance and excitement.'"[20]

Lucile Mann's account of the voyage differs, as she recorded an icy departure from New York. She needed "a couple of stiff drinks to make [her] forget Carveth Wells [sic] gloomy remarks on life at sea. He considers that one always takes ones [sic] life in one's hands when one sets out on a ship…I don't think he really expects ever to see us again." She awoke to calm seas on February 18 and took the opportunity to explore the ship, describing the tiny room packed with their equipment and the dining room, with seating for all twelve passengers (mostly missionaries bound for the Congo) plus the captain. Unfortunately, on February 19 (the entry in her field journal reads Feb 19-23), Mann awoke to the freighter pitching and rolling; she was "hurled from the bunk to the washstand and back again." However, four days of thunderstorms at sea could not dampen her enthusiasm, and by March 6 her journal records barely contain the excitement of landing at Dakar. Although the Manns remained on board, Lucile was fascinated by the ships in the harbor:

> "A small Polish freighter set us all to speculating; what would be the home port of this ship-without-a-country? [...] But the theme of the harbor was war, not commerce, with British airplane carriers, warships, destroyers [...] and airplanes around and above us. The *Uhenfels*, once a German merchant ship, was being coaled under the British flag; it had been captured somewhere between here and South America only a few months ago."[21]

Although the Manns appeared to have anticipated no trouble in their neutral port-to-port trans-Atlantic journey, the winds of war had incredible visual impact on

---

[20] "Dr. Mann describes Ships That Passed Quietly in Night," *The Washington Post*, 13 Apr 1940, p. X3.

[21] Field journal: Lucile Mann,1940, p. 6, William M. Mann and Lucile Quarry Mann Papers, SIA RU 7293.

Mrs. Mann: the description of the scene at the port at Dakar took an entire page in her field journal.

The *S. S. West Kebar* anchored off the coast of Liberia on the "hot, liquid morning" of March 10. Surf boats rowed out to the *Kebar* to transfer the travelers to shore as the shoreline was devoid of a curve deep enough to make a harbor. By the time the passengers stood on dry land, night had fallen, and Lucile Mann recorded the sights illuminated by the car's headlights: "…I could recognize such old friends as sugar cane, palm trees, and miles and miles of rubber. It was the first time I had ever seen rubber in the flowering season, and the perfume was so strong and sweet that it was almost overpowering."[22] The Smithsonian-Firestone expedition arrived in Liberia after 22 days at sea.

From the beginning of their trans-Atlantic journey, the Manns anticipated their expedition with excitement and scientific fervor. Barely affected by the developing conflict in Europe, it is only as they arrived on West Africa's coast that considerations of war entered their field notes. The Manns used travel to establish long-reaching networks and grow the zoological collections at home and abroad. It was necessary to inspire other Americans to visit the zoo's collections. They did this in a number of ways. One way to garner public attention was through the personalities of rare and unique animals, such as public investment in the personal life of Billy, a former presidential pet. The second way was through publicity they generated going on expeditions and speaking to audiences of all ages and intellectual levels, mixing education and entertainment at every stage of travel, including planning their trips, setting the stage for the actual journey and the eventual return home, victoriously shepherding a new menagerie.

Travel in Difficult Places: Negotiations between Traveler and Native

The relationship between foreign traveler and native populations is often fraught with tension due to issues related to differences in language and customs. In the case of travel to Africa there was (and, indeed, still is) the added complexity of power disparities in the relationships between traveler and native. Liberia was an independent nation and not colonized like the majority of West Africa after the Berlin Conference. Still, both the foundational and recent histories of the nation set up power relationships that the Manns had to navigate. In their field notes and journals, however, the Manns cite difficulties stemming from cultural and

---

[22]   Ibid., p. 9.

language issues, avoiding the history of Liberia and Firestone in telling their travel narrative.[23] This is not unexpected as Firestone funded the expedition and the government facilitated the collecting project, but it does underline power disparities that underlie travel in a developing country. Often, these inequalities in power are posited as one-sided. After a general discussion of the Manns' travel within the country, I will highlight two episodes of the Manns' journey that shaped Lucile Mann's travel narratives. These two sets of experiences demonstrate the negotiations between travelers and natives that illustrate power disparities and the agency of native people in response to foreign visitors, especially during the escalating global conflict.

The Manns worked through the administrative structure set up by the Liberian government and Firestone. Both the Liberian government and Firestone had historically complicated relationships with the general population. Liberian-American settlers, who established the modern nation in the mid-19th century through support from the American Colonization Society, ran the government, and their relationship with interior populations was generally tenuous, if not outright hostile. It was not until the first decade of the 20th century that citizens of the interior part of the country were granted degrees of citizenship in the state, resulting in the creation of paramount chief positions to manage hinterland populations. Firestone's relationship with its Liberian employees was also

---

[23] Lucile Mann never criticized Firestone in her field journals or articles. In one instance, she recorded a conversation between herself, Dr. Mann, Paramount Chief Boima Quae and his brother during which they discussed problems between local populations of the hinterland and the Liberian government. She wrote: "They dislike and mistrust the government, saying that although they pay a hut tax of eight shillings a year they get absolutely nothing for it. The natives are forced to work on the roads for nothing, and then the government claims to be too poor to build bridges, so that the roads are of no use for carrying produce down to the Coast. They say the officials are corrupt…Boima Quae told us a little about the Gola War, which he led, and said sadly that their knives and cutlasses were of little use when the government turned a machine gun on them." From this small section, it is apparent that the Manns were not unaware of the political tensions in the republic. Lucile Mann, field journal, 23 May 1940, William M. Mann and Lucile Quarry Mann Papers, SIA RU 7293. For more on the Gola rebellion, see Warren L. d'Azevedo, "The Tenth County: From Myth to Reality in the Gola Concept of Historic Destiny," presented at the 27th annual meeting of the African Studies Association, 1984, p. 1-4.

fraught, mainly due to policies and negotiations with the national government, especially the labor ministry.[24]

The Manns encountered challenges in Liberia that they had not experienced in other places. There was no infrastructure for collecting live animals. Animal collecting in Liberia had been mainly accidental, when animals wandered onto plantation grounds as they were cleared for rubber tree planting. The Manns spent most of their time explaining expedition objectives to county superintendents and paramount chiefs, getting permission to collect specimens nearby, and recruiting local aid. In an article Lucile wrote: "On such a trip as ours much depends on native assistance. Natives, after all, are the best hunters and trappers."[25] In her field journal, Lucile Mann indicates that most of their native counterparts did not believe that Dr. Mann was interested in the flora and fauna; instead, they thought him to be a missionary or to hold out for a position with Firestone.[26] The Manns also dealt with natural obstacles; namely, shooing their animals out of harm's way as colonies of driver ants moved through their storage spaces. The driver ant columns devoured any living thing in their path, and the expedition lost several deer to a single ant column.

From their headquarters at the Harbel Plantation, the Manns made five separate trips into the hinterland, to places that Lucile Mann characterized in her field journal as "beyond the end of the road."[27] They traveled by hammock and rickshaw (on the shoulders of native people), by river (dugout canoe, launch, and boat), but mostly by foot. They carried all of their scientific and collecting equipment, and food, although they purchased fresh food along the way. Often they stayed in a village for several days, and then moved on to the next, relying on chiefs and locals to house them in a "mud hut" or "palaver kitchen…[a]

---

[24] The Liberian government was subject to a League of Nations investigation into human rights abuses in 1930. For the entirety of the 1920s, allegations of misconduct were made against the Liberian government, Firestone, and their mutual contracts and agreements regarding land use and labor. For a comprehensive discussion of the decade of conflict and the League of Nations investigation, see Phillip Johnson, *Seasons in Hell: Charles S. Johnson and the Liberian Labor Crisis*, dissertation, Louisiana State University, 2004, p. 54-170.

[25] Article draft: L. Q. Mann, p. 1-3, William M. Mann and Lucile Quarry Mann Papers, SIA RU 7293.

[26] Newspaper interviews also confirm this narrative. Gerald G. Gross, "Dr. Mann Back With Rare Beasts: 300 New Tenants for Zoo Here: Odd Animals in Collection from Liberia," *The Washington Post*, 11 Aug 1940, p. 25.

[27] William M. Mann and Lucile Quarry Mann Papers, SIA RU 7293, Box 6, folder 6.

council hall…[with] a raised floor and a thatched roof."[28] Generally, most of the collecting occurred on the way back to Harbel as they revisited villages and towns and purchased animals from people with whom they had spoken on their outbound trek. Mrs. Mann describes the daily routine of trekking, collection and socializing, with the Firestone officials and families or with the native Liberians who hosted them while out in the field. Lucile Mann documented everything in the daily routine, from their housing to culinary experiences. The Manns ate local cuisine, the "classic dish of West Africa—palm oil chop." She goes on to describe the dish:

> "To make this the cook takes about sixpence worth of palm nuts, scalds them, crushes them, and pours hot water over them. Two products result, one a rich palm oil, one a palm butter about the consistency of applesauce. Chicken, or preferably game, is cooked in the palm oil. Hot native peppers are cooked in the palm butter, and both are served, with the chicken, poured over rice."[29]

They also purchased coconuts, bananas and pineapples along the road.

Mrs. Mann considered the ordinary equally worthy of record as the extraordinary experiences they encountered while on the road. Her accounts detail Liberian textiles, like the finely woven indigo and white strip woven cloth that populates museum collections today. She also describes the formal handshake and snap characteristic in greeting new acquaintances in the villages. Her day-to-day accounts also describe a number of performances the expedition crew saw and documented. They asked and received permission to photograph and film a number of dances of young women returning from the bush schools, scenes featured briefly in their finished film of the expedition. She participated in much of the dancing and made it a priority to spend time with the elder women in each village. The majority of her field notes concern the cataloging of animals and their care; a voracious baby hornbill who was "equal parts of beak, appetite, and pin-feathers" and a dormouse pocket pet given to her by Paramount Chief Joseph Barclay of Dobli's Island being two highlights.[30]

The Manns were experienced animal collectors, and fiercely negotiated animal prices when they knew an animal may require extra work. On the way to Belleyella, they acquired a baby chimpanzee. In her field journal, Lucile Mann

---

[28] Article draft: L. Q. Mann, p. 7-8, William M. Mann and Lucile Quarry Mann Papers, SIA RU 7293.

[29] Article draft: L. Q. Mann, p. 8, William M. Mann and Lucile Quarry Mann Papers, SIA RU 7293.

[30] Article draft: L. Q. Mann, p. 9, William M. Mann and Lucile Quarry Mann Papers, SIA RU 7293.

expressed her reluctance to purchase the animal, knowing that it would have to be carried for several days, and require care for in camp. Negotiating the chief down to just above half the asking price because the animal was "dry," or thin, the Manns took the baby chimpanzee and taught it to drink milk from a rubber syringe. It eventually "put on weight and made an amusing camp pet." [31]

Two episodes during the trip stand out in the travel narrative, both in Mrs. Mann's field journal and in articles written about the expedition. They illustrate some of the particular cultural negotiations the Manns had to make while traveling. These stories depict different types of traveling experiences. One illustrates the Manns' initiation into a local society, conferring authenticity (and also authority) of the Manns through their acceptance into a foreign culture's private society, especially as it was related to their collecting project. The second episode demonstrates the effects of the escalating conflict in Europe trickling down into West Africa during the summer of 1940.

Lucile Mann highlights one trip to the interior in particular, and it became a regular part of her travel narrative when writing or speaking about the expedition to American audiences. On March 23, the Manns and their party (including about 80 local men working for them) entered the town of Belleyella. According to Lucile Mann's field journal, on March 24:

> "Three members of the local Snake Society came to see us, and we tried to put them to work collecting snakes for us. However, they said it would be impossible for them to sell snakes to anyone who did not belong to the Society. If we cared to spend eight shillings apiece, we could become members and we accepted the invitation with alacrity."[32]

In a later article, the Manns also comment that the men, "realizing from the Explorers' Club flag and the Women Geographers' flag and the [William Mann's] Masonic ring that we were 'joiners,' invited us to join the Snake

---

[31] Article draft: L. Q. Mann, p. 8, William M. Mann and Lucile Quarry Mann Papers, SIA RU 7293.

[32] Mann does not describe if this payment was standard or specifically for tourists. A contemporary Harvard expedition report cited a number of similar remedies, plants, and figurines described by the Manns. However, Richard Strong's report from the 1926–1927 Harvard African Expedition to Liberia (94-95) does not describe how local experts and guides were compensated for their aid in identifying indigenous plants and explaining their use in medical treatment. Lucile Q. Mann, field notes, SIA RU 7293 William M. Mann and Lucile Quarry Mann Papers.

Society."[33] The Manns needed no "added inducement," as "opportunities for white men to learn something of the native mysteries are rare."[34]

After dinner, the members of the Snake Society called again at the Mann's temporary housing and led them out of the village to a house in the forest, with a dozen locals. Mrs. Mann asked for and was granted permission to take notes, (and they photographed and filmed portions of it as well) and she proceeded to do so, phonetically spelling local words. The Manns paid their 8 shillings and agreed to an oath of secrecy and were duly read into the rules and bylaws, passwords and grip of the society.

Mrs. Mann describes the Snake Society initiation in general terms, but excludes details, noting in an article for National Geographic that "We have not yet betrayed any secrets of the Snake Society, nor do we intend to break our promise to our friends in Belleyella. What follows…give[s] only a general idea of what the Snake Society means to the men who take it seriously."[35] The Manns did, indeed, take their participation in the local society seriously. About the initiation, she wrote: "The fetiches were arranged on a large tray on the floor, and the Gli…picked them up one by one and told us their symbolism." This is an interesting point in the field notes, as Mrs. Mann explains a problem of translation – each lesson was given in the Mano language, translated into Belle, then into Kpelle, then into Liberian English by Bobor, one of the Manns' Liberian assistants, then repeated to the group in American English by Silas Johnson, Firestone official and friend of the Manns who accompanied them. Afterward, the group is told the uses and combinations of different plants, some of which are used to effectively handle poisonous snakes and others to manage a variety of human relationships. Mrs. Mann, in a 1980 narration of the film footage shot in 1940, says: "I was given a title, it was Yangwa, and my special power was to cut a palaver [end an argument]…I was given an antelope horn covered in cowrie shells and feathers and when I proudly carried it back to the village, everyone

---

[33] Article draft: William Mann and Lucile Q. Mann, "Expedition to Liberia," p. 2, William M. Mann and Lucile Quarry Mann Papers, SIA RU 7293.

[34] L. Q. Mann, "The Smithsonian-Firestone Expedition to Liberia," draft for *National Geographic*, 1941, p. 11, William M. Mann and Lucile Quarry Mann Papers, SIA RU 7293. Mann's comment is interesting, as the early anthropologists (George Harley and George Schwab) working in the Liberian hinterland are roughly contemporary to the Manns expedition. Harley published the earliest anthropological accounts, *Notes on the Poro* and *Native African Medicine, with special reference to its practice in the Mano tribe of Liberia*, in 1941.

[35] Draft for *Nat Geo:* L. Q. Mann, 1941, p. 11-12, William M. Mann and Lucile Quarry Mann Papers, SIA RU 7293.

knew what it meant." The horn, now in the collection of the National Museum of Natural History, is called a "Bakuna", and is filled with medicine to deter snakes. It is decorated with cowrie shells and cuckoo (dudu) feathers, because the cuckoo eats snakes. The legend on the origin of the Bakuna was duly explained and recorded. The Manns then returned to their house to sleep and the next morning received a second lesson. Thus convinced of the Manns' training and ability to handle venomous snakes, the local men began to sell snakes that they caught to the Manns.

Through the gift of the Bakuna, Lucile Mann attained special status, revealed to her through societal rituals: she was re-named, given information, and finally an object through which she could powerfully use her newfound knowledge. She was given the special power to "break the palaver," or to settle disputes. The story of her initiation became a part of her travel narrative as soon as she wrote it into her field notes. Joined with the local Liberian community through the transfer of knowledge, Mrs. Mann situates her newfound status within that community by noting that "everyone" knew the meaning of her horn as she returned to the village from the bush.

This travel experience was cabled to the United States and picked up by the papers immediately. It was June, and just in time for the first shipment of Liberian animals to reach New York, destined for the New York World's Fair Firestone pavilion; the propagandistic element of the story is evident. Furthermore, the event resonated after the Manns returned to the States. Mrs. Mann, in her narration of the film, described the reception of the story at the White House: "when we showed this film at the White House, there was a filibuster going on in the Senate and finally Roosevelt turned to me and said 'Mrs. Mann, may I appoint you to the Senate next week?'"[36] The presidential exchange was incorporated into Lucile Mann's future narrations of the expedition. Though almost certainly meant as a tongue-in-cheek remark, Mann took her experiences in Liberia seriously, and that people at home engaged with her foreign status-marker demonstrated that the experience retained some meaning across the Atlantic as well.

The second episode that dominated the field notes and travel correspondence while in the field never appeared in any of the Manns' published works. Beginning on May 10, Lucile Mann's field journal included ever more frequent records of the war's progress. That morning, the Manns walked over to one of the Mission houses and heard from a British broadcast about Germany's invasion of Holland and Belgium. She wrote: "Our neighbors are flying a big Nazi flag this morning." That same evening, they hosted a dinner party attended by two Dutch

---

[36] Voice recording: L. Q. Mann, n.d., Box 27, William M. Mann and Lucile Quarry Mann Papers, SIA RU 7293.

guests and a number of the Manns' friends, including two German doctors. Lucile wrote: "[Mrs. Bodewes] had not been told of the German invasion of Holland, so for the last time probably in many years we entertained Dutch and German guests at the same time." The progressing war changed the social climate of European ex-patriots in Liberia and their American counterparts.

The Manns made their last trip to the interior in May, arriving at the town of Bendaja on May 14. Their German doctor friends joined them, "full of news of new German victories in Europe, and confident that Hitler would shortly win the war." The Manns close association with the German doctors proved to be politically unwise. Boima Quae, the paramount chief at Bendaja, received a missive on May 17 from the Superintendent of Grand Cape Mount County, T. Elwood Davis, regarding the Manns' movements. He shared this letter with the Manns:

> "I received your verbal query about the foreigners operating in your section. I wish to inform you that I only heard of their arrival by rumour [sic]. I am addressing a letter to Dr. Mann and his party to remain at Bendaja pending their sending down to me their papers before the proceed further. If they have gone beyond Bendaja you will invite them back to Bendaja.
>
> In the case of Mr. Paul, West agent, the German doctor and the other doctor, you advise them not to go near the British boundary. You will take note secretly of the number of guns they have and laborers as well as their general activities and report to me immediately. Any information that you may have not contained in this letter you will please forward them.
>
> I think it advisable that you place an intelligent messenger with them to observe their activities."

The Manns had tried to present their papers at Cape Mount, but did not find the superintendent at home and so moved on to Bendaja. By May 30, when the Manns finally reached Superintendent Davis, their activities in the area, namely their association with the Germans, had already caused political problems. An "alarmist," as characterized by Lucile Mann, had written the president about it. The Manns found a letter from the American Charge d'Affaires in Monrovia, recalling them to the capitol. From local residents, the Manns learned that they had:

> "been accused of heading a German expeditionary force into the hinterland and towards the English border; that we were armed with eight high-powered rifles; that Bill, suspiciously enough, spoke German! Evidently the requested spies had been on the job, for Davis

knew all about our trip, even to the fact that we had been digging something or other out of bug-a-bug nests."[37]

The Manns sent a flurry of letters to Monrovia fully detailing their actions and whereabouts while in and around Bendaja. Outraged and bewildered that the rumors had been taken seriously in Monrovia, the effects of escalating conflict had penetrated their American expedition on neutral soil.

The expedition narrative, objects and animals are all interrelated. As publicity for the exhibits, as regular features of the lecture Dr. and Mrs. Mann took on the road, and finally, as part of the permanent collections at the Smithsonian, each object, animal and episode illustrated the difficulties and rewards of trans-Atlantic travel through this tumultuous moment in history. The bits of narrative that are excluded from the public one, such as the political incident in Bendaja, are interesting to note. Most important, however, is the agency of local people in these interactions. The arrangement between the Manns, Firestone, and the Liberian government set up a system of unequal exchanges between the travelers and local populations. Even within these constraints, the local people the Manns encountered exercised agency authority within this structure by divesting cultural knowledge or demonstrating the effectiveness and power residing in local communication networks.

Although each document, animal, specimen or object ended up in separate files and exhibition spaces (and today, in storage), the pieces of the Manns' travels are interrelated and accrue meaning because of their relationships with the whole body of material. They also continue to exist in new contexts, as part of the larger exhibition and collecting history of the Smithsonian. Although primarily scientific in motivation, the social and cultural aspects of the Mann's expedition are an integral part of their work and a critical lens through which to consider their travel experiences. Without making intercultural connections, they would have been unable to accomplish their goal of collecting rare animals for the fair and the zoo. Moreover, the subsequent publicity, film commentary and lecture circuit material demonstrate the necessity of meshing the didactic with an element of entertainment in order to convey deeper contexts and meanings to their audiences. This idea will be further investigated in the section on staging the travel narratives.

---

[37] Field journal: L. Q. Mann, 1940, p. 58, William M. Mann and Lucile Quarry Mann Papers, SIA RU 7293.

The Ark Returns: Crossing back with the Spoils of Travel

The journey from New York to Monrovia was characterized by gaiety and anticipation, with Dr. Mann summoning images of the freighter lit up like the Fourth of July. The return journeys across the Atlantic took quite a different tone. As the conflict in Europe escalated, bits of news that came over the radio concerned the Manns as they prepared for the journey home. Before resuming the Manns' narrative, it is important to briefly examine the first shipment of animals sent to New York to participate in the Firestone exhibition at the World's Fair.

The first shipment destined for the Firestone Exhibit at the New York World's Fair departed Monrovia on the *S. S. West Kebar*. Roy Jennier, one of two zookeepers who traveled with the Manns, escorted 135 animals (including 46 snakes, a number of birds, along with the mammals). While aboard ship, keepers had to maintain constant vigilance in caring for the animals, especially since some, like the pangolin, were the first of their species to ever make the journey to America. The first return trip lasted 18 days, a long time for keeper Jennier to deal with seasick animals and their highly specialized diets. For instance, "the chimpanzees…required cream with their warm breakfast food. The menagerie menu called for… mockingbird food, sunflowers and pumpkin seed, wheat, corn, bran, rice, crushed oats, raw meat, fresh fish, eggs, milk, bananas, oranges and fresh vegetables."[38]

Of this first shipment, Lucile Mann records the inventory of animals on April 24, 1940, and added, "we are praying that most of the things will survive the voyage and reach New York alive." She continued: "It is not enough, as far as results of the expedition go, but it's not bad for a little over a month's collecting, and Bill feels more cheerful. It is certainly enough to make a nice show at the Firestone exhibit in New York."[39] The preparations continued for the rest of the week. On April 29, Mann recorded that the animals were being brought down to be loaded onto the freighter. Additionally, food and objects were loaded onto the ship: bananas, avocados, pineapples and greens for the animals and several bags of souvenirs containing masks, country cloth and native knives.

On the western side of the Atlantic, the first shipment due back from the expedition was met with excitement and anticipation. A May 4 article in the *New*

---

[38] "Dr. Mann's 'Ark' Arrives in Boston from West Africa." Unidentified newspaper clipping: Manns' scrapbook, n.d., William M. Mann and Lucile Quarry Mann Papers, SIA RU 7293.

[39] Field journal: L. Q. Mann, 24 Apr. 1940, William M. Mann and Lucile Quarry Mann Papers, SIA RU 7293.

York Times had advertised the addition of the animals to the Firestone pavilion, juxtaposing this addition with the announcement of the withdrawal of several national pavilions, including Venezuela and Cuba: "Live wild animals, captured by the Smithsonian-Firestone expedition to Liberia, including a pygmy hippopotamus…will give the exhibit a menagerie air."[40] The *Washington Post* ran an article on May 17, 1940 that exclaimed: "Wild Cargo Sent Home by Dr. Mann Due in U.S. Today." The shipment, which "officials hope survived the rough voyage," contained "exotic wild beasts." Their destinations, the National Zoo and World's Fair, were noted as well.[41] On May 24, the Post ran its first interview with Jennier.

Jennier characterized his trans-Atlantic travel experience by saying, "I feel like a regular globe trotter already…though until I went to Africa the largest boat I'd ever been aboard with a moonlight excursion steamer."[42] The travel experience, especially to such an exotic location, conferred upon Jennier a special status granted to those who managed to make such a trip. While the majority of the article discussed the business of collecting animals (especially the capture – by the tail – of an 8-foot black cobra), Jennier also juxtaposes the familiar and foreign to convey the strangeness of the place he visited: "Nor will [Jennier] forget…the strange situation in which housewives on the vast Firestone rubber plantation, which is equipped with a golf course and electricity and all modern conveniences, have to watch where they tread when hanging up clothes lest the step on a deadly viper or cobra."

The Post brings the experience of a Firestone housewife into familiar territory of the American housewife. Jennier also brought reminders of his travels back with him. An "elaborate tribal headdress, three hand-carved dolls, several spears and other trinkets" adorned his residence in Alexandria, Virginia.[43] Nelson Graburn writes that mementos and objects can function as mnemonic devices to relive the travel experiences and that objects like these serve as symbols that confirme the experienced reality of travel. These same objects and ended up in Smithsonian and local university collections where they afford contemporary visitors and scholars the opportunity to consider expeditions in historical context, serving similar roles to museum visitors who experience both the original culture and the travel by the collectors through these objects.

---

40   "Venezuela, Cuba Lost to 1940 Fair," *New York Times*, 4 May 1940.
41   "Wild Cargo Sent Home by Dr. Mann Due in U.S. Today," *The Washington Post*, 17 May 1940, p. 8.
42   "Zoo Keeper Tugs Cobra Out of Tree by Tail, Gets Gooseflesh at Sight of a Rat or Spider," *The Washington Post*, 24 May 1940, p. 8.
43   Ibid.

The media feted the animal travelers as well. Two days after Jennier's interview, the Post ran a large photograph of two chimpanzees cradled in Jennier's arms. The article began: "A colorful collection of West African wild life moves moved into the Washington Zoo yesterday and immediately started *playing to the galleries*."[44] The paper addressed how the new residents adjusted to their novel surroundings, and also their reception by the public: "those...uncrated in Washington yesterday attracted immediate attention from a big week-end crowd of Zoo-goers." The article also reported that Dr. Mann would return as well a few weeks later with another cargo hold full of animals, and the animals on display at the World's Fair, "including the rare pygmy hippopotamus," would return to D.C. in the fall, after the close of the fair. Unreported in these accounts but documented in the Manns' logs and veterinary quarantine reports, are the animals that died en route to New York and Washington, a loss felt poignantly by the Manns and their staff.

The Manns were welcomed home with equal anticipation from the American media. However, their re-crossing of the Atlantic was fraught with anxiety over the war news on the eastern side of the Atlantic. On June 14, Lucile Mann recorded: "The war news continues to grow worse and worse. Today the Germans entered Paris. We keep wishing Roosevelt would stop promising aid to the Allies until we get safely home."[45] The anxiety of crossing back across the Atlantic is palpable in Lucile's field note from June 19:

> "This has been a tense week, with everyone sitting over the radio to get the latest news from Europe and the States. So far the peace plans have not been announced. American ships are said to be running arms to Lisbon and flying planes to England...We can't find out...when our ship is due. The more we hear about ships at sea right now the more we wish there were some way of getting home without them. We have never been so anxious to be in Washington. Everybody here is speculating as to what will become of Liberia if Germany takes over the West Coast, as has been hinted."

Nearly a month later, Mann recorded: "day after day drags by while we wait for news of the *West Irmo*," and she wrote that May 12, 1940, they still waited for news of when their ship would arrive so that they could begin the journey home.[46]

---

[44] "Rhinos and Rats, New Animals From Liberia Augment D.C. Zoo", *The Washington Post*, 19 May 1940, p. 14. Emphasis mine.

[45] Ibid., p. 63.

[46] Field journal: L. Q. Mann,, p. 63-69, 12 May 1940, William M. Mann and Lucile Quarry Mann Papers, SIA RU 7293.

The *West Irmo* left Monrovia on May 16, carrying an incredible load: $400,000 worth of mahogany logs, nearly 300 live animals, thousands of specimens for the US National Museum, and, of course the remaining members of the Smithsonian-Firestone Expedition team, Dr. and Mrs. Mann along with Ralph Norris, the second zookeeper. The Evening Star reported the loading of a pygmy hippopotamus "hauled 40 miles" through the Liberian jungle so as to not miss her boat, noting that the *West Irmo* was expected to dock at American shores in Norfolk the next month. The Smithsonian Institution issued a press release announcing the arrival of the expedition to Norfolk on August 6. The release related basic information about the expedition and ends by stating: "Dr. Mann had many thrilling experiences during his treks through the jungles. One of these was his initiation during the blackness of a jungle night into one of the most mysterious of West African secret societies," and another newspaper headline characterized the ship as Dr. Mann's "ark," inviting comparisons to the Biblical Noah and highlighting Dr. Mann's transformative journey.[47]

The Manns were no strangers to hosting a menagerie at sea. Lucile Mann wrote in her autobiography that, "I had grown so accustomed to reptilian chaperonage that it was something of a shock to me to learn that other people regarded it as a reprehensible habit."[48] She wrote that the routine at sea was similar to their daily routine at the zoo, consisting of cleaning cages and regular feedings. Traveling with birds and mammals was a more difficult task than the reptiles and fish, whose maintenance consisted of sprinkling with water to maintain humidity or scooping and pouring cups of water in the fish tanks to aerate them. Occasionally, the Manns even found themselves giving guided tours of the storage spaces, especially if they sailed the animals back on a steamer or cruise ship.[49] When sailing from Central America or the West Indies, the Manns often stopped to refresh their food supply along the way to ensure that the animals maintained as regular a diet as possible. The reptiles were the exception (especially on shorter journeys from Central America), as they often remained in their bags, not needing to eat until they arrived in Washington. The 1940 return journey was different, as the opportunities to stop along the West African coast were hampered by war. The Manns had to manage mainly with the supplies they took on from Monrovia, no small task with companions like the voracious hornbills and hippopotami Lucile describes in her field journals and in the Manns' expedition film. According to Lucile Mann,

---

[47] "For immediate release, from the Smithsonian Institution, N.d. [1940], William M. Mann and Lucile Quarry Mann Papers, SIA RU 7293.
[48] L. Q. Mann, *From Jungle to Zoo*, 1934, p. 232.
[49] Ibid., p. 240-246.

"Loading and unloading of animals is always an exciting business, whether one is saying good-by [sic] to a country that one has learned to love during a brief visit, or whether one is coming into New York harbor, bursting with impatience to bore the friends at home with accounts of the journey."[50]

The Manns' voyages were never boring. Both the Washington Post and Evening Star covered the *West Irmo*'s arrival in Norfolk. After a second 22-day trans-Atlantic journey, the travelers returned to the States. The Post ran photographs of Ralph Norris' wife and son waiting for him and holding sculpted elephant tusks he brought back with him after the ship arrived. Upon arrival, Dr. Mann was ill with malaria and hurriedly unloaded and taken to the naval hospital in Norfolk. However, he and Mrs. Mann fulfilled their publicity obligations, posing for a photograph with assistant director of the Smithsonian, Dr. Alexander Wetmore, who met them on the wharf. The caption reads: "Dr. Mann, recovering from an attack of malaria aggravated by his African Expedition, is shown shaking hands with Dr. Alexander Wetmore…Mrs. Mann, sun-tanned and in excellent health after the trip, looks on."[51] Mrs. Mann and Norris were photographed supervising the animals as they were transferred and loaded onto trains to take them to Washington.

For the travelers, the return voyage across the Atlantic was much more difficult than the initial crossing. Not only did the Manns have to manage the menagerie at sea, they were concerned with the effect of the global conflict on their safety. Their triumphant return, however, was cause for celebration in the media. From the photographs run in news stories, it is apparent that their return drew visitors flocking to see the animals touted so highly over the summer. The arrival in the U.S. signified a change for both human and animal travelers. The animals, formerly trans-Atlantic travelers, became the main event at the sites, zoo and fair, to which audiences traveled. Their physical crossing merged into a different type of crossing, from traveler to attraction. Likewise, the Manns' position changed as well. As travelers returned home, their travel narratives and souvenir collections became attractions to public and scholarly audiences. The staging of these travel experiences allows us to turn our attention to the American traveler who experienced a particular representation of Liberia through exhibition and imagination.

---

[50] Ibid., p. 241.
[51] Photograph and caption from Mann scrapbook, n.d. [1940], William M. Mann and Lucile Quarry Mann Papers, SIA RU 7293.

Staging Travel Narratives

The theme of the 1939-1940 New York World's Fair was originally "the World of Tomorrow," but after the first season and the outbreak of conflict all over Europe, the second season was re-themed "Peace and Freedom."[52] Marco Duranti argues that the shift from utopian to nostalgic themes offers narratives attempting to neutralize the implications of war in Europe, especially in the wake of both the Great War (First World War) and Great Depression in the United States. No study considers a travel and collecting project quite like the Smithsonian-Firestone Expedition; a travel, collecting and exhibition project that brought together multiple types of travelers, audiences and exhibitionary practices.

Other scholarship on the fair focuses on specific national pavilions or on the corporate and technological features isolated from the international spaces.[53] One reason for this is the layout of the fair, which privileged the corporations in both space and architectural aesthetic, and promoted a future world in which corporations improved and modernized life in the United States through the use of technology. Like other 1930s fairs, the architecture and exhibitions were at once nostalgic and forward-looking, attempting to produce a blended vision of modernity for Americans.[54] The fair was divided into seven "sectors," each one a functional part of modern life: Production and Distribution, Transportation, Communications and Business Systems, Food, Medicine and Public Health, Science and Education, and Community Interests. Unlike 19th-century and other early 20th-century fairs, in New York the Government section (containing the national pavilions and League of Nations building) were pushed to the periphery of the fair, the architectural unity and space privileging the corporate and technological pavilions. Upon the withdrawal of some of the nations in the second

---

[52] Marco Duranti, "Utopia, Nostalgia and World War at the 1939 – 1940 New York World's Fair" in: *Journal of Contemporary History* 41:4 (Oct 2006), p. 663-683: 663-665.

[53] Duranti, p. 663-664. Robert Rydell, the leading scholar on American World's Fairs, has also written on the technological features of the 1939 fair in New York.

[54] Robert W. Rydell, "Making America (More) Modern: America's Depression-Era World's Fairs" in: Robert W. Rydell and Laura Burd Schiavo (Eds.), *Designing Tomorrow: America's World's Fairs of the 1930s*, New Haven 2010, p. 1-22.

season, the sparseness of some of the government building exhibitions ran counterpoint to the concept of the fair.[55]

The Firestone pavilion was part of the World's Fair organism, but also belonged to a broader project in conjunction with other exhibition spaces and audiences.[56] Together with the National Zoo and Smithsonian museums, both the expedition adventurers and exhibition visitors created a network of American travelers and travel experiences. Firestone's pavilion resembled other buildings in the transportation section. Robert Bennett describes the "penchant for streamlined modernist designs" in the architecture and landscape design in New York's fair.[57] He connects the distilled American version of European modernist aesthetics to broader trends in the art world. Certainly, there was a strain of formalist modernism that appreciated the clean lines and simple shapes that arranged visions of urban spaces. The infusion of color at the fair also demonstrates the embrace of this aesthetic. Essentially a campus, the pavilion area covered three and a half acres. According to archival records:

> "The exhibition building with house a full scale [sic] tires factory in actual operation, producing a finished tire every four minutes. To demonstrate the part that rubber has played in the modernization of the American farm there will be a life-sized reproduction of a fully equipped farm with a farm house, barns, silos and other farm buildings. Live stock [sic] roaming the fields will complete the rural scene. Dioramas, historical pagents [sic], and scientific demonstrations will dramitize [sic] the history of the rubber industry. Visual demonstrarions [sic] will portray the fascinating story of rubber

---

[55] Duranti examines the pavilions of countries invaded by Germany, particularly Czechoslovakia, Denmark, and Finland to analyze national responses to World War II at the NYWF, p. 667-683.

[56] In *Designing Tomorrow: America's World's Fairs of the 1930s*, Rydell and the other authors featured in the book discuss how American modernity featured at the fairs, concentrating on the sectors of the fair related to modern life. These studies primarily examined the technological and corporate entities as they related to modern art and architectural movements. As suggested in the first part of this paper, examining the Firestone pavilion individually or as part of the larger Transportation section of the fair does not push the analysis of the exhibition to its limits. These studies primarily examined the technological and corporate entities as they related to modern art and architectural movements.

[57] Robert Bennett, "Pop Goes the Future: Cultural Representations of the 1939 – 1940 New York World's Fair" in Robert W. Rydell and Laura Burd Schiavo (Eds.), *Designing Tomorrow: America's World's Fairs of the 1930s*, New Haven 2010, p. 177-192: 178.

from the time it is gathered as latex, on the Firestone Plantations in Liberia, West Africa, until it becomes a finished product on the wheels of America. At the top is shown a great rotunda entrance to the exhibit. The illuminated fin which surmounts the rotunda towers 100 feet in the air."[58]

The campus incorporated different types of buildings to demonstrate the links between modernity and America's past as well as the differences between the source of rubber, West Africa, and the tire production in American factories. The sleek building with its contoured exterior and "towering" fin contained the most technologically advanced equipment, churning out tires in front of the millions of visitors to the pavilion. Visitors were also treated to charming scenes on America's farms, complete with "farmer's daughters" seated in wheelbarrows. Furthermore, visitors to the pavilion were treated to images and a recreation of the source of the natural materials necessary to make the product.

A number of scholars have included Firestone exhibits in broader considerations of corporations at Depression-era fairs. Lisa Schrenk, writing about the 1933 Chicago Century of Progress fair, examines the way that corporations presented their technical processes and products to educate the American public about corporations' "beneficial contribution to modern society."[59] She describes how many corporate leaders, including Harvey Firestone, used the expositions to launch large-scale marketing campaigns linking American industry and financial recovery throughout the decade. At the back entrance to the 1940 pavilion, a "jungle" was populated with lush trees and indigenous Liberian architecture. Inside, visitors were treated to the ubiquitous museum display, a diorama of plantation life. This particular diorama first made its appearance in 1933 at the Chicago Century of Progress Exposition and the package traveled to New York intact.[60] During the 1933 fair, Firestone contributed three separate exhibits: a general display in the Hall of Science, a service station situated near the entrance on 23rd street, and constructed a model factory in their corporate pavilion.[61]

---

[58] New York World's Fair 1939 – 1940 records, 1935 – 1945, bulk (1939 – 1940), VIII. Promotion and Development Division, VIII.B. News Dissemination, VIII.B.6, Photographs, Firestone, Firestone Brothers. Manuscripts and Archives division, New York Public Library, Image ID: 1672778

[59] Lisa D. Schrenk, "Industry Applies: Corporate Marketing at A Century of Progress" in: Robert W. Rydell and Laura Burd Schiavo (Eds.), *Designing Tomorrow: America's World's Fairs of the 1930s*, New Haven 2010, p. 23-40: 23-24.

[60] James Weber Linn, *The Official Pictures of a Century of Progress Exposition Chicago 1933*, Chicago 1933 (no page numbers designated in the catalogue).

[61] Schrenk, p. 32.

Although dioramas had been used in anthropological exhibitions during the 19th century, according to Schrenk, the 1933 Chicago fair is the first time that miniature, three-dimensional scenes are used to promote corporate interests. The dramatization of industrial processes through dioramas, murals, re-created factories, and architecture attracted crowds and ensured that the corporate perspective was conveyed through design.[62] Seven years later, Firestone collapsed these exhibits into the large corporate pavilion space, eventually adding greater context for the natural resources in the form of Liberian architecture, foliage, and animals.

During the fair's second season, the exhibit featured a small zoo with the animals caught during the expedition; the previous section had examined the circumstances under which they traveled to New York. The first shipment of animals arrived at the fair mid-summer, and they were immediately incorporated into Firestone's pavilion. Publicity materials commemorated particularly appealing moments at the fair; for example, a photograph showing a 'junglette' pavilion employee bottle-feeding one of the baby pygmy hippopotami.[63] The animals drew crowds, and a September program for the fair published in the *New York Times* included the 4:30 pm feeding time for the Firestone animals alongside lectures, concerts and art exhibits.[64] The audience of the Firestone pavilion was huge; the 5,000,000th visitor was captured on film and introduced to local celebrities.[65] The Firestone campus was a complex exhibition space, and the possibilities for different types of visitor experiences were infinite. It is an exhibition space ripe for multivalent readings and analyses.

In a study of African performance and placement at American world's fairs between 1893 and 1940, Robert Rydell addresses how representations of Africa change over the half century. He includes the Firestone pavilion in an analysis that sees African representation change from incorporating African people in exhibits to focusing on corporate management of African environments, natural resources, and labor forces. According to Rydell, between the late 19th century

---

[62] Schrenk, p. 28-29.
[63] Manuscripts and Archives Division, The New York Public Library. "Firestone – Woman feeding hippopotamus at Firestone Zoo" New York Public Library Digital Collections. http://digitalcollections.nypl.org/items/5e66b3e8-a721-d471-e040-e00a180654d7, accessed 26 Apr 2017.
[64] "Today's Program At The Fair", *New York Times*, 3 Sept 1940.
[65] "For Immediate Release" – this photograph, of the 5,000,000th visitor to the Firestone Pavilion and actress Judy Canova, is one example of the publicity materials Firestone released throughout the Fair, New York World's Fair, 1939 – 1940, NYPL Image ID: 1672629 and 1672630.

and mid-20th century, American fairs prominently represented Africa, but with less and less of a human presence. Rather, American fairs reduced Africa to its essential resources in a neo-imperialist manner. He compares the Dahomean village at Chicago's 1893 fair to two pavilions in New York: the British South African Company and the Firestone pavilion. In the British South African Company pavilion, the company promoted the leading industries of agriculture (including tobacco) and gold mining, and features a replica of Victoria Falls. Visitors could also peruse native arts and crafts, and native architecture. Rydell writes: "What distinguished this show from its antecedent was that Africans were nonexistent, rendered extinct, as it were, from a continent that tourists could enjoy and corporations could exploit at will."

He follows this argument by discussing the Firestone pavilion as a parallel example. In the Firestone Pavilion, Rydell writes, the visitors walk through the jungle inside the pavilion, encountering the animals and environment that challenged the Firestone engineers, and emerge at the factory, where they are awed by its technological wonder.[66] Several questions arise from Rydell's analysis. The first is whether or not the comparison between the native village arrangements and the corporate pavilions is as linear as presented, considering the reorientation of the fairground space between 1893 and 1940. Additionally, to compare the earliest example, a Dahomean village, with the latest examples, corporations in South Africa and Liberia, ignores the unique French, British, and American/Liberian colonial histories and the separate modes of engagement with audiences. Firestone's economic imperial interests in the independent republic of Liberia, especially considering the League of Nations inquiry into human rights abuses, required a determinedly positive marketing campaign.

Secondly, it is impossible to separate the co-sponsored expedition, its publicity and public narratives, from the miniature zoological park set up in New York. The National Zoo did not merely "help" Firestone as the company "upgraded its exhibit…by organizing a fake jungle habitat," but created an entire travel experience for visitors through the expedition's planning, execution, and resulting exhibits, lectures and films.[67] Firestone also published a book in 1937, *Views in Liberia*, promoting the cooperative nature of the Firestone-Liberian alliance to create necessary consumer products. I would suggest that the Firestone pavilion does not present a representation of Africa or Africans more generally, but specifically plays on the communal history and ties between the United States

---

[66] Robert Rydell, "Darkest Africa: African Shows at America's World's Fairs 1893–1940" in: Bernth Lindfors (Ed.), *Africans on Stage: Studies in Ethnological Show Business*, Bloomington 1999, p. 135-155: 149-152.

[67] Rydell, 1999, p. 150-152.

and Liberia to accomplish its neo-imperialistic goals in that specific place. It speaks more to strategies of American imperialism than it does to representations of Africa.

The objectives and designers for the village and the exhibits also differed. The Firestone pavilion, for instance, had an entire public relations team creating a corporate brand. The representation needed to incorporate national and international contexts and present an image of intercultural cooperation and benefit for everyone involved to promote its modernity. The designers did so through the display formulae available at the time in both fairs and museums: dioramas, architectural installation and miniature zoological park. The animals were showcased as entertainment for the visitors, but were also posited as educational. Furthermore, they were scientifically essential to a national project, that of building the collection of the National Zoo.

Rydell also describes how "Africans put on display at America's fairs often rewrote scripts and turned showcases of empire into theaters of resistance."[68] While nineteenth-century ideas about race and Africa shaped the discourse around cultural practices, by examining the archives more closely it is possible to extrapolate previously silenced voices. If the entirety of the Smithsonian-Firestone expedition is taken into account when considering the resulting exhibitions, local Liberian agency is present in the travel narratives. Of course, the discourse around cultural practices was neither politically correct by today's standards, nor was it even wholly devoid of white paternalism. However, sprinkled in throughout the narrative, Liberian voices are both present and important in shaping the narratives of the 1940 exhibitions.

Additionally, the Republic of Liberia sponsored a pavilion at the 1893 Chicago World's Columbian Exposition and contracted to produce a national pavilion at the 1939-1940 New York World's Fair. Is a comparison of the latter two pavilions and the Firestone pavilion more appropriate to analyze how Liberia specifically, and not as part of a generalized "Africa," was represented over time? The country's unique history fights compression into a general travel or exhibition practice of going to or representing Africa. How broadly, then, can the African exhibits be lumped together? Liberia, as a sovereign nation from the first quarter of the 19th century (albeit with a contentious history), may not be the strongest comparative case study because of its unique history. It is also one of the only sub-Saharan African nations to sponsor (or enter into contracts for) its own pavilion at both of these American fairs. At both the 1893 and 1940 fairs, Liberia

---

[68] Rydell, 1999, p. 136.

(like most nations and states) sponsored a Liberia Day at the fair. [69] Consider the sketch and model for the Liberian government building. Based around a central "Hall of Goodwill," the building was designed to occupy a 15,000 square-foot plot, and included two roof terraces adjacent to the restaurant.[70] The architect and designer of the building was Vertner W. Tandy, the first black architect licensed to practice in New York. Though not part of this study, a comparison of the concept and design of the two 1939-1940 pavilions might provide fruitful fodder for discussion of the presentation of the Liberian nation and its own modernization process during this transitional period.

The visitor response and ultimate design of the fair exhibit was positive, at least to the designers and collectors involved in its creation. On August 23, 1940, C. D. Smith, Firestone's exhibit manager, wrote to E. P. Walker of the National Zoo to tell him that the baby hippo had been put on display: "The whole thing is working out fine and she is drawing a lot of attention. Thanks a lot for letting us have her." He goes on to tell Walker about the photograph of the 'junglette' feeding the baby hippo: "We obtained some nice publicity…in fact we got a four-column picture of the Hippo being fed…here in the jungle in the Journal American and the Brooklyn Eagle." He segues into asking Walker to send some duiker antelopes and chevrotains to New York in order to create a "better show." Walker must have sent them right along because Smith's next letter details how well the animals are settling in: "they are just as calm and unperturbed as they can be—it may be the fact that they are back in the 'jungle' that makes them feel so much at home." Smith goes on to describe the alternating animals of the exhibit. His letters make it clear that Firestone continuously rotated the animals in and out of the exhibit to keep the space fresh for visitors. Even as they became attractions, the animals continued in their initial role as travelers. If we consider the animals as active agents creating and experiencing travel encounters, our notion of what constituted trans-Atlantic and American travel in the early 20th century expands. Perhaps other studies of animal travelers, rather than people who travel to zoological attractions, can illustrate networks and travel experiences that are missing within the literature.

William Mann wrote to Smith in September to compliment him on the exhibit: "The more I think of it, the more pleased I am with your show in New York. It is easily one of the finest small zoo collections I have ever seen—beautifully

---

[69] David J. Bertuca, Donald K. Hartmann and Susan M. Neumeister, *The World's Columbian Exposition: A Centennial Bibliographic guide*, Westport, London 1996, p. 96, 205, 220, 364. New York Public Library Manuscripts and Archives Division, 1939 – 1940 World's Fair materials, Box 698, folder 4.

[70] NYPL Manuscripts and Archives Division, 1939 – 1940 World's Fair materials, Image ID: 1677084.

exhibited and cared for." He also thanks Smith for sending on a chevrotain that did not survive the journey and quarantine process; Mann will accession this animal into the permanent collection at the US National Museum. In a letter to George Seybold, the plantation manager in Harbel, Mann wrote:

> "The exhibition at the World's Fair is a complete success. The architect and decorator did a beautiful job and everything is maintained in A-1 condition. I saw it last Monday and afterwards had a visit with Harvey Firestone, Jr., who seems equally delighted about the show. I have received many comments on the exhibition—all favorable and some from professional showmen, friends of mine.[71]
>
> The exhibition this year is getting a much larger share of the Fair's attendance then it did last year, and I believe ranks second only to General Motors in popularity.
>
> One of the chevrotains and one of the pigmy hippos died there, and we are planning to make a Liberian group in the National Museum. This will consist of pigmy hippos and 'water deer' in a naturalistic setting and will be a permanent affair.
>
> Practically all of the skins and other knickknacks I picked up have been grabbed by the National Museum. Usually when you show a flattened skin to a mammal curator he kicks you out of the office. We brought back about a dozen mammals hitherto not represented in the National Museum Collection—that is, the skins. (Many of them you remember as having perfumed your kitchen.)
>
> The fish collection numbers more than 2500 specimens and with the other alcoholic material is being assorted for study. There will be numerous new species and material for more papers than I thought at first.
>
> The movies are in the hands of the Geographic Society at present for editing. It is probably that we shall show them at one of their formal lecture dates. In addition, there will be several supplemental reels mostly personal stuff on the plantation, and I am making up a reel for Bishop Kroll to use in his lectures here. He reaches an audiences entirely different to mine and the Expedition will, of course, be acknowledged on the films."

Mann ended the letter by urging Seybold to continue to collect and send animals his way. This letter, reproduced nearly in its entirety, reveals several interesting points. One is to reinforce the multiple networks at play before, during, and after

---

[71] Here, Mann refers to another animal showman, Frank Buck, who socialized with both the Manns and the Firestones.

the expedition. Mann clearly expects the trans-Atlantic animal travel to continue. Another is collection development, and the fluidity of moving the animals and objects between fair, zoo and museum. Publicity and the presentation of research related to the expedition and exhibition remained paramount to Mann, alluding to the multiple objectives of persons involved in the expedition and exhibition. Another interesting point is that Mann discusses the potential audiences for the variety of exhibitions deriving from the same source material. Not only does he note an increase in fair traffic, but discusses his own scholarly audience for his research, and Bishop Kroll's "different" audience, indicating that the imagined travel experiences of trans-Atlantic travel extend beyond the fair and zoo.

Additionally, a follow-up letter to the Firestone plantations in Monrovia includes a number of photographs. Thus, the technology the Manns brought with them travels back across the Atlantic to the land and people it captured as part of the travel narrative in the first place. Mann directs that they be given to his main assistants: "Pay-Pay, Bo Bo and Flomo, requesting that you give the pictures to [them] and distribute the Zoo books to…some of your boys." Mann's insistence that photographs go to his field assistants are typical of his and Lucile's relationships with their local, native aides, and suggest something of the network he developed with Liberians as well as the Americans working on the plantations.[72] Mann also published a zoo book, and urged Firestone to send one on to one of the missionary schools that the Manns visited: "…this one can go to the library of the girls who are going to have frogs named after them."[73] The Manns brought native knowledge back to Washington, and sent their own back across the Atlantic. Thus, neither animal nor expedition trans-Atlantic travel ceased, even though physical bodies may have remained on home coasts.

Conclusion

The theme of crossing is deeply rooted within the Smithsonian-Firestone expedition. Explorers and animals crossed the Atlantic physically, allowing visitors in New York and Washington to follow along through articles and exhibits by using their imagination. Newspaper audiences crossed through print, and countless audiences did so through film and the Manns' narrations. The collection did not stop crossing boundaries once it hit America's eastern coast.

---

[72] The Manns kept diverse company. They corresponded with their native field assistants and foreign zoo directors and government officials alike. See L. Q. Mann *From Jungle to Zoo*, 1934, p. 37-62, 243.

[73] William M. Mann to Harvey S. Firestone, 1943, William M. Mann and Lucile Quarry Mann Papers, SIA RU 7293.

Once in the States, the animals and objects collected by the Manns travel through exhibition spaces, representing Liberia and Firestone to tourists at the World's Fair, the National Zoological Park and US National Museum. The collection also crosses temporal boundaries. Many of the animals lived at the zoo for decades and their descendants (especially the pygmy hippos) still educate and entertain visitors in Washington and zoos across the country. The Manns gifted pieces from their personal collections to the Smithsonian over the second half of the 20th century. Animal specimens and some ethnographic objects still are in the National Museum of Natural History, and textiles, bracelets, and a carved stool went to the National Museum of African Art. Their films and papers are in the Smithsonian Institution Archives. These various crossings illustrate the networks that developed after travel in the interest of creating travel experiences for American audiences who made both physical trips to the New York World's Fair and Washington and vicarious journeys to Liberia. The travelers' experiences – the Manns, their crew, and the animals - reveal the complexity of trans-Atlantic travel on the eve of the Second World War.

10. Innocence Aboard

Lynn Bloom

The Eternal Sunshine of the Spotless Ship

Luxury liners, mobile Shangri-las, are designed to inculcate innocence in even their most sophisticated passengers. Even in the 1950s, when the trans-Atlantic voyages discussed here are taking place, travelers are isolated from the outside world throughout the course of the voyage. Although ship-to-shore communication is available to select crew members, passengers - even on student ships – are cocooned in a floating paradise. Having paid for passage in advance, everyone, regardless of income and obligations in the outer world, can live free of care for the duration of the voyage; on well-run ships they're expected to do so. Although on dry land the rich are very different from you and me, on shipboard many of these differences are erased. On board, no one has to worry about whether or when the next ample meal will be served, let alone who will buy and prepare it, or who will wash the dishes. Hot and cold running waiters can be summoned to fill hunger gaps between meals if the ever-available bouillon and biscuits don't suffice. Passengers don't have to make their beds, change the sheets, do the laundry, clean the bathroom – or anyplace else. Disorder disappears, whisked away by invisible hands – whose bodies are seldom seen, whose quarters never observed, whose wages never questioned. Minions are at the ready to do one's personal laundry and perform a variety of other services; cosseted passengers need not lift a finger except to exercise, to gamble, or to sign chits at the bar. That all reckonings are postponed until land is in sight enhances the illusion that everything is free – including shipboard romances, whose consequences will not be tallied on the high seas, but only on dry land.

Passengers are free to penetrate the illusion, to gain information, leverage that will help to rectify the inequities which underwrite such travels, but if any such socially aware people are on the two trans-Atlantic voyages I'm discussing in the narrative that follows, I am unaware of their presence. I understand only that to fulfill my heart's desire upon graduating from the University of Michigan in 1956, I want to spend the summer traveling throughout Europe, my first trip outside North America, and that this will require a week's voyage each way.

What little we students know of contemporary Europe we glean from newsreels, the *New York Times*, and foreign films; we don't yet have TV. As an English major I have taken the requisite two semesters of British history, but Trevelyan only goes as far as Queen Victoria, and the professor's book, William B.

Willcox's *Star of Empire: A Study of Britain as a World Power, 1485-1945* doesn't sink in; kings and battles just aren't my cup of tea. The Second World War has been over for a scant decade, yet our immediate images of "the Old World," mostly in black-and-white, are battle footage – Kristallnacht, Pearl Harbor, D-Day landings; bombed-out buildings – York Cathedral, Dresden, Kurfürstendamm; and Karsh's brooding photographs of Winston Churchill and Charles de Gaulle. Ringing speeches, Roosevelt's designation of the bombing of Pearl Harbor as "day that will live in infamy," threats of Communist takeover (Nikita Khrushchev's "We will bury you") mingle with the irresistible scores of *An American in Paris* and *Lili*, and TS Eliot's very British rendering of "*Four Quartets.*" My college major and New England heritage skew my view of Europe toward the British perspective; I am even anticipating the joys of toad-in-the-hole and bubble and squeak. As I become a better cook, my food preferences will change (vive la France!), but I will always have a tender heart for the terroir of the trifle.

Freshman honors students are introduced to existentialism – a thrilling concept our parents never heard of – via Camus's L'Étrangèr, and Sartre's No Exit, with its world weary, war weary observation, "l'enfer, c'est les autres." We discover art films for the congnoscenti that never play in my New Hampshire home town, and we always wear black turtlenecks and tall leather boots to the auditorium with splintery seats where we view *Open City, The Bicycle Thief, Jeux Interdit, La Silence de la Mer*, all with subtitles. We consider ourselves sophisticates; some even wear shades to the films (never movies) and take up smoking. Though I do not smoke, I appreciate the romance of cigarettes in long holders or adhering to sensuous lips, as in *Casablanca* . I am primed for travel.

1956. The Road to Adventure

Eager to light out for the territory of my own choosing, I have been saving money for this trip to the British Isles and the Continent since freshman year, waitressing in the dorm, reading to a blind student, working in a bookstore, guiding school tours through the science museum. Another English major, Trish, and I hatch a quick plan for a cheap trip. Preoccupied as we are with trying to finish our honors theses, our sketchy arrangements are on the order of E.B. White's practice for the phone call to invite the girl next door for his first date: "I had rehearsed my first line and my second line. I planned to say, 'Hello, can I please speak to Eileen?' Then, when she came to the phone, I planned to say, "Hello, Eileen, this is Elwyn White.' From then on, I figured I could ad lib."

On one train trip from New Hampshire to Ann Arbor, I have met kindly Marius J. Broekhuisen, whose job is to welcome Dutch immigrants to the United States. When he learns I am going to Europe, he not only sends a letter of introduction to his relatives in Gorinchem, who have returned postwar from an administrative post in the Dutch East Indies, but helps me to get a last-minute ticket on a single-class student ship, $320 from New York to Rotterdam and return, one-third of my travel budget. The *Groote Beer* (the Dutch name for Ursa Major, the constellation which contains the Big Dipper) is a Holland-American line vessel that has been a troop ship during the Second World War, and used afterward to transport emigrants from Rotterdam to New York, Halifax, Australia, and New Zealand. Known as a "Victory Ship," this boat weighs 7316 gross tons and is 455 feet long. Yet even with dormitory accommodations for eight hundred students, it's too late for Trish to book a berth on the same boat. So she arranges to take a different ship. She will arrive in Rotterdam the day before I do, and meet me at the pier. We will rent bicycles and off we'll go – through the Netherlands, France, the Alps (we have not figured out how, with no training and balloon tires, we will attempt this version of the Tour de France), Italy – at least Rome and Naples, and then back north through Switzerland to Germany, before crossing the Channel to spend at least a month in England, Scotland, and Wales. As English majors, we can do no less in the two months we have allocated. How I will carry the thirty-inch hard-sided suitcase (my prize in a contest in which I have explained why I have my heart set on a European trip) never occurs to me. Nor can I fathom why I take an extra duffel bag with more clothing – what am I thinking, dresses, ballet flats, tight skirts – do I really expect to wear these while biking?

After traveling alone by train from my parents' home to New York City, I take my first solo cab ride ever, to the Port of New York Authority. Unaccustomed to tipping for anything except 10% for infrequent meals out, I do not tip the driver, who clearly expects more than I know to give him. No one sees me off at the ship, and I am surprised to see farewell parties on the deck, families bearing bouquets and fruit baskets for their departing offspring. My second surprise is that I do not carry my own luggage to my cabin; a porter does this. This small, wiry man – I do not think he is Dutch despite the ship's Holland-American affiliation – drops the bags with a thump onto the narrow space between the double decker bunks of the cabin for four to which I am assigned. No tip for him either. As a child whose parents came of age during the depths of the Depression, and who worked their way through college and indeed life with nothing to spare, I am unfamiliar and uncomfortable with both the concept and the practice of tipping. If most of my fellow passengers were as innocent and as impecunious as I, the baggage handlers, like the rest of the crew, must have felt they were being stiffed right and left, but they remained gracious to the point of invisibility.

Although I am accustomed to living in cramped dormitory quarters – Michigan is full to bursting and my roommate and I have been sharing a single room in the most posh dorm on campus for two years, with big leaded casement windows overlooking a walled garden – the small size of this space threatens claustrophobia even when the door is open. The cabin is dark, despite the ceiling fixture and small lights designed for reading in bed; the absence of a porthole means we can't tell night from day. Two sets of double decker beds hug the side walls, blankets drawn tight as drumheads; the ladder to reach the upper bunks gets in the way and it's easier just to hang onto the iron bedstead bolted to the wall, vault into a top bunk, and shimmy down under the covers. The beds are flanked by skinny wardrobe closets holding lifejackets, and separated by a narrow path leading to the door that opens into the hall corridor. Although the cabin has a marble-backsplash sink large enough to wash lingerie in, just as in our college dorms the bath and shower rooms are down the hall, equipped with laundry tubs in lieu of automatic washers.

In 1956 I don't miss what I can't imagine, so although I would appreciate a shower and a chair, the only aspect of the cabin that really bothers me is the absence of light. Whether or not I have mild seasonal affective disorder (an affliction that hasn't been invented yet) gloom makes me morose, and to enter that cabin is to encounter an eclipse of the sun, every single time. In the gloaming I can discern two bodies bulking up in the lower bunks. They belong to two friends from New Jersey, Daisy and Dottie, with big hair and voices to match. These early arrivals have also snared prime wardrobe space, so I shove my suitcase under the bed, and send the already-cumbersome duffel bag to the hold. Soon our fourth cabin mate arrives, Lana, a lissome, long-limbed Georgia co-ed whose Southern drawl, like her pale blonde hair, exudes charm. The unspoken suspicion among us Yankees is that anyone that pretty and charming must be dumb, but Lana is not, and she remains ever gracious amidst the lumpenproletariat.

"Would you like to play bridge?" asks Daisy.

"I don't know how," I reply, having resolved not to join the incessant nightly bridge games in the dorm, which I knew would impede my writing sessions that usually began at 10:30, after women residents were safely locked in for the night. But I am on vacation. "We'll teach you," offers Dottie, and Lana and I settle in for lessons. In the absence of chairs – the cabin's folding backless camp stools are models of efficient discomfort – we sit on the edges of the lower bunks, but have to bend over to avoid getting our hair tangled in the iron mattress webbing from the upper bunks. Somehow we novices catch on, but as soon as Dottie has taken four tricks for the team I remember that half of the passengers on this ship are men, and they are out and about on deck. I signal to Lana, and we are out the door.

Every ship, each voyage has its own culture and its own cultural nuances, which we travelers discover as the ship plows steadily across the Atlantic. (I refuse then, as now, to refer to this ocean as "The Pond," with pseudo-British nonchalance or in the fake Oxford accent adopted by my more affected English major peers.) In fair weather the *Groote Beer*'s top two decks, of the three above water (two are below) are crowded with college kids, most of us on our maiden voyage, milling about to see and be seen. Our clothing is decorous. Knee length skirts for the women, khakis for the men; Bermuda shorts, preferably in patchwork or pastel plaid; white bucks or boat shoes without socks; and drip dry shirts for both sexes. This travel discovery of the decade is so significant that the pair costumed as "Drip" and "Dry" at the farewell sock hop win the prize. No one wears sunblock; everyone wants to tan. Sunglasses are optional for some, but de rigueur for the Gauloises-smoking Francophiles whose black berets are in perpetual danger of being blown overboard in the strong wind. One older man, he must be at least twenty-five, clad in black from head to toe, stands watch at the rail, smoking cigars. "Daddy tastes good tonight," he opines in gleeful pop-psych jargon when anyone comes near. I keep my distance.

If there is a bar scene, as there must be on this Dutch ship with Heineken as a national beverage, I am unaware of it. If co-eds are cohabiting in cabins not their own, I am unaware of this as well; I know that my own cabin hosts a nonstop bridge game and that I will be invited to join if I arrive before Daisy and Dottie go to bed. Though most of us are college students, the ship's personnel treat us like full-fledged grownups. Waiters in formal dress serve us sit-down meals at tables for eight or sixteen, covered in heavy white linen. The food is hearty, Dutch, and much tastier than it looks on the menu: robust soups, thick pea soup is a favorite; Edam and Gouda cheese, a mild but distinctively favorable contrast to the pasteurized process American not-real-cheese most of us are used to; a variety of breads, dark thinly sliced pumpernickel, whole wheat, even white – all home-baked and crusty with creamery butter instead of the wartime margarine we're still eating after the war; and lots of fish. Though the menu is light on fresh fruits and vegetables, we eat with gusto.

Echoes of prewar maritime elegance survive in the serving of bouillon on deck in thick mugs at eleven. Moreover, a string quartet, working their way across for free passage, it is rumored, plays concerts every afternoon in the salon at four to the tinkling obbligato of tea served with tiny sandwiches. Not long ago I was an aspiring violin player, until my music teacher at Michigan suggested that I should consider becoming a professional writer – although he had never read a word I'd written. So I am entranced, particularly when I notice a dark haired preppy type with a lean jaw, drawing occasionally on a briar pipe, absorbed in the music. I move unobtrusively to the chair next to his, and stare straight at the musicians. Brandenburg Concerto #3, an obvious crowd pleaser, is music to my ears.

We whisper briefly when the musicians pause to tune, and then after the last notes fade away, and soon we are talking as often and as long as possible. He too is an English major, at Princeton and therefore an expert on F. Scott Fitzgerald. We love Shakespeare, Donne, the Romantic poets. I am not so sure about Hemingway, he about Virginia Woolf, but we agree that James Joyce is the best contemporary writer in English. We can quote *Dubliners* and *Portrait* by heart, but the ship's small library lacks *Ulysses* so we can't check our interpretations. We drink tea with crisp cookies saved from the concerts. He has promised his grandfather that he will not touch alcohol until he is twenty-one, which means I keep silent about my age, though now we both understand that I am older than he. This knowledge, and the fact that I am being faithful to the two men I am dating concurrently at Michigan, means that although we stay up later and later night after night, our relationship is more chaste than might be expected even in the bourgeois 1950s. As the voyage nears an end, he cajoles me into washing some of his shirts by hand; had I been a year wiser, I'd have refused, even though we make a game of it, with a procession of sodden garments dripping water down the corridor from the women's lavatory to his cabin. He promises to treat me to chocolate and pastries at the Rijksmuseum after we have made our respective ways to Amsterdam. Our sumptuous repast, delivered after he has led me, eyes closed until they open in awe at the sight of Rembrandt's *Night Watch*, signals the ecstatic beginning of Lynn's Excellent Adventure, made even better by the fact that Trish has not met the ship at Rotterdam as planned, and indeed is nowhere to be found. But that is another story.

The voyage out, like all outbound voyages for pleasure rather than exile, is full of excitement, the promise of escape and adventure, anticipation of the unknown. Even if I'm too excited to sleep much in transit, I arrive relaxed by the stately pace of ship travel, with no jet lag (a term not invented until a decade later) when the clock is set forward an hour each night. I'm full of energy, my suitcase is full of clean clothes, my Youth Hostel pickpocket-proof pouch contains my life savings, converted to traveler's checks.

Best of all, I am filled with the sense of freedom that has been building throughout the voyage. I have been released from four years of deadlines, papers due, exams, jobs and housekeeping. Everything – food, shelter, exercise, entertainment – has been free; I haven't spent a cent. On the ship no one but my Princeton pal knows where I am at any given time, and no one cares, good preparation for ten whole freeform weeks in Europe. There no one will know where I am, either, given my uncertain itinerary – not parents; not boyfriends, including one I have ditched on departure and another who will dump me on return; not, for better or worse, my erstwhile traveling companion, who – out of sight, becomes truly out of mind. The obligations and responsibilities that will descend on my return to the States and enrollment for a MA in grad school, where I will be self-supporting for the first time in my life, are in blissful abeyance. Empowered to travel light by the voyage's incredible lightness of being, I stuff the duffel bag with cumbersome extras and ditch it at the dock in Rotterdam to await the return trip, which comes all too soon.

Return to Reality, 1956

If the outbound voyage is a trip to the moon, the return brings us back to earth even while we're at sea – out of time, out of money, out of patience with the ship's slow pace. Gone is the string quartet, Mr. Princeton, even the guy with the big cigar, but Dottie and Daisy return laden with souvenirs: garish velour wall hangings, precursors to Elvis on velvet, which in attempting to be polite I refer to as bath mats; fragile figurines for glass menageries; perfume-filled replicas of the Eiffel tower. At our cabin show-and-tell session (my thirty-six rolls of film have yet to be developed) I proffer a delicate Swiss watch and two pewter pitchers – one for myself, and one for Martin – as it turns out, the man I will return to England to marry on my next trans-Atlantic voyage.

1958. Escape Route

Two years later I have spent my last dollar on a one-way ticket to England on the *S.S. America*, the United States Lines' 663-foot 26,454 gross ton answer to the *Queen Mary*, requiring a crew of 643 to accommodate 1202 passengers on 11 decks. The *America*, considered "the most beautiful of all American passenger ships," is a ship with a distinguished history. Launched as a luxury liner on August 31, 1939, the day before Hitler invaded Poland, in May 1941 in anticipation of entering the war, the US Navy converted this fast, easily maneuverable vessel to a troop transport. Her initial capacity of 5272 was eventually raised to 7678; during the Second World War this nimble vessel safely carried over 350,000 troops (plus Red Cross and UN personnel, USO entertainers, prisoners of war, returning civilians) all over the world. By 1946 the *America* was restored to prewar elegance, intentionally designed to provide an atmosphere of charm and friendly good cheer, in contrast to its stuffy rivals.
Boarding with but a single objective that I expect will change my life, I am largely impervious to this history. Although I appreciate the cabin's firm bed and the ship's pervasive cleanliness, I am scarcely aware of the names or the number of my assigned cabin mates. With a wedding dress, a sage green silk chemise; a

trousseau I have sewn myself; a Grecian Goddess nightgown from Saks, discreet omen of the wedding night to come; and new braces on my teeth, I am en route to marry Martin, my fiancé, who is finishing his University of Edinburgh diploma in social study with a psychiatric internship in Sutton, Surrey. After two months of European travel, we'll return to the University of Michigan, where we both have fellowships, to begin our doctoral work.

My parents have been badgering me for months, "Break it off." "What good is a doctorate in social psychology?" sneers my father, a chemical engineering professor. "If you get married you won't finish your PhD," in English literature, even worse. "We'll boycott your wedding," so why not get married in exile? The real reason for their harassment erupts at my departure: "As Martin's wife you'll be the victim of anti-Semitism for the rest of your life. If you marry him" – they proceed to prove their claim – "we will have nothing to do with him, or you, or any children you might have."

So I seldom sleep on this voyage either. Although much faster, five days at sea, than my previous trip, this outbound vessel seems to crawl through the waves; I spend considerable time in the bow on the tourist open promenade deck as if energetically facing into the wind will make the ship go faster. Having left home for good, how can I be certain I will have another? Will this man I have not seen for ten months, whose blue air-letters have arrived erratically, really be ready to marry me? How do I know that I myself, at twenty-three a veteran of several serious boyfriends, can make such a grown-up commitment? The weather is fair, and without a soupçon of seasickness I interpret the ship's smooth sailing as a favorable omen.

Whereas on my first voyage *Don Quixote* is my reading material of choice, this time I take the *Bible*, both *Old and New Testaments*. Although this makes me appear more pious than I am, it is an inadvertently fortuitous selection because the ship abounds with Anglican bishops, and nuns too, en route to the Lambeth Conference, an international convocation held every ten years at the University of Kent in Canterbury.

Having spent all my life in small college towns, the *America* provides my first experience of overt class segregation. The areas of this sleek ship ensconced in Art Moderne are reserved for First and Cabin class passengers, as is the swimming pool amidships where the water sloshes with dangerous emphasis. Yet we in Tourist Class are well-served and well-fed. Although the upper classes get "Corn on the Cob with Melted Butter" while Tourist Class corn is "off the Cob," we all can choose "Roast Young Tom Turkey," or "Grilled Sirloin Steak with Mushrooms Sauté," among other options. In my innocence it seems to me that the class barriers are porous, for the *S.S. America* is throbbing with clergy – witty, well-read, urbane, philosophical, not given to pontificating, but conversing a mile a minute – with each other, and with me. What is the meaning of life? What is the nature of God, and why does it matter? What is truth? Beauty? Justice? Love, divine and human? Contrary to my parents' dire predictions of anti-Semitic ostracism, I am enveloped in ecumenical empathy, and I arrive at Southampton showered in blessings that count.

From a porthole just at the water line I have to crane my head upward to look above the pilings to the dock. Through the loud beating of my heart, I hear stevedores shouting, the thumps of cargo being unloaded, bang onto the dock. Finally I catch sight of Hush Puppies pacing the pier, a Burberry knockoff flapping in the wind, and finally a familiar crewcut as I race off the gangplank. A porter follows behind, carrying a travel gift from my future in-laws, a large state-of-the-art American Tourister tri-taper fiberglass-reinforced suitcase soon to hold clothing for two, and a matching hatbox as retro as the fancy hat I have chosen for our wedding. We will marry in July on my birthday, at a registry office in Epsom, Surrey, with seven psychiatrists (Martin's mentors at Belmont Hospital), their five wives, two babies, and three of our college friends in attendance.

The Incredible Lightness of Voyaging: Return to the New World, 1958

Martin has secured return passage on the *SS Ile de France*, a sophisticated Art Deco ship that attracted celebrity clientele such as Lena Horne and the Grand Duke of Monaco from its maiden voyage in 1927 until the onset of the Second World War in 1939. After serving the British admiralty during the war, by 1949 the *Ile de France* has been retrofitted as a high style passenger ship. The only tickets available that will enable us to return in time for the wedding of Martin's brother Bob are in first class, which my new father-in-law is happy to spring for. We will have a second, intimate family wedding on the morning of Bob's big afternoon gala so Martin's parents can ensure that we've been properly married according to Jewish law, the only observance they've requested from me, the shiksha in their midst, and I am pleased to comply.

Having successfully navigated the summer on and off Europe's beaten paths by train, tube, bus, foot and a daring flight to West and East Berlin before the Wall has been erected, we arrive once again at Southampton. We believe we are now sophisticates, world (well, almost) travelers who can handle anything, despite the fact that although we have been staying in youth hostels and B & Bs and lunching on bread, cheese, and fruit, we are nearly out of money; our Teaching Assistantships at Michigan won't begin for another month. As we embark, I wave our yard-wide wedding certificate in the purser's direction in an attempt to explain why my new name is different from the name on my passport. His shrug of Gallic indifference leads me to wonder whether the stereotype of French character is, in fact, true.

That the *Ile de France* is slated for decommissioning and demolition two months after our return is a fact perhaps known to its former social register clientele who choose to fly rather than sail, but we are clueless and realize that everyone we meet in first class, to which we are restricted, is incredibly older, more worldly, and many social rungs richer than we. They wear evening clothes to dinner, stylish and impeccably crisp, with which even our wedding clothes – Martin's heavy wool winter suit and my silk sack dress – can't compare. They wear sailing ensembles on deck, with matching boat shoes; we wear the rumpled residue of our summer on the move, and sneakers. Our windowless cabin, tucked under a stairwell, although perhaps furnished with Porthault (a name I would not recognize at the time) sheets, and towels as thick as bathmats, does not match the individual designer-decorated cabins shown on the brochures; it's Spartan white, perhaps intended as accommodation for servants traveling with their employers. Nevertheless, we are assigned to tablemates whose company we can escape at breakfast and lunch. At breakfast I order the rainbow panoply of freshly squeezed juices, all of them, every morning. Otherwise, we scarcely drink, even when in the presence of our more bibulous dinner companions. Snookered into buying a bottle of champagne "for the table" by a solo high flyer determined to undermine our abstemiousness, we spend our last $20 (a week's grocery money) out of courtesy. There will be – again – no tips for the wait staff; if they or for that matter our tablemates are snooty they are nevertheless flawlessly mannered and we are as oblivious as we are impecunious.

After two days at sea, these distinctions cease to matter. A hurricane, directly in our path, is roiling the Atlantic, and although radar enables the captain to avoid sailing directly into the eye of the storm, the ship pitches and rolls, precipitating many, including Martin, into major seasickness. The dining stewards have installed heavy metal rims on the tables to secure the dishes; now I, undeterred from my place at the table, understand the reason for the heavy crockery and unskiddable furniture. I continue to enjoy the array of breakfast juices, augmented by pancakes and poached salmon.

When I'm not tending to Martin, who mostly wants to sleep, I spend the time in a dimly lit, upper deck lounge reading. The journey of our lives together was begun in innocence and continued throughout Europe with incredible lightness of being, an insulation – however illusory – fostered by the *Ile de France*'s First Class service which continues flawlessly throughout the storm, an attempt to sustain the ship's serenity amidst turbulence. But the book I am reading is *Moby Dick*, a dramatic contrast to our idyllic summer. Should I be interpreting this turbulent narrative of powerful natural forces, maritime cataclysm, identity lost and found, as an emblem of our lives to come? Will we experience, as Ahab does, an inability to control either the universe or our own destiny, either in marriage or in graduate school? Should I pitch the book overboard, or trade it for, say *Robinson Crusoe*? The storm subsides; we realize that no man, no couple, is an island. And so we debark in New York with confidence, heading into a new life in this world which as Shakespeare's Miranda, heroine of *The Tempest*, understood with hope and trepidation, is as brave as it is new. We will learn from experience just how much innocence we can retain in the fifty-four years (at this writing) of marriage, but the experience will come on dry land. Every voyage will be a return to innocence.

11. Conclusion

Birgit Braasch and Claudia Müller

We started this collection with the example of the *Queen Mary 2*, Cunard's most current ocean liner. Puzzled by the observation that the practice of waving to and from the ship at its landing and departure in Hamburg is still very important for both, the people on board and on shore, we posed the following questions:
What informed and shaped practices on board an Atlantic liner?
Which practices were important for ocean-travel tourists and how did they appropriate them?
How have on-board tourist practices been appropriated in other contexts of travel, every day routines or leisure?
Following these questions our authors found specificities of tourist settings which shaped tourist practices, and they found tourist practices which shaped settings. The entanglement of both tourist settings and practices led our authors to observe the transformative potential of sea voyages. This transformative potential is the major narrative our authors encounter and pursue. In the following we would like to elaborate on the practices, settings and the notions of transformation our authors examine.
Before going into the details of this argument we would like to highlight one specificity of our approach. In this collection we included not only what one might consider typical tourists but also encounters of non-tourists, like soldiers, with tourist settings and practices.
We found that drawing on such ambiguous cases and relating tourist and non-tourist examples can prove methodically productive for our endeavor to understand the relationship between a tourist setting and tourist practices. The contributions show in how far the tourist setting of an ocean liner, partially with its crew, enforced tourist practices even among non-tourist soldiers, and vice versa they show how tourist practices helped, for example soldiers, to make sense of their sea-voyage in a non-tourist setting.
The ship and also its entertainment offers are settings which shaped tourist practices. The authors of this collection found that the shipping companies organized the tourists' practices on board through the ships' architecture, advertisements and the structure of the daily activities on board. For example, Emma Roberts shows how shipping companies tried to create unique spaces which were meant to have an impact on passengers' practices. The spaces were meant to facilitate certain behaviors and feelings, like the imagination of luxury and feeling pampered. Other elements of the architecture were there to restrict practices, like crossings from one class to the other.

This structuring influence of the great liner even continued in the Falklands conflict. As Jo Stanley shows, some officers used the same cabins as passengers in peace times. In contrast to the usual barracks the officers prominently experienced the cabins' luxury. Even just being on the "great liners" gave some soldiers the feeling of upward social mobility.

There was however no unidirectional influence of the ships' spaces on the tourist practices. The tourists with their practices also heavily influenced the ships architecture and the tourist settings. In her article Emma Roberts hints that the shipping companies built the ships as a reaction to assumed passengers' desires. The companies created a fantasy for the passenger according to their fantasy of the passenger, so the passengers indirectly influenced the development of practices on board.

The tourists also directly influenced these practices as Dagmar Bellmann shows in her article. She argues that many of the practices on board the ocean liners were attempts to deal with passengers' feelings and needs. The game of betting on the daily progress can be seen as a way to deal with the uncertainty related to the in-between situation of being on the ship. Furthermore, she analyzes how the activities on board which were at first organized by passengers were appropriated by the shipping companies. Her examples show a double influence of the passengers: Their direct inventions were adopted and the shipping companies reacted to passengers' emotional reactions to the crossing.

Tourists onboard practices were not only adopted by shipping companies, but also resonated on shore in literature, like travel reports, and art. An example of a very strong narrative on shore and on board centered around the desire for luxury. Eric Sandberg shows in his contribution about how P.G. Wodehouse caricatured the aspect of social elevation on board in his novels. Similarly, in Lynn Bloom's essay about her personal journey the aspect of social distinction is taken up as an annoyance. Accordingly, on-board practices and their meanings found their way into shore narratives in literature, art and film. The narrative around on-board luxury was so widely distributed that soldiers and peace-time passengers alike found the vocabulary to talk about this luxury.

It were tourists' practices and experiences of dining for example, which expressed and fed this narrative of luxury, as Birgit Braasch shows. For dinner passengers often dressed in their best in order to live up to the expectations of their dining partners. Passengers also took photographs of these events in order to document the importance. Dinner was not only served to still hunger but also turned into a meaningful practice for the passengers as proof of their social elevation.

Through the exchange with the shore the tourists' practices and narratives even persisted on the ships in war time. Jo Stanley and Mark van Ells show in their contributions the dissemination of on-board tourist practices on shore or rather in other seafarer contexts. In his contribution van Ells impressively shows how even in war times soldiers had a knowledge of tourist practices which they might have gained on shore. On a war ship soldiers referred to practices like writing a travel diary and taking pictures and appropriated them in the context of their own crossing of the Atlantic from the USA to Europe during World War II.

Not all on-board practices can be traced to have disseminated into other social contexts. A comparison of Dagmar Bellmann's findings with those of Mark van Ells rather indicate that those specific practices related to common emotions and experiences on board the ocean liner, like boredom or fear of sea travel. Thus, Mark van Ells shows how soldiers appropriated specifically those practices which helped them to structure the days on board and which supported their transition from one continent to the other, from peace to war, and helped them deal with fear, like e.g. a daily entertainment program consisting of movies or shows performed by the passengers or sporting events and competitions between the soldiers. Thus, soldiers appropriated tourist practices in this new context while pertaining some of the meanings related to ocean liner tourism. Since Casey Orr did not travel on an ocean liner but on a container ship, such an entertainment program was not available to her and boredom remained one of the most prominent emotions connected to her journey across the North Atlantic, also because her unusual mode of travel made long distances visible and the space of the North Atlantic bigger.

By analyzing the relationships between touristic space and non-tourists as well as tourists' practices and narratives all authors found a notion of transformation to describe the relationship. Jo Stanley's analysis of ships as heterotopic spaces that are the habitat in which people with different habituses meet is one way to approach the ships on the Atlantic as a specific space which contributes to transformation in the passengers' practices and beliefs. In his analysis, Eric Sandberg emphasizes the carnivalesque characteristics of ship space which allows to try out the illicit and Dagmar Bellmann and Emma Roberts point out the liminality of this space.

Despite their different approaches, the authors have found some common ground and recurring themes in their characterization of ship space on the Atlantic Ocean in that it enabled certain specific practices and changed them. Concerning the society on board the ocean liners, two, at first sight opposing, trends for practices stand out. These opposites are the freedom of societal interaction on the one hand and strict surveillance by the crew and a strong structuring of the space on the other.

On the ships tourists could try out other practices. The transformation Eric Sandberg finds in P.G. Wodehouses' novels manifests itself in the rejection of traditional authorities and the defiance of traditional gender roles. The characters use the ensuing personal freedom to pursue new romantic possibilities. Similarly, Jo Stanley depicts ship space as a space that allowed for new romantic possibilities and gender roles in that men could be openly camp on board. However, because of the presence of military personnel on board, gendered practices which were common on passenger ships needed to be re-negotiated during the Falklands conflict.

While Dagmar Bellmann takes up the specific romantic possibilities on board in her analysis, these possibilities also serve as an example for practices that induce fear as part of the liminal and are channeled as part of the liminoid to reduce ambivalences.

In the attempt to keep up structures on board the crew played an important role. This strong role of the crew becomes especially evident in Jo Stanley's analysis of the relationship between crew and soldiers. During the conflict the crew maintained certain habituses and an entertainment program which originated from the ocean-liner crossings. A similar role of the crew holds true for Dagmar Bellmann's observation. Whereas it was considered indecent in the 19th century that the sexes were so close together on one ship, flirts on board were expected and explicitly allowed at the beginning of the 20th century. Some common games even played with the romantic possibilities on board. It might be argued that because the ocean liners enabled practices that did not conform to the societal order on land, shipping companies put an emphasis on surveillance by the crew. This surveillance reached from simply organizing practices, for example, in games, to rigorously controlling whether everyone stayed in the class they had booked in order to keep the hierarchical order on the ship.

The Atlantic Ocean as a space played an important role in enabling such a heterotopic setting of transformation. The authors in this collection show that the unusual encounters of people with differing practices were possible on the ships since these were not on land but moved across the Atlantic Ocean. The characters in P.G. Wodehouse's novels delve into their romances on board and fulfill them on land; they mostly revert back to ordinary life as soon as they are on land since the opportunities for carnivalesque behavior are missing on dry land. Dagmar Bellmann seconds this analysis in her discussion of the liminality of sea voyages by emphasizing that the voyage is only temporary and that normal life will be resumed once the voyage is over. According to Jo Stanley, the conversion of merchant vessels into war ships overturned the passengers' expectations; most of them probably knew that "everything's queer once you've left that pier" and therefore expected practices out of the ordinary.

The transformative potential of sea voyages that Dagmar Bellmann and Emma Roberts emphasize in their analyses of the liminal state during Atlantic crossings also becomes evident in the figure of Noah's ark. In her analysis of the Manns' excursion to Liberia, Stephanie Beck Cohen shows that their ship was compared to Noah's ark and their transformation emphasized. Similarly, one of the soldiers that Mark van Ells follows felt like being on Noah's ark. The relief of leaving the ship and reaching land evident in this metaphor emphasizes the contrast between touristic journeys and war-time voyages. Whereas the tourists could enjoy their time on board, the Manns as well as the GI were glad to have reached the other side, either because they felt safe again or because they could finally leave the bad conditions on board.

In spite of this contrast to other journeys across the North Atlantic, the space of the ocean continued to hold some of the fascination it had for tourists on their crossing. Some GIs were fascinated by the animals they could see in the ocean and perceived the Atlantic as a beautiful natural space. Others shared the ambivalences of crossing the ocean which Dagmar Bellmann found because the vast and empty ocean offered no orientation in time and space. This disorientation was even more relevant for the GIs because in contrast to tourists who had booked the voyage some of them did not know where they were going.

Whereas most passengers mentioned in the different contributions did not have a choice but to cross the Atlantic Ocean by ship, Casey Orr specifically picked a container ship over the easier possibility of crossing the North Atlantic by plane. The role of the watery space of the Atlantic Ocean as a link between spaces and times fascinated her and the journey by ship allowed her to explore the intriguing space of the North Atlantic and its extension to the inland in her photographic essay. Although she emphasizes the boredom she felt on board, her photographs capture some of the fascination with and beauty of the Atlantic that the soldiers expressed, in that the artistic rendering of the vastness of the space leaves room for one's imagination. The interplay of sun, wind and water in her photographs shows the ocean as a space with changing colors and moods that might be related to the romantic connotations that shipping companies expressed in their advertisements in connection with the North Atlantic.

We looked at the Atlantic and the ships, animals, soldiers, employees and tourists who crossed, and we found that for all of them the Atlantic was a space which they inhabited with their specific and sometimes contradicting practices. Their ways of interacting with each other led to the experience of transformation which might be related to the ongoing myth and magic attributed to the great Atlantic liners.

List of Figures

Cover: Queen Mary (ship), 2004 – State Library of Queensland.
Figure 1: Aquitania First Class Lounge with Clock.- University of Liverpool Library, Cunard Archive.
Figure 2: Cunard Menu Card – Gilded galleon scene. – University of Liverpool Library, Cunard Archive.
Figure 3: Cunard Menu Card – Cottage Garden.- University of Liverpool Library, Cunard Archive.
Figure 4: Chinoiserie Room with African Sculptures. University of Liverpool Library, Cunard Archive.
Figure 5: Bedroom with Lucienne Day 'Calyx' Fabric.- University of Liverpool Library, Cunard Archive.
Figure 6: Tourist Class Smoking Room. University of Liverpool Library, Cunard Archive.
Figure 7: First Class Smoking Room. University of Liverpool Library, Cunard Archive.
Figure 8: *Aquitania* Dining Room Ceiling University of Liverpool Library, Cunard Archive.
Figure 9: *Aquitania* Soda Fountain in Garden Lounge. University of Liverpool Library, Cunard Archive.
Figure 10: Pyramid, 1907 Cunard Brochures University of Liverpool Library, Cunard Archive.
Figure 11: *QE2* in the Falklands: The Neptune Ceremony takes on a new form when hundreds of troops were involved. (Right: Nursing Sister Jane Yelland). Picture courtesy of Cunard Line, kindly loaned by Jane Yelland.
Figure 12: Neptune ceremony on *Norland*: steward Mimi poses as Queen Amphitrite. Picture courtesy of Wendy Gibson.
Figure 13: "One of our war's leading characters": Roy 'Wendy' Gibson at the Falklands. Picture courtesy of Wendy Gibson.
Figure 14: Surreal ways of going to war. Cartoon by Roy Carr in *Up the Falklands: Cartoons from the Royal Marines*, Roy Carr, Arthur Huddart and John R Webb, Blandford Press, Dorset, 1982.
Figure 15: Paratroopers sunbathing en route to the Falklands on North Sea ferry *Norland*. Picture courtesy of Wendy Gibson.
Figure 16: Merchant seafarers had to be dressed for trouble; Kevin Smith poses in his gas ask on *Canberra*. Picture courtesy of Kevin Smith.

Figure 17: Gurkhas practice aboard *QE2* by the world map usually used by passengers to revel in their distance from home. Picture courtesy of Cunard Line, kindly loaned by Brian Smith.
Figure 18: Stewards looking after passengers in new ways: "More caviar! Where would sir like it, down his flak jacket, or up his nose?" Cartoon by Raymond Jackson, *Evening Standard*, London, 13 April 1982, picture courtesy of Associated Newspapers Ltd/ Solo Syndication/ British Cartoon Archive, University of Kent.
Figure 19: Shopping in the ship's shop on *QE2:* picture kindly loaned by Brian White
Figure 20: Returning home wounded on *QE2*. Picture kindly loaned by ship's nurse Jane Yelland.
Figure 21: Wendy Gibson and Frankie Green welcome home their shipmates who went again to the Falklands, 2.2.1983. Picture courtesy of *Hull Daily Mail*.
Figure 22: Lydia DeGuio, Lydia on Sundeck of *United States*. Image courtesy of Independence Seaport Museum (Philadelphia, PA).
Figure 23: Lydia DeGuio, Mid Atlantic: Image courtesy of Independence Seaport Museum (Philadelphia, PA).
Figure 24: Lydia DeGuio, Lydia in Bed (with breakfast tray). Image courtesy of Independence Seaport Museum (Philadelphia, PA).
Figure 25: Lydia DeGuio, *S.S. United States*, Lydia, Theresa, Gene (at the dinner table). Image courtesy of Independence Seaport Museum (Philadelphia, PA).

List of Archives

DSM: Archive of the Deutsches Schiffahrtsmuseum, Bremerhaven.
DTA: Deutsches Tagebucharchiv, Emmendingen.
EUA: Emory University Archives, Atlanta, GA.
ISM: Independence Seaport Museum, Philadelphia, PA.
MMM MAL: Merseyside Maritime Museum, Maritime Archives and Library, Liverpool.
NMM: National Maritime Museum, Greenwich.
NYPL Manuscripts and Archives Division: New York Public Library Manuscripts and Archives Division, New York, NY.
SIA RU 7293: Smithsonian Institution Archives, Record Unit 7293, William M. Mann and Lucile Quarry Mann Papers, Washington, DC.
UoLSC&A: University of Liverpool Special Collections & Archives, Liverpool.
WVM: Wisconsin Veterans Museum, Madison, WI.

Selected Bibliography

Amit, Vered, "Structures and Dispositions of Travel and Movement," in: Vered Amit (Ed.), *Going First Class? New Approaches to Privileged Travel and Movement,* New York, Oxford 2007.
Andrews, Hazel, and Les Roberts (Eds.), *Liminal Landscapes. Travel, Experience and Spaces In-Between,* Abingdon 2012.
Archbold, Rick, and Dana McCauley, *Last Dinner on the Titanic*, New York 1997.
Armstrong, John and David M. Williams, "The steamboat and popular tourism", in: *The Journal of transport history* 26: 1 (2005).
Baker, Paul and Jo Stanley, *Hello Sailor! The Hidden History of Homosexuality at Sea*, Harlow, London 2003.
Bakhtin, Mikhail, *Problems of Dostoevsky's Poetics.* Caryl Emerson (Ed. and Trans.), Minneapolis 1984.
Bakhtin, Mikhail, *Rabelais and His World.* Helene Iswolsky (Trans.), Bloomington 1984.
Bicheno, Hugh, *Razor's Edge: The Unofficial History of the Falklands War,* London 2007.
Boelhower, William, "'I'll Teach You How to Flow': On Figuring Out Atlantic Studies", in: *Atlantic Studies* 1 (2004), p. 28-48.
Bourdieu, Pierre, and Wacquant Loïc, *An Invitation to Reflexive Sociology*, Chicago 1992.
Bourdieu, Pierre, *Outline of a Theory of Practice,* Cambridge 1977.
Bourdieu, Pierre, *The Logic of Practice,* Cambridge 1992.
Brinnin, John Malcolm, *The Sway of the Grand Saloon. A Social History of the North Atlantic,* New York 1971.
Brinnin, John Malcom, and Kenneth Gaulin, *The Transatlantic Style,* New York 1988.
Butler, Daniel Allen, *Warrior Queens: The Queen Mary and Queen Elizabeth in World War II*, Mechanicsburg/Penn. 2002.
Carr, Jean, *Another Story: Women and the Falklands War*, London 1984.
Cartwright, Roger, and Carolyn Baird, *The Development and Growth of the Cruise Industry*, Oxford, et al 1999.
Coleman, Terry, *The Liners: A History of the North Atlantic Crossing,* London 1976.
Coons, Lorraine, and Alexander Varias, *Tourist Third Cabin: Steamship Travel in the Interwar Years,* New York 2003.

Culler, Jonathan "The Semiotics of Tourism" in: Jonathan D. Culler, *Framing the Sign: Criticism and Its Institutions,* Norman/OK 1990, p. 1-10.

Dawson, Philip, *British Superliners of the Sixties: A Design Appreciation of the Oriana, Canberra and QE2,* London 1990.

Dawson, Philip, *Cruise Ships: An Evolution in Design,* London 2000.

Dawson, Philip, *The Liner. Retrospective & Renaissance,* London 2005.

de Certeau, Michel, *The Practice of Everyday Life,* Steven Rendall trans. Berkeley, Los Angeles, London 1988.

Dowling, Ross K. (Ed.), *Cruise Ship Tourism.* Oxfordshire, Cambridge/Mass. 2006.

Edington, Sarah, *The Captain's Table: Life and Dining on the Great Ocean Liners,* London 2005.

Endy, Christopher, *Cold War Holidays: American Tourism in France,* Chapel Hill/NC, London 2004.

Fitzgerald, Warren, *All in the Same Boat: The Untold Story of the British Ferry Crew who helped win the Falklands War,* London 2016.

Fletcher, R. A., *Traveling Palaces: Luxury in Passenger Steamships,* London 1913.

Foucault, Michel, "Space, Knowledge and Power" in: Paul Rainbow (Ed.), *The Foucault Reader,* Harmondsworth 1986, p. 239-256.

Foucault, Michel and Jay Miskowiec, "Of Other Spaces" in: *Diacritics* 16, (1986) p. 22-27.

Fox, Stephen, *The Ocean Railway: Isambard Kingdom Brunel, Samuel Cunard, and the Revolutionary World of the Great Atlantic Steamships,* London 2004.

Frow, John, "Tourism and the Semiotics of Nostalgia" in: *October,* 57 (1991), p. 123-151.

Fussell, Paul, *Abroad: British Literary Traveling between the Wars,* Oxford 1980.

Galligan, Edward L., "P. G. Wodehouse Master of Farce", in: *The Sewanee Review 93* (1985), p. 609-617.

Gardiner, Robin, *The History of the White Star Line,* Hersham 2001.

Geddes, John, *Spearhead Assault: Guts and Glory on the Falklands Frontlines,* London 2008.

Gerstenberger, Heide, "Men Apart: The Concept of 'Total Institution' and the Analysis of Seafaring", *International Journal of Maritime History,* Vol. VIII, no. 1, June (1996), p. 173-182.

Gottlieb, Alma, "Americans' Vacations," Annals of Tourism Research 9 (1982), p. 165-187.

Graburn, Nelson H.H., "Tourism: The Sacred Journey" in: Valene Smith (Ed.), *Hosts and Guests: The Anthropology of Tourism,* Philadelphia 1977, p. 21-36.

Green, Benny, *P. G. Wodehouse: A Literary Biography,* London 1981.

Griffiths, Denis, *Power of the Great Liners – A History of Atlantic Marine Engineering,* Sparkford 1990;
Harrison, Julia, *Being a Tourist: Finding Meaning in Pleasure Travel*, Vancouver, Toronto 2003.
Hart, Douglas, "Sociability and 'Separate Spheres' on the North Atlantic: The Interior Architecture of British Atlantic Liners, 1840-1930" in: *The Journal of Social History* 44, (2010), p. 189-212.
Hillier, Jean and Emma Rooksby, *Habitus: A Sense of Place,* Aldershot 2002.
Johnson-Allan, John, *They Couldn't Have Done It Without Us*, Woodbridge 2011.
Jolly, Rick, *The Red and Green Life Machine*, Liskeard 2007.
Kennett, Lee, *GI: The American Soldier in World War II*, New York 1987.
King, Benjamin, Richard C. Briggs, and Eric R. Criner, *Spearhead of Logistics: A History of the United States Army Transportation Corps*, Washington 2001.
Klein, Bernhard and Gesa Mackenthun (Eds.), *Das Meer als kulturelle Kontaktzone: Räume, Reisende, Repräsentationen*, Konstanz 2003.
Kludas, Arnold and Dietmar Borchert, *Das Blaue Band des Nordatlantiks - Der Mythos eines legendären Wettbewerbs,* Hamburg 1999.
Kludas, Arnold and Karl-Theo Beer, *Die glanzvolle Ära der Luxusschiffe: Eine illustrierte Kulturgeschichte im Spiegel zeitgenössischer Quellen*, Hamburg 2005.
Lévi-Strauss, Claude *Structural Anthropology*, Claire Jacobson and Brooker Grundfest Schoepf (Trans.), Garden City/NY 1967.
Lukowiak, Ken, *A Soldier's Song: True Stories from the Falklands*, London 1993, p. 174.
Magee, Richard M., "Food Puritanism and Food Pornography: The Gourmet Semiotics of Martha and Nigella" in: *Americana: the Journal of Popular Culture*, 6 (2007).
McCart, Neil, *Atlantic Liners of the Cunard Line: From 1884 to the Present Day,* Wellingborough 1990.
McCracken, George, "Wodehouse and Latin Comedy", in: *The Classical Journal, 29* (1934), p. 612-614.
McCrum, Robert, *Wodehouse: A Life*, New York 2006.
Miller, William H. and David F. Hutchings, *Transatlantic Liners at War: The Story of the Queens*, New York 1985.
Miller, William H. Jr., *Picture History of British Ocean Liners, 1900 to Present*, Mineloa 2001.
Morgan, Cecilia *'A Happy Holiday': English Canadians and Transatlantic Tourism, 1870 – 1930,* Toronto 2008.

Morgan, Linda "Diplomatic Gastronomy: Style and Power at the Table" in: *Food and Foodways: Explorations in the History and Culture of Human Nourishment*, 20 (2012), p.146-166.
Muxworthy, John L., *The Great White Whale Goes to War*, London 1982.
Peter, Bruce, and Philip Dawson, "Modernism at Sea: Ocean Liners and the Avant-garde", in: Lara Feigel and Alexandra Harris (Eds.), *Modernism on Sea: Art and Culture at the British Seaside*, Oxford 2009, p. 144–57.
Pugh, Nicci, *White Ship, Red Crosses*, Ely 2010.
Quartermaine, Peter and Bruce Peter, *Cruise: Identity, Design and Culture*, London 2006.
Rennella, Mark and Whitney Walton, "Planned Serendipity: American Travelers and the Transatlantic Voyage in the Nineteenth and Twentieth Centuries" in: *Journal of Social History*, 38 (2004), p. 365-383.
Satchell, Alister, *Running the Gauntlet: How Three Giant Liners Carried A Million Men to War*, Annapolis 2001.
Schnurmann, Claudia, "Frühneuzeitliche Formen maritimer Vereinnahmung: Die europäische Inbesitznahme des Atlantiks," in: Bernhard Klein and Gesa Mackenthun (Eds.), Das Meer als kulturelle Kontaktzone: Räume, Reisende, Repräsentationen, Konstanz 2003, p. 49-72.
Scholl, Lars U. (Ed.), *Technikgeschichte des industriellen Schiffbaus in Deutschland Bd. 1: Handelsschiffe, Marine-Überwasserschiffe, U-Boote*, Hamburg 1994.
Seer, Mike, *With the Gurkhas in the Falklands*, Barnsley 2003.
Simpson, David, "Tourism and Titanomania" in: *Critical Inquiry 25* (1999), p. 680-695.
Smith, Crosbie, Ian Higginson, and Phillip Wolstenholme. "'Avoiding Equally Extravagance and Parsimony': The Moral Economy of the Ocean Steamship", in: *Technology and Culture 44,* (2003), p. 443-469.
Stanley, Jo, "Queered seafarers in heterotopic spaces", in: Richard Gorki and Britta Söderqvist (Eds.), *The Parallel Worlds of the seafarer: Ashore, Afloat and Abroad, Papers from the 10th North Sea History Conference*, Gothenburg 2012.
Stanley, Jo, *From Cabin 'Boys' to Captains: 250 Years of Women at Sea*, Stroud 2016.
Steinberg, Philip E., *The Social Construction of the Ocean*, Cambridge 2001.
Throop, Jason C., "Articulating Experience", in: *Anthropological Theory* 3 (2003) p. 219-243.
Turner, Victor W. and Edward M. Bruner, *The Anthropology of Experience*, Urbana/Ill. 1986.
Turner, Victor, *From Ritual to Theatre: The Human Seriousness of Play*, New York 1982.

Turner, Victor, *The Forest of Symbols. Aspects of Ndembu Ritual,* New York, London 1967.
Turner, Victor, *The Ritual Process – Structure and Anti-Structure,* New York 1995.
Tye, Larry, *Rising from the Rails: Pullman Porters and the Making of the Black Middle Class*, New York 2004.
Urry, John, *The Tourist Gaze*, London, Thousand Oaks and New Delhi 2002.
Van Gennep, Arnold, *The Rites of Passage,* Chicago, London 1972.
Villar, Roger, *Merchant Ships at War: The Falklands Experience*, Annapolis 1984.
Wheeler, Reginald W., *The Road to Victory: A History of the Hampton Roads Port of Embarkation in World War II*, New Haven/Conn. 1946.
Wheelwright, Julie, *Amazons and Military Maids*, London 1994.

List of Contributors

Stephanie Beck Cohen earned her PhD in Art History from Indiana University in 2016. Most recently she curated the exhibit *Soft Diplomacy: Quilting cultural diplomacy in Liberia* at the Fine Arts Museum at Western Carolina University, and *Liberia in stitches: Quilts from Sinoe and Montserrado counties* at Cornell University. She lives and works in Singapore.

Dagmar Bellmann completed her thesis about transatlantic passenger travelling from 1840 to 1930 at the Technical University in Darmstadt in 2014 as scholar in the DFG-Research Training Group "Technology of Topology". Her thesis was published in 2015 at the German publishing house Campus under the title "Von Höllengefährten zu schwimmenden Palästen".

Lynn Z Bloom, University of Connecticut Board of Trustees Distinguished Professor Emerita, held the Aetna Chair of Writing 1988-2015. She is the author of *Doctor Spock: Biography of a Conservative Radical* (1972), *The Seven Deadly Virtues* (2008), *Writers Without Borders: Writing and Teaching Writing in Troubled Times* (2008), and 175+ articles. An inveterate traveler, she has recently taught creative writing in Florence and held a creative writing Fulbright in New Zealand, where she is an Honorary Professor at the University of Waikato.
e-mail: Lynn.Bloom@UConn.edu

Birgit Braasch earned her PhD from Leeds Metropolitan University (now Leeds Beckett University). Her research interests are in the historical construction of different land- and seascapes, especially through tourism. For her PhD she analyzed the construction of the North Atlantic seascape through Atlantic crossings in the time following World War II.

Mark D. Van Ells is professor of history at Queensborough Community College of the City University of New York. He received his Ph.D. from the University of Wisconsin, and is the author of several books, including *To Hear Only Thunder Again: America's World War II Veterans Come Home* and *America and World War I: A Traveler's Guide*. Dr. Van Ells is currently writing a history of the U.S. 32nd Infantry Division during World War II. e-mail: MVanElls@qcc.cuny.edu, website: markdvanells.com

Claudia Müller in her academic work bridges the gap between History and Economics. For her PhD thesis she explored tourists' experiences during the Cold War.

In another attempt to mediate between historians' methods and economic application she now works as a project and quality manager in the German Health Care sector.

Casey Orr is a photographer, researcher and Senior Lecturer in the school of Art, Architecture and Design, Leeds Beckett University. She is also a member of the feminist art collective, F=. She has shown in various galleries in the US (Jen Bekman, New York, the University of the Arts, Philadelphia or San Antonio College Gallery, Texas), as well as in galleries, museums and festivals in the UK including Look Liverpool International Photography Festival, Brighton Photo Biennale, The Yorkshire Sculpture Park, The Observer Magazine, The Royal Photographic Society Contemporary Photography Magazine, and The Yorkshire Sculpture Park and (the first time the walls of a prison have been used as a space for art) at HM Prison Leeds.
She considers photography not only as "a tool to document" but also in its poetical relationship to metaphor in a continually changing world. See her work at caseyorr.com

Emma Roberts runs the BA (Hons) History of Art course at Liverpool School of Art and Design, Liverpool John Moores University, U.K. She completed a Ph.D. on the sculpture of Barbara Hepworth in 1997 (University of Liverpool). A sample of her publications include *The Public Sculpture of Cheshire & Merseyside* (2012); *The Liverpool Academy: A History and Index* (1997); 'Barbara Hepworth within an International Context' in Tate's *Barbara Hepworth Reconsidered* (2003); and 'Representation and Reputation: Barbara Hepworth's Relationships with her American and British Dealers' (2013) in *Tate Papers On-Line*. Emma Roberts has also curated exhibitions. The focus of her research lies in three areas: public sculpture; maritime history and design and utopian, 'New Urbanist' architecture and environments.

Eric Sandberg completed his PhD at the University of Edinburgh, and is currently an Assistant Professor at City University of Hong Kong and holds a Docentship at the University of Oulu, Finland. His research interests range from modernism to the contemporary novel, with a particular interest in the borderlands between literary and popular fiction. His monograph on Virginia Woolf appeared in 2014. He co-edited *Adaptation, Awards Culture, and the Value of Prestige* for Palgrave in 2017, and edited *100 Greatest Literary Detectives* for Rowman & Littlefield in 2018. He has published essays in numerous edited collections, and in journals including *Ariel, The Cambridge Quarterly, the Journal of Modern Literature, Critique*, and *Neohelicon*.

Jo Stanley is an internationally recognized expert on the gendered sea, including queer seafarers. Recent books include From Cabin "Boys" to Captains: 250 Years of Women at Sea (2016) and Women and the Royal Navy (2017). A creative historian she works with museums, visual arts projects, TV and theatre to represent diverse histories accessibly. She is Honorary Research Fellow in the University of Hull's Maritime Historical Studies Centre. Her blog can be found at http://genderedseas.blogspot.com.

Atlantic Cultural Studies
edited by Prof. Dr. Claudia Schnurmann (Universität Hamburg)

Claudia Schnurmann
Brücken aus Papier
Atlantischer Wissenstransfer in dem Briefnetzwerk des deutsch-amerikanischen Ehepaars Francis und Mathilde Lieber, 1827 – 1872
Die ebenso amüsant-ehrliche wie lehrreich-lebensnahe Korrespondenz des Ehepaars Francis und Mathilde Lieber der Jahre 1829-1872 fungierte als ein Brückenschlag über den Atlantik. Mit ihren Briefen verbanden die Wahl-US-Amerikaner, der gebürtige Berliner Franz Lieber (1798-1872) und seine Frau, die gebürtige Hamburgerin Mathilde Lieber geb. Oppenheimer (1805-1890), über den Atlantik und sechs Dekaden hinweg Generationen und Gesellschaften, Demagogen und Denker, Milieus und Meinungen, Kaufleute und Genies in Europa und Amerika in einem dichten Beziehungsgeflecht. Aus der Analyse von circa 11 000 Briefen gewinnt man neue, unerwartete Einblicke in die Kultur-, Wirtschafts-, Sozial-, Familien-, Bildungs- und Politikgeschichte von Hamburg und Berlin, Preußen, England, Puerto Rico und den USA ebenso wie in emotionale und intellektuelle Befindlichkeiten der Menschen, die ihre Beziehungen in Briefen erlebten.
Bd. 11, 2014, 560 S., 89,90 €, gb., ISBN 978-3-643-12678-8

Hermann Wellenreuther
Heinrich Melchior Mühlenberg und die deutschen Lutheraner in Nordamerika, 1742 – 1787
Wissenstransfer und Wandel eines atlantischen zu einem amerikanischen Netzwerk
Bd. 10, 2013, 728 S., 99,90 €, br., ISBN 978-3-643-12358-9

Claudia Schnurmann (Hg.)
Clio in Hamburg
Historisches Seminar Universität Hamburg 1907 – 2007
Bd. 9, 2010, 208 S., 24,90 €, gb., ISBN 978-3-643-10746-6

Hermann Wellenreuther (Ed.)
Jacob Leisler's Atlantic World in the Later Seventeenth Century
Essays on Religion, Militia, Trade, and Networks by Jaap Jacobs, Claudia Schnurmann, David W. Voorhees and Hermann Wellenreuther
Bd. 8, 2009, 248 S., 29,90 €, br., ISBN 978-3-643-10324-6

Claudia Schnurmann
Europa trifft Amerika
Zwei alte Welten bilden eine neue atlantische Welt, 1492 – 1783
Bd. 7, 2009, 208 S., 24,90 €, br., ISBN 978-3-8258-1907-1

Sabine Heerwart
Verlassene Dörfer
Auswanderungsverläufe des 19. Jahrhunderts am Beispiel der deutschen Dörfer Ürzig und Wolfshagen
Bd. 5, 2008, 320 S., 29,90 €, br., ISBN 978-3-8258-1293-5

Susanne Lachenicht (Ed.)
Religious Refugees in Europe, Asia and North America
(6th—21st century)
Bd. 4, 2007, 304 S., 29,90 €, br., ISBN 978-3-8258-9861-8

Sabine Heerwart; Claudia Schnurmann (Eds.)
Atlantic migrations
Regions and Movements in Germany and North America/USA during the 18th and 19th Century
Bd. 3, 2007, 272 S., 29,90 €, br., ISBN 978-3-8258-9862-5

LIT Verlag Berlin – Münster – Wien – Zürich – London
Auslieferung Deutschland / Österreich / Schweiz: siehe Impressumsseite

Geschichte Nordamerikas in atlantischer Perspektive von den Anfängen bis zur Gegenwart
Herausgegeben von Hermann Wellenreuther

Norbert Finzsch
Konsolidierung und Dissens
Nordamerika von 1800 bis 1865
Bd. 5, 2005, 944 S., 86,90 €, gb., ISBN 3-8258-4441-2

Hermann Wellenreuther
Von der Konföderation zur Amerikanischen Nation
Der Amerikanischen Revolution zweiter Teil, 1783 – 1796
Mit diesem Band findet die Arbeit an der langen Entstehungszeit der Vereinigten Staaten von Amerika und der kürzeren Zeitspanne der Amerikanischen Revolution ihren Abschluss. Erstere hatte mit der Besiedlung des nordamerikanischen Kontinents vor mehr als 15.000 Jahren begonnen, letztere schien mit dem Friedensschluss von Paris 1783 für die Zeitgenossen abgeschlossen zu sein. Denn keiner der Zeitgenossen erwartete im Frühjahr und Sommer 1783, dass der Konföderation der amerikanischen Freistaaten eine Krise bevorstand, aus der sie als Bundesstaat mit einer Verfassung hervorgehen würde, die die zentralen Lehren moderner republikanischer Verfassungen beherzigen und zugleich Bürger-und Menschenrechte festschreiben würde. Mit der Wahl von George Washington zum ersten Präsidenten der Vereinigten Staaten von Amerika und der Umsetzung der Bestimmungen der Verfassung von 1787 war dieser revolutionäre Prozess der Umformung der britischen Kolonien in das zu jener Zeit modernste republikanische Staatswesen abgeschlossen. Der „Amerikanischen Revolution zweiter Teil" hatte sein Ende erreicht.
Bd. 4, 2016, 624 S., 86,90 €, gb., ISBN 978-3-8258-8795-7

Hermann Wellenreuther
Von Chaos und Krieg zu Ordnung und Frieden
Der Amerikanischen Revolution erster Teil, 1775 – 1783
Bd. 3, 2006, 608 S., 59,90 €, gb., ISBN 3-8258-4443-9

Hermann Wellenreuther
Ausbildung und Neubildung
Die Geschichte Nordamerikas vom Ausgang des 17. Jahrhunderts bis zum Ausbruch der Amerikanischen Revolution 1775
Bd. 2, 2002, 808 S., 86,90 €, gb., ISBN 3-8258-4446-3

Hermann Wellenreuther
Niedergang und Aufstieg
Die Geschichte Nordamerikas vom Beginn der Besiedlung bis zum Ausgang des 17. Jahrhunderts
Bd. 1, 2. Aufl. 2004, 744 S., 86,90 €, gb., ISBN 3-8258-4447-1

Hermann Wellenreuther
Niedergang und Aufstieg
Die Geschichte Nordamerikas vom Beginn der Besiedlung bis zum Ausgang des 17. Jahrhunderts
Bd. 1, 2. Aufl. 2004, 744 S., 34,90 €, br., ISBN 3-8258-7672-1

LIT Verlag Berlin – Münster – Wien – Zürich – London
Auslieferung Deutschland / Österreich / Schweiz: siehe Impressumsseite